Praise for *Corbynism from Below*

'Corbynism promised the end of a top-down Labour Party and the start of a mass movement to change society for good. This is no easy task. *Corbynism from Below* describes the detours and difficulties along the way, without losing sight of the movement's prospects and possibilities.'

Laura Parker, National Coordinator, Momentum

'It is the grit, tenacity and creativity of activists, both inside and outside the Labour Party, which has kept the Corbyn project alive … The success of Corbynism will depend on the mobilisation of these activists, and this book accounts for how we have achieved so much so far, without forgetting all that remains still to be done.'

Holly Rigby, founder of 'Abolish Eton', grassroots Labour campaign against private schools

'The last few years have seen a plethora of ideas bubbling up from the grassroots movement that underpinned Jeremy Corbyn's dramatic rise to be leader of the Labour Party. It fills me with hope that this ecosystem of thinkers on the left just keeps growing and growing – and these essays are a hugely important contribution to that.'

Sam Tarry, Campaign Director, Jeremy Corbyn 2016 leadership campaign

GW00585092

From the reviews of Mark Perryman's *The Corbyn Effect*

'An invigorating addition to what is still a pretty thin literature about Corbynism.'

Andy Beckett, *The Guardian*

'These essays extend Corbyn's "effect" into a clear-eyed contemplation of what his project should be: whether that's deepening democracy and reconnecting the civic levers of change; rebuilding business along social and co-operative lines; or reimagining immigration policy to put optimism and humanity at its core.'

Zoe Williams, *Times Literary Supplement*

'*The Corbyn Effect* offers a window into a movement trying to shape a rush of ideas and excitement into a programme for government, and doing so in the knowledge that, should it win power, its success or failure will have profound implications for the future of European social democracy.'

Justin Reynolds, Social Europe

'*The Corbyn Effect* is a very welcome, highly topical and in some ways innovative contribution to ongoing debates about left-wing politics, the Labour Party and the re-shaping of British politics, packed with insights into recent political history, especially the turmoil in the Labour Party and its social and political roots.'

Alex Snowdon, Counterfire

'There are some excellent contributions here. Jeremy Gilbert examines how alternative ideas to the neoliberal consensus were marginalised for so many decades. Des Freedman quantifies the scale of the media hostility against Corbyn ... In an important piece, Eliane Glaser distinguishes between populism – a negative bashing of elites aimed at disrupting the political system, and a popular left politics ... The stand-out chapter for me is Maya Goodfellow's essay on immigration, debunking the pseudo-sociology of the so-called "white working class", "a mythical bloc of people who are all assumed to hold the same views".'

Mike Phipps, *Labour Briefing*

For an open left!

Corbynism from Below

[signature]

For all who dreamed and danced of a change from below at the Rock Against Racism Carnival, Victoria Park, Hackney, 30 April 1978. For those who have ever since, but most of all those who do today, and will tomorrow too.

Corbynism from Below

Edited by

Mark Perryman

Lawrence & Wishart
London 2019

Lawrence and Wishart Limited
Central Books Building
Freshwater Road
Chadwell Heath
RM8 1RX

Typesetting: e-type
Cover design: Peter Brawne | matter@pobox.com
Printing: Imprint Digital

British Library Cataloguing in Publication Data.
A catalogue record for this book is available from the British Library

ISBN 9781912064250

Contents

History in the Remaking

Below the Line

Afterwords

INTRODUCTION

Corbynism from Below

After Labour's much-better-than-expected 2017 general election result, with 'Oh, Jeremy Corbyn!' ringing out around Glastonbury that year, and a party more united than at any time since Corbyn's election as leader, came the Brexit impasse.

Remember the Conservatives' election mantra of 'strong and stable government'? Or the spectre they tried to summon, of a 'coalition of chaos' between Labour and the Scottish National Party (SNP)? As reality unfolded, the first devolved into a Tory government in meltdown, the latter, a Conservative-Democratic Unionist Party coalition from hell. But, in spite of the Tories' woes, much of Labour's 2017 optimism of the will has been replaced by a rising tide of intellectual pessimism.

The kind of radical break that Corbynism promises does not make for an easy political ride. *Corbynism from Below* seeks to explore the breadth and depth that is required for a project of transformation of party and political culture to sustain and develop the momentum for change.

This is an edited collection, not a manifesto – the clash of points of view, experiences and writing styles is intended. The aim is to bring together different perspectives so that we can learn from one another. Not a bad starting point for a political project that seeks not to simply function, but to succeed on an unimaginable scale.

In his keynote essay, Mark Perryman describes Corbynism as 'the party turned upside down'. He argues that what is needed is a movement that seeks an ideological change as profound as those of Attlee in 1945 and Thatcher in 1979. This means that the party itself, its organisational culture in particular, cannot remain, as it has done hitherto, virtually unchanged since its foundation in the early twentieth century. A radical shift in the party's culture would help it fulfil what Perryman, quoting Gary Younge, identifies as the central political objective in the Brexit era: that of replacing a harmful division of 'them and us' with a popular 'we'.

Following this keynote essay, the collection is divided into four sections. The opening section, 'Top to Bottom', explores various models of Labour leadership, while the next section, 'Building Blocs from Below', concerns models of Labour membership and campaigning. The third section, 'Morbid Symptoms', seeks to identify the causes and effects of the setbacks Labour has suffered since the 2017 general election, and proposes some possible solutions. The fourth, and closing, section, 'History in the Remaking', looks forward more optimistically towards the remaking of Corbynism, using 'from below' as the matrix for how this might be achieved. The section includes an analysis of changing voting patterns that provides the all-important electoral context.

Opening the first section, Lorna Finlayson offers an invaluable contextualisation of Jeremy Corbyn's leadership of the Labour Party and all things Corbynism. She surveys long-term trends in Labour history, the party's record in government under Blair and Brown, and finally how the party has changed since Corbyn became leader in 2015. This last period, she argues, represents a fundamental challenge to the status quo.

Andrew Gamble suggests today's era of political change is best understood in terms of authoritarian populism versus a plural left. The revival of authoritarian populism will not be effectively resisted, still less rolled back, by a left overly dependent on the ways, means and ideas on which it has always relied. The voting population is far more flexible in its choices now; as seen in the surge in support for the Liberal Democrats, the Green Party, the SNP, and Plaid Cymru, while on the right, Nigel Farage's Brexit Party poses a different kind of threat. A 'no compromise' position has its appeal among leftists, but without a pluralist outlook, Gamble suggests, Labour will condemn itself, firstly, to a narrowing of its appeal, losing support to other parties and, secondly, it will become incapable of meeting the challenge Farage poses. The result: defeat snatched from the jaws of victory.

Phil Burton-Cartledge frames Labour's current predicament in terms of the twin crises of decomposition and recomposition. Facing up to decline, while discovering how not only to recover, but grow, is a painful yet necessary process. Jeremy Gilbert has helped to pioneer one very particular route through this challenge: 'Acid Corbynism'. This is a mode of understanding and explanation that challenges conventional political thought, and Gilbert's 'beginners guide' helps to explain why we need to do precisely that.

'Acid Corbynism' probably doesn't appear as an agenda item at many Constituency Labour Party meetings, and if it does, the *Daily Mail* will probably want to know about it for the paper's next front-page splash. Nevertheless, it is vital that we make the connection between ideological change, and the necessary transformation of Labour's organisational culture. This is a key theme of *Corbynism from Below*. In the opening chapter of the second section, Jess Garland examines the implications of Labour becoming a 'multi-speed party', one in which there is a broad spectrum of depth of loyalty and affiliation among members, quite unlike the 'my party, right or wrong' tribalism that has traditionally been symptomatic of both Labour's left and right. This is not to suggest that a 'multi-speed' membership cannot be an active one, but if it is, it won't be in response to a simple call to political arms. Adam Klug and Emma Rees argue that what is needed is 'big organising'. They draw on their own and others' experience of the 2016 Bernie Sanders presidential campaign in the US in particular to show how effective such organising can be.

It is Labour's organised roots in the trade unions that not only makes it different among the political parties, but also illustrates the scale of what a party rooted in both workplace and community can achieve. Heather Wakefield makes the argument that this isn't of simply historical interest: what we need now is a 'Corbynised' trade unionism. This would be a trade unionism shaped by grassroots initiatives, and often led by women, young, migrant and part-time workers, rather than the traditional, male, full-time employees that trade union culture and the left are more used to.

Such a transformation in how Labour organises 'from below',

whether in communities, workplaces, or, best of all, both, will take place in a much changed mediascape. Anne Coddington's chapter maps the innovations being made by the Corbynist left to link the political to the communicative.

The Corbynism 'wave', first emergent in 2015, then breaking over the party again in 2016, and again for a period after the general election of 2017, has inspired a huge growth in Labour Party membership. But has the 'wave' exhausted itself? Is it adequate to the tasks that now face it? Is it capable of being revived, or have Brexit, the antisemitism crisis, and breaches within the left shown that Corbynism's flaws outweigh its usefulness? Neal Lawson asks these difficult but necessary questions in his essay opening the third section, 'Morbid Symptoms'. He offers answers that might make uncomfortable reading for diehard Corbynites – but since when has a left politics worthy of the name offered only comforting answers?

Lindsey German's chapter in this section of critiques is concerned with how Corbynism could fall victim to 'parliamentary socialism'. To prevent a divorce from the movements and campaigns from which it grew – a split which would harm its chances of effecting change – Corbynism must find ways to be both in and against the corridors of power. This is, she argues, vital to the durability of Corbynism's potential.

If it fails, the obvious threat is of a resurgent populist right with the spectre of racism never far away. Satnam Virdee's chapter describes how racism flourishes in a vacuum where class politics, capable of unifying different and diverse communities with 'more in common', is in retreat. Virdee outlines the urgent necessity of facing up to this challenge before it is too late. This reckoning takes place on an entirely different terrain to the one Labour is familiar with. Labour can no longer simply depend on what Gerry Hassan in his chapter calls 'the Labour nation', a paradigm of national and political identity of the same vintage as the 'spirit of 1945'. The union is broken, Britain is breaking up – a civic, broadly social democratic Scottish nationalism bringing about its downfall, accelerated by Brexit. For how much longer, Hassan asks, will Labour ignore the implications of all of this for its own, unionist, politics?

Despite these reservations, the core argument of the book is that the potential for a 'Corbynism from below' remains both obvious, and possible. The bedrock of support for it in Labour's ranks has never gone away. Sure, there's been a battering or three. And that is not unique to Labour – the Brexit impasse has forced a rupture upon the entire British body politic. Now is not the time to retreat, though altered circumstances do demand a rethink. In the final section, 'History in the Remaking', James Meadway's chapter takes Corbynism's break with the ruins of neoliberalism as an opportunity to revive an economic strategy to end austerity, one that is sustained by renewables, and by a belief in sharing the wealth of our society for the benefit of us all. What is needed is a politics that is shaped by Labour at every level from top to bottom or, even better, from bottom to top. A party with this kind of strategic profile will, Paul Hilder argues, be 'networked' – not run from a single national, regional or even local central command, but empowering and engaging the entire membership. This kind of radical inclusivity is perhaps the biggest – as yet unfulfilled – potential of a Corbynism from below.

In the medium term, what all this adds up to is how Labour campaigns at the next general election. Paula Surridge's chapter offers the research and the figures to enable us to navigate the changes in the electorate that Labour must contend with. This will mean reorienting, where necessary, the target-seat strategy in the context of Liberal Democrat and SNP revivals – not forgetting, too, the Brexit Party eruption. Surridge's analysis can help activists understand these changes, to shape a grassroots strategy to win.

Of course not everything that Corbynism must face, learn from and be transformed by is entirely new. Hilary Wainwright's concluding essay contrasts the experiences of feminism remaking socialism, and Labour as a tale of 'two parties' since the first Bennite insurgency of the 1980s, of which the young Jeremy Corbyn was a part, with the social movements of the early twenty-first century from which Corbynism has drawn such support. Come what may, these various fragments, old and new, remain our resources of hope.

At the back of the book can be found Mark Perryman's A-Z of Corbynism for those new to the coded language of Labour left activism. Plus his handy guide to reads, Twitter feeds, websites, campaigns and think tanks, to help readers fulfil Corbynism from below as more than just a book.

In these hard times, Labour transformed is more necessary than ever before. Who ever said it was going to be easy?

Keynote Essay

The Party Turned Upside Down

Mark Perryman

Corbynism [*kawr*bin-izm*) *n*. a movement not an individual; fundamental shift in system of ideas; for the many not the few.[1]

I grew up politically during the 1980s, under the long dark years of another 'ism' – Thatcherism. Though Britain did not change overnight on the day of Thatcher's election victory – no 'ism' can effect change that fast – 3 May 1979 did mark the beginning of the end of the post-war settlement, which was shaped by one kind of consensus, and the early days of another – neoliberalism. Corbynism from below,[2] if it is to mean anything, will at long last break with the latter and initiate another, entirely different, consensus.

Stuart Hall and Martin Jacques, early pioneers of the analysis of Thatcherism, described its project thus:

> It may be that Thatcherism is not finally to be judged in electoral terms – important as these moments of mobilisation are in the political process. Rather, it should be judged in terms of its success or failure in disorganising the labour movement and progressive forces, in shifting the terms of political debate, in reorganising the political terrain and in changing the balance of forces in favour of capital and the right.

As Hall and Jacques also recognised, while Margaret Thatcher herself would at some point go, the political imprint that Thatcherism left behind wouldn't be so easily removed. Politics in future would be grounded in a fundamentally altered 'political territory':

... with the left in disarray, the defences of the labour movement weakened, the progressive social movements demoralised and the overall balance of political forces tilted much more favourably towards a hegemony of the right.[3]

And that is more or less what Thatcher did leave us with – until now. Corbynism is thus not about any one individual. Instead it has to become a movement initiating change from below on the scale of Attlee in 1945 and Thatcher in 1979, to create a fundamental shift in ideas, rooted not only in the way we are governed, but in the way we live.

RECOVERY OR MORE DESPAIR?

It was to be the mid 1990s before there was even a smidgen of a suggestion that Thatcherism might be coming to some kind of sorry end. There's no mistaking the fact that the 'new' prefix that Blair gave Labour was a powerful antidote to the eighteen years of Tory misrule that predated Labour's 1997 landslide victory. Blair stood as a bright, spanking – and, yes, 'new' – contrast to what Thatcher's successor John Major had come to symbolise. David Stubbs conjures well the mood associated with the outgoing prime minister:

> Major's wistful visions of a Britain of warm beer and 'old maids cycling to church in the morning mist' seemed to belong to the credits of some Sunday evening middlebrow period drama rather than a Britain whose heartbeat was pounding assertively with the delirium of the End of History. This was a dead man talking.

By 1995 Blair's commitment to the 'new' already included the proposal, overwhelmingly adopted by a special party conference, that Labour should abandon the original Clause Four and all those troublesome words about the common ownership of the means of production, distribution and exchange. Having won the support of the conference for this change, when Blair was summing up, he mentioned he'd had a new idea – the name of the party. There was a pregnant pause. The delegates were not sure whether to stand up and cheer, or walk out in disgust. Blair grins, 'only joking' – but he knew right then he could get away with just about anything.

Stubbs also sums up very neatly the broader popular mood that embraced New Labour – a desperate desire for something, anything, other than what we'd been forced to endure for far too long: 'There was simply a crying need for new faces at the helm, to displace an old guard who felt disassociated with the sense of self-confidence and triumphalism of Cool Britannia.'[4]

Blair's genius was that for a moment he came to personify this 'crying need', and by association Labour did too, or more particularly New Labour did.

At Labour's final party conference before the 1997 general election, Blair was in fine form, making all the necessary connections – England at Euro '96, a chart-topping football song, Labour:

> Seventeen years of hurt never stopped us dreaming. Labour's coming home! (Applause) As we did in 1945 and 1964. I know that was then, but it could be again – Labour's coming home. (Applause) Labour's coming home.[5]

We may cringe now, but in October 1996, with Labour enjoying something like a thirty-point lead in the polls, and a general election less than a year away, few were going to mutter anything resembling words of discontent and doubt.

And, to be fair, Blair had some other words in his speech that two decades on might just as well have been said by Jeremy Corbyn in his leader's speech to Labour Conference: 'For all the people or for a few? That is the difference between us and the Conservative Party that governs Britain today. That is the choice before us.'

But, as we know, words are not enough. The political economist David Held described the philosophy that underpinned New Labour as 'hyper-globalist' – founded on a single over-arching belief: that 'internationalisation of economic processes ... both of production and of financial transactions ... is the central force of our times'.[6] As Held argued, this belief was linked to the idea that social democracy had to adapt to these forces, and this, in turn, would determine almost everything Labour might achieve, or not achieve, in office:

One of the political consequences of this line of reasoning is that social democracy in its traditional form is inevitably undermined: the Keynesian, welfare-oriented state, with considerable capacities for economic and social management, will not survive in the new circumstances. States no longer have the policy instruments they require to run the gauntlet of global economic change.[7]

This critique appeared in a special one-off issue of *Marxism Today*, published in November 1998. The front cover of this issue was filled by a portrait photo of a youthful Tony Blair, full of all that initial promise, with a single word of text – 'Wrong'. At the time, the producers of the issue (of whom I was one) were criticised for indulging in premature accusation.

So whatever did happen to that 1997 landslide – when Labour won a near historic 43 per cent share of the vote? (Thatcher in 1979 had mustered an identical 43 per cent, Wilson in 1966 reached 44 per cent, Attlee in 1945 got 47 per cent.) Things did not, in the end, get better. In 2001 the Labour vote went down to 40 per cent. In 2005 it was 35 per cent, barely a percentage point better than Kinnock had managed in 1992. And in 2010 it sank to 29 per cent, more or less the level of Michael Foot's disastrous 1983 showing.

THE LONG MARCH OF BENNISM HALTED

In 1981 Tony Benn had made a challenge to the incumbent postholder in elections for the deputy leadership of the party – Shadow Chancellor of the Exchequer, Denis Healey. Benn set out his reasons for standing as:

Labour was not established by its founders just to manage capitalism. We exist to bring about a transformation to socialism, using the ballot box; all the experience of past Labour governments proves that if that objective is set aside, Labour governments will be forced back onto policies that harm working people and lose us electoral support. That must never happen again and the campaign for more democracy in the party is our best guarantee that it will not.[8]

Benn lost by the narrowest of margins, with a 49.6 per cent share of the vote versus Healey's 50.4 per cent, but his defeat began the eventual turning of the tide against what until then had been a rising Labour left. It has been a very long march back for the Bennite left of the early 1980s, the length of which – and the outcome of which – few would have dreamt of at the time.

Some never doubted the happy ending. Alan Freeman, writing in 1982, the year following Benn's defeat, provides the reasoning for a faith shared by many of his fellow believers:

> Firstly, the Benn movement, though a minority current, is none-theless deeply popular. It has swept the Constituency Labour Parties. It won over two million votes in the unions. In December 1981 a poll indicated that forty per cent of Labour voters in the unions wanted Benn to continue his campaign in the Labour Party. Wherever he speaks, Benn attracts record audiences. This is a new, mass, popular social movement.[9]

There were still many reasons to be hopeful at that time. The 1981 People's March for Jobs from Liverpool to London had electrified anti-unemployment campaigning. In 1982 the NHS workers' action for better wages mobilised hundreds of thousands, both on strike and in hugely supportive local demonstrations. The Campaign for Nuclear Disarmament (CND) remained a potent protest movement with enormous crowds joining marches against Trident and cruise missiles, helping to ensure Labour remained committed to unilateral nuclear disarmament. And wherever and whenever these protesters gathered it was virtually guaranteed that the most popular speaker would be Tony Benn. Despite his failure to defeat Denis Healey in the Labour poll everywhere else he was the left's undisputed leader.

In *Three Letters to a Bennite*, however, Paul Foot put forward what proved to be some well-founded reservations:

> I don't know whether or not the industrial downturn will go on through 1982. But I do know that there will be a struggle, whatever the pitch of it. There will be strikes and occupations and sit-ins and demonstrations. Are you really going to spend

your time locked in Labour Party meetings, digging in for long resolutionary trench warfare, waiting to go over the top at the Winter Gardens in October?[10]

If Paul was sounding a bit miffed, he had good cause, given his advocacy of mass struggle outside the Labour Party. The Bennite tide was yet to turn, tens of thousands were flocking to hear Benn, and many thousands were digging into their local Labour Party for what still seemed to be a much shorter haul than the one it turned out to be.

Within a year of Paul writing his three letters, a thirty-something trade union organiser by the name of Jeremy Corbyn had been elected Labour MP for Islington North, as part of the continuing Bennite surge.

What happened next? For three decades, not a lot. Corbyn spent many years in the relative wilderness of the back benches as the tens of thousands of people who'd signed up to be part of Benn's transformation of the party were ground down. Heads first knocked against an impenetrable wall of resistance as Neil Kinnock steered the party away from being associated with support for, and the fallout from, the 1984-5 miners' strike. Then Kinnock's 1992 defeat was followed by Labour inexorably moving further rightwards, first with the soft social democracy of John Smith, and then the shock treatment of the new with Blair. By 2001, as Blair was setting out on the road to the Iraq war in 2003, it was all over for the left: the drip, drip, drip of mumbled discontent and disillusion had become an angry flood, with something like 100,000 members exiting Labour, the vast majority leftwards. But there was nowhere else to go, and the odd march was more like a reunion of old-timers than a movement to do something about a collective political plight.

By 2015, five years after the Tory comeback that brought an end to New Labour, this outside left did not resemble any sort of movement at all, and counsels of despair – and grumpiness – were everywhere. Typical of its rejectionism was Tariq Ali, who on the eve of the May 2015 general election described what so many of us had turned our backs on as 'the extreme centre':

We live in a country without an opposition. Westminster is in the grip of an extreme centre, a trilateral monolith, made up of the Conservative-Liberal Democrat coalition plus Labour: yes to austerity, yes to imperial wars, yes to a failing EU, yes to increased security measures, and yes to shoring up the broken model of neoliberalism.[11]

The catalogue of political wrongs done to two generations of the left was legion. Hopes of something, anything, being different were dashed over and over again for thirty years or more. Ali concluded his argument with a 2015 version of Lenin's 1905 pamphlet 'What is to be done?': 'It will require alliances from above and below to cement changes. We are many, but the few control the wealth, and have a military to back up that control.'[12] And then he dutifully quoted the old Bolshevik, and the ferment that created 1917, to cheer us all up – or not, given that the likelihood of any kind of change remotely resembling the scale and nature of the Russian revolution had receded further and further into the history books. There seemed to be no hope, and not much of a future. Keeping on keeping on was about all we could possibly look forward to.

'SINCE DAY'

There's a best-selling T-shirt available via Momentum that features a headshot pic of Jeremy Corbyn with a headline splashed across it – 'Since day'. Most who've bought it weren't even born when the picture was taken, in 1984, when Corbyn was being arrested on a protest picket outside apartheid South Africa's London embassy.

Corbyn, now in his early seventies, has been around a long time. And a significant part of his appeal is an unwavering set of principles dating back four decades or more. Of course, that can be a problem – times and circumstances change. But his appeal remains rooted in his refusal to waver over a long period of time, a period that stretches from the social-democratic consensus of his youth to the neoliberalism that may now be drawing to an end.

The year that Corbyn was elected to Parliament, 1983, the socialist dream was decisively quashed in France, much as it had already been in the UK, the difference being that the change was being wrought by a Socialist Party president, François Mitterrand, who made the U-turn towards austerity (*rigueur*). Mitterrand was also later to play a major role in the European Union's shift towards neoliberal policies. It is worth pausing here to note that Europe's neoliberal consensus depended on this kind of capitulation from the left, every bit as much as it did on its architects from the right.

In contrast, 'Since day' Corbyn would have no truck with any accommodation of this sort. Ben Tarnoff has described the movements that Corbyn's kind of oppositional politics produces as the 'next left':

> The movements [figures such as Corbyn] have channelled and inspired are at an interesting stage of development: no longer in their insurgent phase, they have succeeded in pushing formerly fringe ideas into the mainstream, but don't yet wield power on the scale required to put those ideas into practice.[13]

The insurgency is in the process of becoming, but it hasn't yet reached the mainstream stage. Doing so will be full of possibilities but also fraught with the risk of setback and defeat. To fulfil the former and avoid the latter it is doubtful that policies based on any kind of absolutism will have the flexibility of purpose required. Rather, the collective ability to distinguish strategy from tactics, in order to identify politics as the art of the possible, is what will help us shape a practical progressivism – one that is liberated from impossibilism masquerading as idealism.

One promising possibility in this vein – and one that some view Corbynism as very much part and parcel of – is 'left populism'. This 'populism' has some commonalities with the slogan of 'taking back control' – whose only real problem was those who mouthed it. (And it has a whole lot more going for it than the slogan of 'keeping things as they are', otherwise known as Remain. The marketing guru who came up with the latter as a means to win a campaign against the dynamic of 'Leave' really should be banished to the stationery cupboard for ever.)

Left populism is a politics confident in its strategy but unafraid of getting its hands dirty in the tactical. But that doesn't mean that it should become a politics of fudge and nudge, with each side using slogans virtually indistinguishable from the other. Political theorist Chantal Mouffe helps us spot the difference:

> Right-wing populism claims that it will bring back popular sovereignty and restore democracy, but this sovereignty is understood as 'national sovereignty' and reserved for those deemed to be true 'nationals'. Right-wing populists do not address the demand for equality and they construct a 'people' that excludes numerous categories, usually immigrants, seen as a threat to the identity and the prosperity of the nation.[14]

And of course right-wing populism poses no effective challenge to the causes and effects of austerity, no substantive alternative to neoliberalism. The discourse of 'anti-elitism' is simply the flim-flam of the same old same old. Nevertheless, as countless examples from the recent period show, it works.

Left populism has to be brave enough to reject all of this in order to become something that is entirely different. Mouffe again: 'A left populist strategy aims at federating the democratic demands into a collective will to construct a "we", a "people" confronting a common adversary: the oligarchy.'[15]

So, is the answer left populism? Perhaps. But really the current ambition is a little bit simpler – to both be popular, and have a cause.

INSIDE AND OUTSIDE LEFTS

Across Europe, in response to the increasing numbers of social-democratic parties that have adopted the path of triangulation in the face of neoliberalism, parties to their left have started to draw support away from them. In some countries, having failed to find alternatives to the neoliberal order, many social-democratic parties have collapsed electorally. This happened most spectacularly in Greece, when Pasok gave way to Syriza, but there have also been challenges from, among others, Podemos in Spain, Left Bloc in Portugal, Die Linke in Germany, the Green Left in Holland and Mélenchon's La France Insoumise. The writer-activist James Doran came up with the term 'Pasokification' to describe the Europe-wide development of this phenomenon. Doran locates the reason for these parties' growth as follows:

> Because these newer radical parties embraced extra-parliamentary activity and sought to give voice to concerns about the rule of elites, they were able to challenge the territory held by social-democratic parties when the established order collapsed during the financial crisis of 2007-08 and the resulting global recession.[16]

But this is not what has happened in the UK. In all the cases mentioned above, the parties fought elections under one version or another of proportional representation. This makes an electoral challenge to rightward-moving social democracy a practical proposition – and it certainly makes it possible to win enough votes to establish a parliamentary bloc. In Greece it was enough for Syriza to form a coalition government with a much smaller partner, in Portugal it was enough for the left to become part of the governing coalition; elsewhere it has allowed the left to be an effective point of pressure from within the legislature. In Britain, the first-past-the-post system effectively precludes any of this. This is why the challenge has arisen inside an existing party, not outside of it.

But that doesn't mean there aren't commonalities between Labour and what's being going on in mainland Europe. Kevin Ovenden captures very well the nature of the mainstream social-democratic politics Syriza was up against, which is not so different from the situation inside Labour before Corbyn became leader:

> A permanent capitulation to the right and abrogation of what you believe in through 'triangulation'. Under that voodoo politics, the left should seek a midpoint between itself and the right in order to win a middle ground. The result is to shift this fabled middle ever further to the right.[17]

DAYS OF HOPE AND POSSIBILITY

What a difference a few weeks can make. On 15 June 2015 Jeremy Corbyn succeeded in getting on the ballot paper for the Labour leadership contest, and the rest is history – though perhaps not quite yet.

Everything changed in that moment. A politics of hope ignited that had scarcely existed for decades. A movement emerged as if from nowhere. Unsurprisingly, it met with wilful misunderstanding and deliberate misrepresentation. Here is Nick Cohen in the *Observer* providing readers with his view of the 2017 Labour conference: 'Cultism has turned Labour into a childish, sycophantic, thuggish and unthinking party.'[18]

I may not have been one of the fans rushing to the Labour Party shop to buy Corbyn-themed knick-knacks, or jumping to my feet in adulation when Jeremy walked on stage. And perhaps these were not scenes in the image of a grown-up party to be broadcast to millions. But the 2017 conference – which took place not long after the election in which Labour had performed so much better than the naysayers had predicted – should surely be understood as a way of identifying with a much-derided politics that we strongly believed in, and signs of a well-deserved emotional release after being lectured at for two years along the lines that Jeremy Corbyn would lead Labour to a crushing defeat, a Tory landslide of historic proportions – and that would be on a good day. No, we hadn't won the election, but we'd come close enough to give the Tories the fright of their lives and had been well enough placed to be considered serious contenders the next time around.

Nick wasn't having any of this, though. Instead, this time writing in the *Spectator*, he described the modern Labour Party as being at the mercy of a 'far left animated by a hatred of the West and fascistic conspiracy theory'. He explained his thinking thus:

> I don't want to overanalyse the Corbyn movement, and worry too much about which box of left-wing thought it fits into. You only have to look at candidates who endorse antisemitism or suggest the murder of Jo Cox was a false flag operation, to dispense with political science and conclude that a portion of its supporters appear mentally ill.[19]

Hold on a minute Nick. If we're 'mentally ill', no wonder you're not worried about what kind of left we might be, and you're probably wise, too, to admit that you're dispensing with 'political science'.

But it is not just Nick. An indecent proportion of the liberal media's salaried commentariat share his view of Corbynism, though most of them are not quite so outlandishly rude. Caricature, ignorance, lazy labelling – the 'Corbynista' and the like – this is the nature of much of what passes for understanding in the media of a phenomenon that has now endured for several years, and which reflects a broader international shift.

'Corbynism' is not a personality cult, and it is not monolithic either. There are various ways to identify the contrasting, sometimes in conflict, elements that make up the contemporary Labour left.

First there are the stay-at-homes – the remnants of the 1980s Bennite left who were in it for the long haul, who never left, whatever the depth and breadth of their differences with what the party became. Part of the party's furniture for longer than they care to remember, these people know how the levers of power work in Labour, it's just that they have never had their hands on them before – and now they are grimly determined not to let go. Their mirror image exists on Labour right – never-say-leave. Neither can abide those they regard as carpetbaggers who desert the good ship Labour when matters don't go their way.

Second are the 'come-back-homes' – people with more or less the same political origins as the 'stay-at-homes', but who bailed out during the Blair-Brown years, especially during the Iraq war. They kept their principles intact if not always their activism. They never expected to rejoin, but are now comfortable once more with the familiarity of the party, feeling like they've never been away.

Third is the 'at last we have a home to call our own' tendency. They are mainly over thirty, and have in the past mostly voted Labour, Green on occasion. Labour membership never really appealed to them though – they were unconvinced that time spent would actually change anything. They were more likely to be found active in their union, campaigns, social movements, or perhaps reading a good left-wing book. The Blair-Brown years put them off Labour. No experience of Labour organisational culture, but they know how this kind of thing works.

Finally, there are the 'home from another homes' – usually under thirty, with an experience of politics exclusively post Blair-Brown. For many their first experience of campaigning was against the

Lib Dems' betrayal, when, in coalition with the Tories, they tripled tuition fees. The power of protest and direct action are core to their activism, and the non-party political, social movement form is seen as the best way to carve a personal political identity. They never imagined there'd be a Labour leader who'd accommodate much of this, but they still find the party itself more than a bit alien and off-putting.

Some might use other labels, or challenge these definitions. The boundaries between them aren't supposed to be hard and fast. A degree of fluidity has emerged, a way of negotiating the differences, as this huge, and highly committed, mass of individuals listen and learn from another. The key point therefore is that there is a wide range of opinion within and between a renewed and lively Labour left. This is something the Labour right and the cynical critics continually overlook.

There are also, however, people who have hardened their identification with one group or another, to thwart the possibility of a common agenda for change. That route spells disaster.

A CONVERSATIONAL PARTY

This hardening of identifications serves to exclude the kind of conversations on which a radical socialist politics should thrive. But there seems also to be something else, at a deeper level within Labour's organisational culture, that prevents these conversations from thriving – or at least doesn't actively encourage them. And this can't simply be put down to politics. I've lost count of the number of events I've done for Constituency Labour Parties for my previous book *The Corbyn Effect*, where, at the end of a robust but well-informed and highly participative discussion, those who have taken part comment on how good it was to talk politics for a change, and how it was not something that usually happens at Labour meetings.

Of course this isn't the whole story: there have to be MPs' and councillors' reports at local meetings, and there are resolutions to pass, delegates to elect, campaigns to support. But this is the business of politics – how we organise it – rather than a discussion about how we effect change, and why. We don't want a talking shop or debating society – that's not what most of us joined the Labour Party for – but we did join it because of a passionate belief that politics matters, and that Labour is the best means to ensure it matters for the common good of all. So we need in addition the space to have debates and discussions.

For most of us, there is a recognition that while we might disagree entirely on ABC, we can nevertheless have a useful discussion about LMN, and as a result find ourselves in agreement, and working together, in the cause of XYZ. This is politics as conversation, the practice of listening to each other – as opposed to socialist sermonising, when shouty, usually male, voices lead the way towards a political cul-de-sac, squabbling at the expense of fruitful thought.

After he had spent time with the crowd at The World Transformed festival running alongside Labour's 2016 conference, John Harris described the bare bones of a very different Labour left that he saw beginning to emerge:

> These were not the hardliners and ideological desperadoes that some people might imagine: their politics felt open, self-critical and realistic about the huge tasks it faces. They may not yet have a clear idea of how a new left politics might decisively cohere – but no one (not even gobby newspaper columnists) does, as yet. The point is to at least begin with a sense of how it might start to mesh, and the breadth of people who will have to be involved.

This was in the wake of a pretty gruesome summer – the Parliamentary Labour Party coup against Corbyn, followed by a second leadership election in two years and all the bitter division that that brought with it, a party that was split two-thirds versus one third. But Harris was of the opinion that this divide was largely meaningless, that too many people have this huge emotional stake in something that has no obvious meaning to the big wide world outside of a Constituency Labour Party meeting; and that Labour's left and right have much more in common than either realises:

> [they are] equally convinced that Labour alone has the answers, that arcane debates about party committees and conference resolutions represent a worthwhile use of human effort, and that absolutely everything always centres on the question of whether Corbyn and his allies should stay, or go.[20]

The unwelcome truth is that John has a point. Labour's organisational culture too often produces no practical outcomes. It is closed, conservative and cautious, slow to catch up with the world outside the party. It subcontracts ideas out to sympathetic think tanks and experts, rather than seeking to engage its mass membership in the political thinking process in any meaningful way – a process that Antonio Gramsci saw as vital to the party developing itself to become an 'organic intellectual' force. There are exceptions to all this, but such discussions are never the rule. And this way of thinking turns the party into the antithesis of a plural, popular left, 'from below'.

NO IFS, NO BUTS

It is harder to think of a more fearsome barrier to this ambition for Labour to become a kind of ideas exchange, a space where experiences are shared and an all-embracing conversation flows about how to change the world, than the idea that Labour might be an antisemitic party. Yet this is a label that has stuck to Labour for the past few years, despite every effort to shake it off, and there are now allegations that the entire apparatus of the Labour Party is institutionally antisemitic.

This is something we must get better at dealing with. Many would vigorously reject both the label and the allegation. But the fact remains, whether we like it or not (to be clear, I do not), that antisemitism is something that has come to be associated with Jeremy Corbyn's leadership of the Labour Party. First of all, we have to be clear that contesting the label is entirely different from endorsing the idea that antisemitism is anything but a foul form of racism. Equally, suggesting that the handling of the issue hasn't been exactly without fault is not the same as giving up on the idea that Labour is capable of doing better.

What is needed is a clear and unequivocal position that antisemitism is wrong, full stop. And here we need to have some courage in our own convictions. Suggestions that those who accuse Labour of antisemitism are indulging in 'smears' or 'weaponising' the subject are unnecessary, unhelpful and too often couched in terms that are downright insulting and serve to undermine any professed opposition to antisemitism. Instead we need clarity of principle on antisemitism, no ifs, no buts – no qualification required and no whataboutery either.

It should be easy for a Labour Party, and in particular a leader who wears his anti-racism as a badge of considerable pride, to find such clarity. But it hasn't proved to be. Instead, the party has been fighting an increasingly bitter rearguard action, almost always on the defensive, with nothing much positive to say in terms of the values it holds dearest – which we might have expected to be our best possible line of attack against the accusation of antisemitism.

Labour's values should also provide the foundation for confronting Labour's sexism, misogyny, racism, Islamophobia, homophobia and transphobia. Please don't tell me that these don't also exist in our ranks and institutions, across all wings of the party, alongside the antisemitism. And whataboutery dressed up as cultural relativism doesn't excuse these either. Being better than most isn't the same – not nearly – as being good enough.

The key to an identity politics that is both educative and transformative lies with a values-led politics – not in definitions, or the enforcement of codes, or working examples, caveats and the like: values that we learn from one another, and are shaped via the lived experience of being in a mass party of countless differences. The commonality of the cause does not subjugate us as individuals but liberates us, both as individuals and as a collective, enabling us to face up to what would otherwise divide us.

David Schneider, a comedy actor who once taught Mr Bean judo, and was co-writer with Armando Iannucci of the screenplay for *The Death of Stalin*, has produced a 'Basic test for antisemitism', whose four questions make a decent starting point for thinking about the issues:

1. Do you accept that millions of Jews perished in the Holocaust? [YES]
2. Do you think that Jews exercise undue influence on organisations/the government/the media/finance/your life? [NO]
3. Do you treat antisemitism in exactly the same way as hatred and prejudice against any other group, condemning it outright

without any qualifying comment about, for instance, the suffering of other groups? [YES]
4. Did you manage to answer 1-3 without moving the subject on to Israel/Palestine? [YES].[21]

David added 'I suggest that anyone who fails this test probably has issues with Jews.' The fourth question is the one that is pertinent to the Labour rows on antisemitism. There is clearly a need, on all sides, to separate out the issue of antisemitism from the issue of Israel.

Yet this does not mean that all criticism of the Israeli state or sympathy for the Palestinians is antisemitic. Indeed Labour was for a very long time supportive of Israel, including the social-democratic values of the state's early years.[22] Nor was this support passive: the party was active in popularising more widely an image of Israel as 'the beacon of progress in the Middle East.[23] Today what Paul Keleman describes as a 'divorce' has occurred, as this historic support for Israel has been transformed in response to a sense of solidarity with Palestinians. But this sense of solidarity should not prevent people from remembering the reasons – which have a persistence that cannot simply be denied – for Israel's original foundation as a nation-state. Keleman calls the contradictions of the situation 'awkward' – which is perhaps putting it mildly. He describes the 'awkwardness' as arising from historical context. On the one hand, 'Israel's establishment emerged out of the triumph over fascism and as a restitution to the Jewish people for the Nazi Holocaust'. But, on the other, it was also 'the product of imperial expansion'.[24]

Largely as a result of each 'side' clinging on to one of these two factors, to the virtual exclusion of the other, opposition to antisemitism – which should of course be universal and unequivocal – has instead become embroiled in the most unseemly of spats between the Labour left and the party's right wing, one which does neither very much credit. At times it has seemed as if each is more interested in the demolition of the other rather than the deadly seriousness of the issue at hand. Opinions are often dismissed simply because of who voices them, instead of being listening to. As with anything in politics, especially left politics, there are issues here to argue over, definitions to contest, motives to question. But, the near instant rush to judgement that social media encourages has amplified the differences, and the debate has become debased and devalued, devoid of moral principle.

Jonathan Freedland, after giving a brief history of antisemitism, taking in Judas Iscariot, Shylock, Fagin and more, made the point that: 'Given the 2,000 year-old history of this equation between Jews and the wickedness of money, it is absurd to imagine any one of us would be immune to it.'[25] This history was not offered to excuse antisemitism, but rather to help us understand its ugly and enduring prevalence, including on the left. And when there was a spat over Jeremy Corbyn writing a foreword to a new edition of J.A. Hobson's 1902 classic *Imperialism*, because of Hobson's antisemitism, Corbyn's defenders unwittingly made the same point when they trotted out a long list of those, like Hobson, who also held antisemitic views, including Virginia Woolf and Sidney Webb.[26] Others that could have been cited include figures central to Labour's history such as Keir Hardie, John Maynard Keynes and George Bernard Shaw. It is an unwelcome tradition that we all need to account for rather than deny.

David Feldman and Brendan McGeever, director of and lecturer at the Pears Institute for the Study of Antisemitism, offer this advice to Labour:

> Labour needs to learn and reflect on how racisms of different sorts have figured in its own past and continue to shape the present. It should be possible to decry global inequality and support justice for the Palestinians without likening Israelis to Nazis, invoking the Jews' special conspiratorial power or holding diaspora Jews directly responsible for the actions of the Israeli state. The challenge for the Labour Party's leadership is to oppose racism unconditionally and without exception, including when its targets are Jews, most of whom do not support the party and who identify with the state of Israel.

And they add, not as an afterthought but as an equal part of their argument:

> There is also a challenge for the Jewish community, especially its leaders. Their alertness to antisemitism in Britain should lead

them to provide greater support to anti-racist campaigns more generally. It might also allow them, even as they identify with Israel, to recognise and censure the racialised inequalities within and beyond its recognised boundaries.

They conclude with a message to bring the two sides together, not drive them yet further apart: 'In their different spheres, both the Labour Party and the leaders of the Jewish community should understand that anti-racism is not divisible.'[27]

THE BREXIT IMPASSE

Brexit has proved to be the biggest, single, at times almost insurmountable, barrier to all the hopes placed in Corbynism reaching any broader fulfilment. It is a problem to which there are no easy answers, no quick-fix solutions: anything Labour chooses to do will result in gains here, losses there. Those who claim that all Labour needs to do is 'X', and then everything will be all right, tend to dismiss the negative fallout from their favoured plan in order to protect their own, sectional, ends – and never mind the consequences.

Navigating this has been tiresomely messy, making for a politics that is both awkward and unappealing – and one to which Corbynism is entirely ill-suited. A vital debate, Britain's relationship with Europe and all that entails, has been reduced to parliamentary arithmetic and politics as a spectator sport – the passivity of the onlooker while the not-so-great and anything-but-good get down to business. This is the complete opposite of what Corbynism sought to break Labour free from – it feels more like a return to the old practices of parliamentary socialism. Any extra-parliamentary activity seems to have been farmed out to the Remain campaign, memorably described by Suzanne Moore: 'from its passion-free name and its inherent self-righteousness ... the worst campaign I have seen in my lifetime'.[28] Moore is no Corbyn supporter, but she knows a hapless and useless campaign when she sees one.

Before the 2016 referendum on Britain's EU membership, the campaign to 'Remain' was entirely lacking in any kind of dynamic; it seemed to be based on the idea that everything with the EU was fine, and any hint of something being wrong was seen as bordering on treachery. And the 'People's Vote' campaign for a further public vote on the issue has continued on this sorry track, deliberately failing to understand why Remain lost, and secure in the apparent knowledge that Leavers didn't know what they were voting for, were duped by politicians' lies, mind-controlled via dodgy Facebook ads. Remainers never for a moment had the necessary self-awareness to realise that what they thought of others said more about themselves than their opponents. Corbyn sits uneasily alongside this, and quite rightly.

To return to the people, via another referendum, the final decision on what kind of Brexit (or not any kind at all) there ought to be, is the popular-democratic position. But it is fraught with pitfalls, though these are lazily dismissed by the politicians and commentators who support it. At the very least its supporters need to account for the seats Labour would lose as a result, and be honest enough to declare this a price worth paying. But that is only part of the problem. What if 'Remain' wins next time round but by the narrowest of margins. Best of three? The democratic credentials aren't as solid as they might first appear. What this amounts to is the ways and means of managing a political crisis, not the answer to it.

Gary Younge has argued better than anyone else what that answer might look like. Corbynism needs to disrupt the existing order of ideas, to break the divisions that have been highlighted by Brexit, and tell better stories than the right about, in his words, 'what this country has been, has become and might be'. It needs stories that turn the old ideas about '"them" and "us" into "we"'.[29]

THE PERSONAL IS HEGEMONIC

Lynne Segal, in her book *Radical Happiness*, describes the 'moments of shared joy' that collective energies can foster.[30] As she argues, such joy is significantly aided by having a shared dream for what a better future might look like. Stephen Duncombe suggests that it is through such dreams that the left might acquire a capacity to 'reimagine' the political via the spectacle of change:

> Our spectacles will be participatory: dreams the public can mould and shape themselves. They will be active: spectacles that work only if people create them. They will be open-ended: setting

stages to ask questions and leaving silences to formulate answers. And they will be transparent: dreams that one knows are dreams but which still have the power to attract and inspire. And, finally, the spectacles we create will not cover over or replace reality and truth but perform and amplify it.[31]

Collective joy? A spectacular politics? The subversiveness of the participatory-creative? No, it doesn't sound much like most constituency and branch Labour meetings I go to either – many of which have been reproducing, for goodness knows how long, an organisational culture every bit as exciting as not merely watching, but rather listening to, paint dry. This culture generates hours of procedure that satisfy Labour's few – the self-selecting activist class – but not the many – the vast majority of its disconnected and disenfranchised membership. And yet it is a process with precious few effective consequences apart from maintaining the emotional wellbeing of its enthusiasts – people who find comfort in a way of running a twenty-first century political party that wouldn't look out of place in a nineteenth-century corresponding society, and who are as likely to be on the Labour left as the right.[32] In short, Jeremy Corbyn's Labour Party, despite all the considerable positives, hasn't done very well at becoming a mass party.

This culture produces non-activism, as the party continues to demand that members fit in with its outmoded structures, never mind the ever-declining response; continues to heap the blame on those put off, alienated, bored by what the party serves up, never mind questioning the cause and effect. The party turned upside down would seek, instead, to adapt the organisation to members' needs and aspirations.

Corbynism is a product of the kind of left from which it first emerged, and from which it has never entirely escaped. It is rooted in what is generally known as the hard left – and language has an uncanny ability to reveal an otherwise concealed intent. We understand 'hard' to mean unflinching, uncompromising, an absolute refusal to be broken.

This approach is often very necessary. It was the cry 'They Shall Not Pass' that stopped British fascism in its tracks at Cable Street in 1936. It was not a question of 'would you mind, ever so much, not being such nasty Nazis or we'll have to report you to something or other'. And four decades on, when British fascism was resurrected in the shape of National Front, it was the Anti-Nazi League's street protests that stopped the Nazis from marching, not a polite request not to do it. In that iconic photo of Jeremy demonstrating against apartheid South Africa, he wasn't gently asking them to desist from their racist practice: he was protesting, picketing, boycotting, and being arrested for the trouble he was causing.

But being hard can produce a brittleness, too, a propensity to snap, to break into fragments, leaving in our wake the broken pieces, on the way to we know not where. And in the process it favours dogmatism, an unwillingness to listen to other points of view. It can lead to a refusal to recognise potentially big advances, if they are dependent on even small compromises; or a dogged defence of each and every tactic while losing sight of the strategic ambition they are intended to serve. We are on the road to nowhere, but never mind, because our principles are intact. Such has always been the fate of the hardest of hard lefts, a politics that all too often puts off for life those who would otherwise be supportive. If Corbynism isn't in the end any different, it will suffer the same fate.

In the 1970s feminists fought to teach a male-dominated left an invaluable lesson: 'the personal is political'.[33] Among other things this means that how we do our politics must be shaped by why we do our politics. This needs to become the bedrock of a socialist politics. This is what should guide our praxis. It is our best guarantee against the historic failings of the hard left becoming our failure too – and the means through which the personal becomes hegemonic.

FOR A POPULAR FRONT OF THE MIND

The left has always depended on making alliances and coalitions between groups and blocs. It is written into the very fabric of our identity – 'The Workers United', 'The Union Makes us Strong', 'Unity is Strength'. It is the product of generations of combined effort, organisationally engineered. But in a political culture that is increasingly both atomised and amplified this is no longer sufficient. What we need today is a popular front of the mind.[34]

Such a project's starting point is a familiar one; it is the core value of Labour – equality. And this is not only a state towards which we aspire, or in the name of which we seek to re-organise society: it should also, surely, be already evident in how we treat others and expect to be treated by others in return. If this is not the case, then what exactly are we signing up to?

This is all the more important for a mass party. Members join with a variety of life experiences and opinions, and membership is thus best understood as a journey for the individuals who join, and one that is travelled by developing these experiences and opinions in the way that best helps us to serve a shared aspiration, both as individuals and as a party. One without the other isn't very much use.

Crucially, Labour has always also been a broad party, and to be successful it must remain so. Differences of opinion are to be expected, and they are expected, too, to be openly expressed. But more than that, they should be positively encouraged, in a manner whereby we can learn from one another even when we choose to disagree.

None of this means Labour shouldn't reject all forms of discrimination: the journey of membership, the breadth of the party, the differences of opinion openly expressed, are all a part of the way we develop the project together. But it isn't a value-free project. A non-exhaustive list of the forms of discrimination that Labour should both disown and campaign against includes ableism, ageism, anti-Semitism, homophobia, Islamophobia, misogyny, racism, sexism, transphobia. The list is deliberately alphabetical. There is no hierarchy of discrimination – Labour needs to oppose all forms of discrimination, equally, while as a democratic socialist party also recognising that class plays a fundamental role in shaping each.

Such opposition to all forms of discrimination isn't unchanging in its nature. This is mostly for good reasons, but sometimes, unfortunately, bad ones. Changes usually occur as definitions of each form of discrimination are contested, or as new constituencies make successful political claims. But change should never be a reason to excuse the discrimination.

Labour should be able to provide a space for open and friendly debate amongst members, and beyond. If it can't then the party has a serious problem that demands urgent attention. And the recognition of equality also means thinking about the way we discuss things. Not so long ago the place where such a culture could thrive, for better or worse, was exclusively through face-to-face discussion in formal or informal party structures. But now a much bigger space has erupted, where opinions are expressed via brevity, everything can be archived, and messages are amplified via sharing. These are the pluses and minuses of social media. Labour is largely a voluntary party, and there are precious few full-time staff, which means that even if we wanted to, it would be impossible to police social media on any kind of effective scale – or in the way that could happen in a meeting, conducted within certain agreed parameters. When we are expressing ourselves on social media we must therefore ask ourselves whether, on joining the Labour Party, we are willing to be responsible for our individual actions, given a situation in which they are likely to be judged, whether that is intended or not, as representative of the entire party – one that aspires to win elections, and form a government. If we're not, then Labour isn't the party we should be joining – and it has no reason to welcome us as members. We all need to take part in the presentation – and reality – of a party that respects everyone in all their differences.

By helping in this way to construct a popular front of the mind, not only amongst our own membership but also in the wider world, Labour will, in the process, be producing a much improved political culture. We need a culture in which, before we press send, we automatically ask ourselves whether what we've written, and the way we've written it, is likely to offend. And if it is, and that is our aim, we need to ask whether that serves the purpose of the debate we're taking part in. This goes way beyond abuse, bullying and all manner of 'isms'. It is about abandoning the instant put-down, the hard-faced quip, the intolerance of others' viewpoints, the attempts to make our 'side' look good and the other lot the worse for wear.

I'm not in any way saying that the circles I move in – the Corbynite left – are worse at this than anybody else. Nor am I suggesting that the Labour right don't also indulge in most of the worst excesses of a broken political culture. They do. But passing the buck is no strategy to achieve the kind of transformation demanded by Corbynism from below. A desperate search for the lowest possible common denominator by which to judge our political effectiveness should be a non-starter. Rather, Corbynism from below begins with individuals who have the ambition to become part of a collective, acting to mend the fractures in the way we do our politics, the things that hold us back, and repel others from joining in.

The aim is not to stop anyone from contributing – what sort of radical, democratic, socialist party would want to do that? But Labour's practice should foster discussion and participation for all, within an organisational culture that actively encourages it, rather than infringes upon it. A party for a self-selecting few with their own very particular baggage of political privileges is never going to be able to serve the interests of the many.

THE POLITICS OF WE

Getting our own party in order, however, can only be the start.

The Brexit impasse has become all-pervasive. It isn't to minimise the importance of this issue, however, to point out that my child's school being threatened with becoming an academy has precious little to do with whether or not we stay in the EU. Or that head-teachers have been driven to this most desperate of measures because of the chronic lack of resources all primary schools now face. I live in Lewes, a small market town of 16,000 persons, but unless Brighton and Hove Albion are at home or it's our annual Bonfire, there is no permanent uniformed police presence in the town. The police station is now a glorified phone box. When the front window of our house was terrifyingly smashed in by vandals, the only advice the police could offer, by email, was to install CCTV. It's not the EU who have reduced us to this, it's austerity-driven politics. Meanwhile our town's high street is increasingly becoming a commercial waste-land of empty shops, so many vacant properties that there's not even enough charity shops to fill them up. And when I catch a train to London I am paying to travel on one of the most expensive railways in all of Europe, and certainly the worst. One day a week I teach at a university. When the Vice Chancellors wrote a letter declaring that Brexit would devastate higher education, they couldn't spare a single sentence to mention their collaboration with the tripling of tuition fees that has spelled not only the marketisation of universities but their destruction too. How will being in or out of the EU change very much of this sorry tale?

Mine is a fairly middle-class, small-town existence, I know. I've checked my privilege. But the same account, of a society divided every bit as much by austerity and inequality as 'Leave versus Remain', could be provided for villages, towns, suburbs and inner cities the length and breadth of the country. And, underpinning all our futures, there is the huge issue of climate change. Just imagine for a moment if all the days, weeks, months and years Parliament has been debating Brexit had been spent on finding the answers to solve that. We can vote to leave or remain in the EU, but there's no exit from a dead planet.

To effect the shift that Gary Younge called for – from us and them to 'we' – demands a politics from Labour that does much more than simply reproducing the much lauded 2017 general election manifesto and the message of 'For the Many not the Few'. However good this was, it didn't win the last general election and it certainly won't win us the next one. The beginnings of a new agenda for change may be there, but it has been entirely submerged by the tidal wave of all things Brexit. To break through demands a practical vision of the state as the provider and defender of the public good; an anchoring of our understanding that life chances in every sector of society are determined by the scales of inequality; and the boldest imaginable break with an economic model that is accelerating us all towards an unmanageable environmental crisis, through putting in its place a sustainable economic strategy.

The kind of break that would be signalled by implementing a 'Green New Deal', for example, also demands the construction of another 'we'.[35] Labour's credibility to deliver any such deal has been hopelessly compromised by the Labour MPs who support the expansion of Heathrow and other airports, the Labour council leaders clamouring for the high-speed rail project HS2 to go ahead, the affiliated trade unions in favour of fracking, and the party policy that remains in favour of nuclear power and the re-opening of coal mines. Neither our relationship with one continent nor that with the entire planet will be settled via this or that procedure or deal: what is needed is an almighty break with the existing political consensus, and a new consensus founded on a new popular majority and a new common sense.

Brexit, a sustainable economy – these are issues that require us to confront the sectionalism that frames both opposition to, and support for, them; in its place we need to put a progressive universalism. For Labour this is doubly urgent because members, allies and supporters find themselves lining up on opposing 'sides' on these matters, while often otherwise sharing the same politics.

At a time when the Conservative Party faced similar deep divisions, what Thatcherism began – and neoliberalism achieved – was the creation of a popular majority and a new common sense.[36] Corbynism, however tough things get, has to set itself the same ambition, albeit in pursuit of an entirely different, progressive, vision. In the not too distant future there will be a general election. We must operate on the basis that the next general election could be the vote that breaks one consensus, neoliberalism, and shapes a new one. We need a break with the past that is as bold as Attlee's spirit of '45, a reinvention that enables us to meet the challenges of our own time, when we face an environmental catastrophe requiring solutions every bit as radical as those needed for winning the peace after a world war.

A Corbynism from below aspires towards a better way of doing politics. And though Labour's direction of travel has changed since the left won leadership of the party, progress in that direction has been too faltering to satisfy this aspiration. A practical, prefigurative humanism wouldn't be a bad way to revive our spirits.

Any such revival would be taking place in conditions where food banks are a commonplace lifeline for millions. At events I help organise for my Constituency Labour Party in seemingly well-heeled Lewes, I always ensure we have a collection of non-perishable food for our food banks; though ours is a small town, we have three food banks, and each is inundated with pressing needs from those who need to eat. Like most blokes of my generation I'm not a natural at showing my emotions in public, but at one event, when explaining why we did this from the platform, I suddenly found myself crying in front of the crowd. I'd started by pointing out that shortly after I came into politics we'd spend most weekends collecting food for the striking miners of 1984-85, and now we were doing the same, but for our neighbours: if it was good enough for the miners, it was certainly good enough for those who live round the corner.

It's because of this toxic mix of austerity, inequality and an unsustainable economic model that we stand on the verge of such momentous change – something that is both terrifying and exhilarating. Down the road from where I live is Hastings and Rye, Amber Rudd's seat, number seven on the list of 66 target seats that Labour must win at the next general election if it is to form a government on its own.[37] Up the road is Crawley, number 45 on the same list – a bigger swing there, 2.44 per cent, will bring us a little over halfway towards the magic 3.69 per cent swing required to win all 66. And a short train ride along the coast, bubbling just under these targets for change, is East Worthing and Shoreham. Thanks to the extraordinary breakthrough there since 2017, which took Labour from more than four decades of zero councillors to its current total of ten, this is also a realistic possible extra seat that Labour could win. OK, Hastings has had its fair share of making history – 1066 and all that. But Crawley, Worthing? Yet winning these seats, alongside others across the country, will be our first stage in making a society where food banks aren't needed any more and climate change is something society is actively reversing.

A collective, a majority, a coalition made up of many individuals. This has to be our beginning for a 'Corbynism from below'. Not me or them, or them versus us – but me, them and us becoming 'we'. Not via this or that parliamentary manoeuvre, procedure or leadership challenge, but via the remaking of the entire body politic. We need to create a socialism of the self that becomes a socialism of our selves – and in the process shapes a new, popular consensus.

We want to win votes, sure, but, this time, the aim is to transform Britain together, for good, forever. It's our moment, let's make some history.

NOTES

1. Definition used at Lewes Labour Party's 'Corbynism: A day making new kinds of politics', 8 June 2018.
2. I first came across the term in Tom Blackburn's 'Corbynism from below?', www.newsocialist.org.uk, 12 June 2017.
3. Stuart Hall and Martin Jacques, 'Introduction', in Hall and Jacques (eds), *The Politics of Thatcherism*, Lawrence & Wishart: London, 1983, p.13.
4. David Stubbs, *1996 and the End of History*, Repeater: London, 2016, p.35.

5. Tony Blair, Leader's Speech, Labour Party Annual Conference, Blackpool, 1 October 1996.
6. David Held, 'The timid tendency', *Marxism Today*, November/December 1998, p.24.
7. *Ibid*.
8. Tony Benn, 'Questions and answers', *New Socialist*, Sept/Oct 1981, p.8.
9. Alan Freeman, *The Benn Heresy*, Pluto: London, 1982, p.14.
10. Paul Foot, *Three Letters to a Bennite*, SWP: London, 1982, p.21.
11. Tariq Ali, *The Extreme Centre: A Warning*, Verso: London, 2015, p.17.
12. *Ibid*, p.191.
13. Ben Tarnoff, 'The Next Left', *The Guardian*, 15 December 2018.
14. Chantal Mouffe, *For a Left Populism*, Verso: London, 2018, p.24.
15. *Ibid*.
16. James Doran, 'An antidote to Pasokification', in Mark Perryman (ed), *The Corbyn Effect*, Lawrence & Wishart: London, 2017, p.214.
17. Kevin Ovenden, *Inside the Labyrinth*, Pluto: London, 2015, p.41.
18. Nick Cohen, 'Labour conference? More Like the cult of St Jeremy', *Observer*, 1 October 2017.
19. Cohen, 'Labour's tragedy is Britain's tragedy', *Spectator* Coffee House blog, 23 April 2018.
20. John Harris, 'A Labour Party of the future is beginning to emerge', *The Guardian*, 29 September 2016.
21. @davidschneider, 8 April 2018.
22. See Paul Kelemen, *The British Left and Zionism: History of a Divorce*, Manchester University Press: Manchester, 2012.
23. *Ibid*, p.9.
24. *Ibid*, p.186.
25. Jonathan Freedland, 'For 2,000 years we've linked Jews to money: It's why antisemitism is so ingrained', *The Guardian*, 9 March 2019.
26. Donald Sassoon, 'Jeremy Corbyn, Hobson's *Imperialism* and antisemitism', *The Guardian*, 2 May 2019.
27. David Feldman and Brendan McGeever, 'Labour and Antisemitism: What went wrong and what is to be done?', *Independent*, 18 April 2018. See also www.pearsinstitute.bbk.ac.uk.
28. Suzanne Moore, 'I won't be marching for a people's vote: There has already been one', *The Guardian*, 19 October 2018.
29. Gary Younge, 'So poorer Brexiters voted to be worse off? There's nothing wrong with that', *The Guardian*, 1 February 2019.
30. Lynne Segal, *Radical Happiness: Moments of Collective Joy*, Verso: London, 2017, p.94.
31. Stephen Duncombe, *Dream: Re-imagining Progressive Politics in an Age of Fantasy*, New York: New Press, 2007, p.17.

32. For two alternative visions, see Aaron Bastani's activist-focused Labour Party reorganisation proposals: Aaron Bastani, 'Labour can only win with Jeremy Corbyn', Open Democracy, 27 July 2016; and Paolo Gerbaudo's wide-ranging survey of how a tech-led organisational revolution is affecting how political parties function: Paolo Gerbaudo, *The Digital Party: Political Organisation and Online Democracy*, Pluto: London, 2019.

33. Sheila Rowbotham, Lynne Segal, Hilary Wainwright, *Beyond the Fragments: Feminism and the Making of Socialism*, Merlin: London, 1979.

34. I first came across this term in the 1980s, when an anti-Thatcherism occasional magazine called *Samizdat* used it as a strapline. Very neat, I thought, though they didn't apply it in the way I am advocating.

35. See the Labour for a Green New Deal website: www.labourgnd.uk.

36. See Sally Davison and Katharine Harris (eds), *The Neoliberal Crisis*, Lawrence & Wishart: London, 2015; and Jeremy Gilbert (ed), *Neoliberal Culture*, Lawrence & Wishart: London, 2016.

37. 'Labour's battleground seats: A smart campaign guide', in Mark Perryman (ed), *The Corbyn Effect*, Lawrence & Wishart: London, 2017.

Top to Bottom

The Corbyn Context

Lorna Finlayson

All commentators seem to agree that something extraordinary happened when Jeremy Corbyn was elected leader of the Labour Party. For the anti-Corbyn side, what's extraordinary is that a relic from the 'hard left' – a faction thought to have been permanently subdued in the 1980s – managed to win the election and promise to alter the party beyond recognition, assisted by social-media-savvy but politically inexperienced young people (plus a smattering of veteran Trots). Labour's political identity and its inheritance of practical knowledge, both the product of long, often bitter experience over more than a century, are consequently seen to be under grave threat. Some of the same facts – the pivotal roles of young people and of social media, for example – also feature in the pro-Corbyn version of the story. But there's a difference: in the first version, Corbynism represents a dramatic deviation in the history of the Labour Party; in the second, a dramatic return to, or resurrection of, its values.

CHANGING DIRECTION

The disagreement about Labour's true identity has more to do with clashing ideals in the present than with conflicting analyses of party history, but the history is often bent to fit a particular agenda. It is a distortion to present Corbynism, as its critics sometimes do, as the second wave of an alien invasion: first the Militant Tendency, now Momentum. Corbyn's politics belong to a tradition that stretches back to Labour's beginnings (something that could never be said of Tony Blair's). But it would also be a distortion to present Corbyn's politics as the dominant strain in the Labour Party pre-Blair. The social democratic values he stands for – a strong welfare state, public ownership and provision of services – were most fully realised by the post-war Attlee administration, but this was, for any number of reasons, mainly relating to the impact and aftermath of the Second World War, an exceptional rather than representative period in Labour's history.

In other words, Corbyn may be atypical of the Labour Party, but his views aren't extreme or unprecedented. He is manifestly not a revolutionary – whatever the papers may say – and only in a highly circumscribed sense can he even be called a 'radical'. While it's true that his roots are in the Bennite 'hard left', this tradition – characterised by a commitment to wealth redistribution and Keynesian economics, as well as by some tentative support for workers' control of industries and a deep scepticism about the European Union – is not to be confused with the 'far left'. These terms are often used more or less interchangeably to describe Corbyn and Corbynism, but 'far left' is more properly used for extra-parliamentary groups and movements committed to the revolutionary overthrow of capitalism. Corbyn is not proposing to replace capitalism, by revolutionary or any other means. He is not even proposing a very radical redistribution of wealth. What he has so far felt able to put forward is moderate by the standards of the Bennite left of the 1970s and 1980s: according to the economist James Meadway, the economic strategy that underpinned the party's widely lauded 2017 general election manifesto is actually less radical than that offered up in 1983 by the Social Democratic Party (SDP)[1] – the breakaway party formed by a faction of Labour's right wing. Labour under Corbyn is promising, among other things, to abolish tuition fees and expand free childcare, reversing some of the cuts imposed by the Conservatives – and by their coalition partners between 2010 and 2015, the Liberal Democrats. It proposes to pay for these measures by raising income tax for the top five per cent of earners – though nowhere near pre-Thatcher levels – and by increasing corporation tax from 19 per cent to 26 per cent.[2] The lowest rate of corporation tax under Thatcher was 34 per cent.[3]

All that said, context and direction of travel matter in politics at least as much as the detail of particular policies – otherwise, it would seem to follow from the facts above that Thatcher was more left

wing than Corbyn. Policies or political positions which, if a contin-
uance of the status quo, would not be a disruptive intervention in
a society, can be exactly that if proposed in a different context. In
one sense, free university education is not a remotely radical policy:
it was, until quite recently, what we had in this country, and of
course many other European countries still have it. But to call for its
reinstatement in Britain now is to challenge an already entrenched
model of education as a private rather than a public good, and of
students as individual consumers and entrepreneurs who must
borrow to invest in their own 'human capital'.

CALLING THEIR BLUFF

The greatest significance of 'Corbynism', though, lies not so much
in its challenge to the status quo as in what it has disclosed about
the political conditions under which we live. The events of Corbyn's
leadership campaigns and of his subsequent embattled tenure have
helped reveal the degree to which the self-appointed political 'centre'
has drifted to the right, leading the spectrum of political possibility
to contract accordingly. Corbyn's left reformism may be mild by
the standards of earlier generations, by the standards of some other
European countries, and relative to public opinion in the UK: the
polls – though admittedly a fallible guide to people's convictions and
voting behaviour – consistently show majority support for a fully
public NHS, for the nationalisation of rail and utility companies,
and for the cutting of tuition fees.[4] But this moderate agenda is,
clearly, totally unacceptable to the British political Establishment.
This includes most Labour MPs, and those who identify themselves as 'left-leaning' or 'liberal' journalists, many of whom remain
wedded to a market-friendly model shaped by the legacies of
Thatcher and Blair.

The advent of Corbynism has called the bluff of those who argue
that the homogeneity of British politics since Blair is simply reflec-
tive of a public consensus. The story we have been told is that we
live in a reasonably open and well-functioning democracy, in which
political decisions reflect, for better or worse, the will of the people.
We have been assured that in this system – in clear contrast to totalitarian societies – political dissent and challenge are possible, and

that the scarcity of advocates for left-wing positions reflects a lack of real appetite for them: people just won't vote for the left. Some say that this is because people have realised that left-wing policies don't work. Others maintain that the problem is that people are too bigoted and irrational to see the merits of a more just and compassionate society. Either way, the message is the same: don't blame 'the system', blame the people.

It has now been demonstrated that people are not only prepared to vote for a left alternative, but are willing to rally in their thousands in support of the chance to vote for it. Shutting their eyes to all evidence to the contrary, Corbyn's opponents maintained from the first that he was 'unelectable';[5] they continued to insist on it right up until the general election of June 2017, which showed the biggest increase in Labour's share of the vote since 1945, the year of Clement Attlee's great election victory. While a few still cling to this line, attributing Labour's performance to the Tories' poor campaign or devising creative theories about the motivations of Labour voters – the political theorist Andrew Hindmoor suggests that people only voted Labour because they were sure the party wouldn't win[6] – the 'unelectability' objection has now largely been dropped. However, electability or public opinion were never the real issues at stake for Corbyn's critics; it is they, not the electorate, who are unwilling to tolerate any serious challenge to the political status quo.

AGAINST THE ODDS

It's worth remembering the extent to which Corbyn's 2015 leadership campaign occurred against the odds and despite almost insurmountable institutional obstacles. That Corbyn or anyone like him would be elected to the leadership of the Labour Party – as opposed to forming a new party or extra-parliamentary movement – happened only thanks to a highly contingent combination of struggle and accident. In the aftermath of the party's 2015 election defeat under Ed Miliband, many on the Labour left – including John McDonnell – were initially sceptical of the wisdom of standing a left candidate at all. The most likely contenders for the role, Diane Abbott and McDonnell himself – both of whom had run unsuccessfully before – were unwilling to take it on at what the latter called the 'darkest hour' for the Labour left since the defeat of the Attlee administration in 1951.[7] When it was eventually decided that a left candidate should stand, and that that candidate would be Corbyn, there were only twelve days remaining until the deadline for securing nominations from Labour MPs. It would have been altogether impossible for Corbyn to make the cut had MPs not universally underestimated the threat that his candidacy would pose. Later, Margaret Beckett would memorably describe herself as having been a 'moron' to lend him her nomination.[8] This complacency may have made getting Corbyn onto the ballot possible, but still not easy or likely. It took not only the usual metaphorical arm-twisting and – in the final minutes before the midnight deadline – some literal genuflecting by John McDonnell at the feet of reluctant MPs.[9] It was also due, crucially, to the exertion of pressure from below, with large numbers taking to online platforms in order to publicly cajole and shame MPs into making good on their avowed democratic credentials and commitment to a 'proper debate'.[10]

But no amount of grovelling or tweeting could have been enough to propel Corbyn all the way to the leadership. His eventual victory – and arguably even his candidacy – could only come to pass thanks to some spectacular miscalculations on the part of his ideological opponents within the Labour Party. The Collins Review of 2014, which raised the number of nominations by MPs required in order for a candidate to stand was, according to Alex Nunns, 'intended to prevent someone like Corbyn joining the field'. But it backfired. As Nunns relates: 'The left bitterly opposed the Collins Review at the time: without it Jeremy Corbyn could never have become leader.'[11] Collins' institution of a 'one-member-one-vote' (OMOV) system for choosing leaders was what made it possible for Corbyn, having cleared the 15 per cent hurdle for MPs' nominations with moments to spare, ultimately to win the race.

Collins had wanted to raise the required number of MPs' nominations to 20 per cent or even 25 per cent of the Parliamentary Labour Party (PLP), which would have made it effectively impossible for a left candidate to enter. But not only was this opposed by the unions, it was also – more surprisingly – rejected by the Blairites, increasingly aware of their numerical weakness and isolation within the broader Labour right of the PLP. It was the Blairites, too, who backed OMOV, and who pushed for extending voting rights beyond the party membership to include 'registered supporters' – non-members who, in exchange for £3, would have a say in leadership elections. In return for the abolition of the MPs' 33 per cent 'block vote' (under the 'electoral college' system that preceded OMOV), the unions were eventually prepared to concede all of this, egged on by Unite's Len McCluskey, who saw in this unpopular reform a chance to reconnect with former members who had become disenchanted with Labour during the Blair years. As McCluskey recalls: 'I saw the prospect, if we could get into a situation where there was a credible left candidate, of appealing to those thousands of people we'd lost.'[12]

Of course, the architects of the reform had rather different hopes. The Blairites, in Nunns' reconstruction,

> thought that opening up Labour's internal elections would diminish the influence of union members and plant the party on the fabled centre ground. They assumed that those availing themselves of the opportunity to vote would naturally be to the right of quixotic political activists. Quite why none of them considered the possibility that quixotic political activists would be the most likely to take up the offer remains a mystery.[13]

The role of registered supporters in Corbyn's rise has been greatly exaggerated: he would still have won – though by a smaller margin – without them. But given the long-standing scarcity of opportunities for pleasure in the happenings of British parliamentary politics, there is no shame in savouring this little addition of self-insult to self-injury.

What happened next is just as instructive. Those who had claimed to be so keen on 'broadening the debate' expressed bitter regret for having allowed Corbyn's voice to be heard. The PLP mobilised to try and nip in the bud that which, it became unmistakeably clear, was never supposed to be allowed to bloom. There were calls to halt the leadership contest, once it began to appear that Corbyn would win. There were purges of the membership, and some of those applying to be registered supporters were prevented from doing so, often on spurious grounds.[14] In the second leadership election, following an attempted coup only ten months after Corbyn was first elected with a landslide, there were retrospective changes to party rules, disenfranchising a whole chunk of the overwhelmingly Corbyn-supporting newer membership. The fee for registered supporters was raised from £3 to £25. None of this was enough to avert a second landslide. Yet it was enough to confirm beyond doubt that the highest levels of the Labour Party had no genuine commitment to 'party democracy' and no tolerance for challenges to their orthodoxy. At an invitation-only event attended by academics and Labour MPs I heard the head of a prominent polling organisation tell his elite, and highly receptive, audience that the newly crowned Corbyn should 'be ejected from the party by any means necessary'.

ON THE OFFENSIVE

The engineering and subsequent ad hoc weaponisation of party bureaucracy against Corbyn has been accompanied by an ideological offensive of such dramatic proportions that it has been described by a former chair of the BBC Trust as 'quite extraordinary'.[15] The extent of media bias and misinformation aimed at discrediting Corbyn and undermining his political project has by now become a subject of academic study.[16] There have been so many twists and turns in this offensive that it would be impossible to document them all here, but I will briefly comment on some of the more recent developments – for the attacks show no sign of abating. The two themes that have emerged as consistent favourites among Corbyn's critics are those of Brexit and antisemitism. Being more or less unrelated except for their shared efficacy as weapons against Corbyn, these twin themes are deployed in an at-times slightly perplexing 'and/or' fashion. Or perhaps 'belt-and-braces' captures it best. The Labour MPs who in early 2019 broke away to form a new 'Independent Group' in Parliament (subsequently named Change UK and splitting soon afterwards) invoked both issues, with varying degrees of emphasis, moving between one and the other in a way more suggestive of opportunism – 'If you don't buy A, maybe you'll like B better' – than of any principled conviction.

Neither argument makes sense as a case against Corbyn. There is no evidence either that antisemitism is more prevalent in the Labour Party than elsewhere in British society – within the Conservative Party, for instance – or that its incidence within Labour has increased since Corbyn became leader. The dispute is really about Corbyn's positions on Israel and Palestine – positions which, like his domestic policies, enjoy broad public support. It has long been apparent that nothing will satisfy those who charge Labour, baselessly, with being 'institutionally antisemitic',[17] short of the removal of the democratically elected leader and the renunciation of his moderately critical stance on Israel and his sympathy with the cause of Palestinians. It is no coincidence that six of the eight former Labour MPs to join Change UK are supporters of Labour Friends of Israel (LFI) – one of the defectors, Joan Ryan, continues to serve as LFI's parliamentary chair, despite having left the party.

As for Brexit, a crucial point that has been overlooked, amidst all the wrangling over whether democracy is best served by holding a second vote or by attempting to adhere to the result of the first one, is that without a parliamentary majority, Corbyn has no power to make a second referendum happen, whether he wants one or not. Few seem to think that the numbers currently exist in Parliament for a bill proposing a second referendum to pass. By now, Corbyn has not only moved, in line with the policy agreed at the 2018 Labour conference, to endorse a second vote as a last resort in the case where the alternative is a 'no deal' Brexit: he has called for any Brexit deal, whether negotiated by a Tory or Labour government, to be subject to a public vote with 'Remain' as the alternative. But despite the ongoing Brexit impasse, no second referendum is as yet on the cards. Nor is it clear that Change UK's formation has made a second vote any more probable than it was before. Without making their stated objective more likely, what Chuka Umunna et al. have done is to make it at least marginally more likely that the next government will be another Conservative one.

THE PATH AHEAD

If the path Corbyn has opened up in British politics is again closed off, there are two foreseeable consequences. The first is that popular anger and disaffection will find another outlet. While frequent reference to a racist and right-wing public opinion has been a convenient device for the protection of the status quo, there is no virtue in maintaining an opposite fiction of the British people as saints and socialists. The appetite for Corbyn's vision of a more compassionate and co-operative society coexists with a counter-tendency that has been well nurtured in recent years: the tendency towards suspicion of strangers and neighbours, the scapegoating of the vulnerable, resentment and a desire to dominate others. This tendency was on full display during the Brexit referendum campaign, and was given a formidable boost by the result. There is no need to choose between the interpretation of Brexit as a protest against a neoliberal political Establishment or as expressive of an ill-informed, racist bigotry: it is both. Islamophobic sentiment and related attacks are on the increase, facilitated by a media which has for years been normalising far-right rhetoric.

The other foreseeable consequence of the defeat of Corbynism is that what remains of the achievements of earlier Labour governments will be undone. The combination of the economic consequences of Brexit and another few years at the mercy of the Tories or the 'centrists' inside or outside of Labour will spell certain death for the NHS. Even without Brexit, the health service would be doomed to an only slightly slower demise in such hands. In this context, the attacks on Corbyn's leadership are attacks on all those whose lives depend, quite literally, on a break with politics as we have known it.

NO GOING BACK

What is no longer an option is a return to politics as usual. Those who claim otherwise are incapable either of acknowledging the scale of discontent or of understanding its basis: they would rather blame 'populists',[18] or the distorting effects of social media 'echo chambers'.[19] From this point of view, the sources of Corbyn's appeal and his success are equally mysterious: it must be a result of infiltrators, nostalgia, a youth fad. 'Democracy' must be defended against this insurgency, but the idea that Labour candidates should be made accountable to the members of their constituency parties through a mandatory reselection process, for example, is 'totalitarian'[20] – even the idea that MPs who have now left the party they were elected to represent should stand again is, apparently, unthinkable. The Brexit referendum must be rerun, because 'democracy' malfunctioned in that case, while decades' worth of neoliberal reforms, carried out against the will of the population, remain safely within the bounds of the legitimate and unquestionable.

Former National Union of Students President Malia Bouattia describes the meaning of Labour for those who grew up under Blairism:

> The Labour Party for my generation is associated with destructive attacks on welfare services, black communities, and the poor. My entry into politics and my first political memories, thoughts, and actions formed around the early stages of privatisation in the health service and the introduction of university fees after being promised 'education, education, education' – both carried out under a Labour government. More than anything else, my generation's formative political experiences were the invasions of Afghanistan and Iraq, and the announcement of the so-called War on Terror... We were faced with violent aggression abroad and increased surveillance and criminalisation at home. It was the Labour Party that justified the bloodshed in the Middle East, while launching the Prevent agenda in the UK.[21]

Bouattia's generation is my generation. The first general election I can remember was in 1997 – with the anodyne, feel-good musical accompaniment of 'Things can only get better' (things didn't). Like Bouattia, the first political movements I was involved in were the movements against the UK's warmongering in the Middle East and against tuition fees – in other words, in opposition to what the Labour government was doing. I was a melancholy kind of activist because I had no expectation at all that anything we did would change anything. I participated out of a kind of deliberate blind faith, and a sense of wanting to announce – to whom, I'm not really sure – where I stood: to declare, again and again, 'Not in my name.' However futile that might have been, it seemed pretty clear that trying to contribute to positive change from inside the Labour Party would be a still more hopeless project. I remember standing at anti-war demonstrations in London and watching an MP called Jeremy Corbyn address the crowds – he was always among the two or three left MPs who would speak at these events – and finding it a somewhat sad spectacle. I wondered how people like that could stand what the Labour Party had become, and what they thought they could achieve by staying in it.

In the event that Corbyn survives to win an election and form a government, what may be hoped from it? It has often been said that we should not expect his troubles to end when he becomes prime minister, and indeed that this may be the moment when his real problems begin. This is probably true, if not very useful. What we may hope for also depends on a more basic and fundamental question. If we think that capitalism can be managed in such a way as to afford a decent life for all, then it is precisely this we should hope for and demand from a Labour victory under Corbyn. If not, the hope must be for something else – whether a step towards a more radical transformation, or at the very least some temporary relief. Perhaps there are little grounds for hope from either perspective. But in immediate practical terms, it doesn't make much difference. After all – to paraphrase a favourite slogan of the right – Corbyn? There is no alternative.

NOTES

1. James Meadway, 'Extreme? Back to the 80s? How Corbynomics compares with the SDP manifesto', www.leftfutures.org, 28 August 2015.
2. BBC News, 'Labour manifesto: Extra £48.6bn in tax revenue to fund pledges', 16 May 2017.
3. 'Corporation tax: Could we have raised more?', Full Fact, 2 June 2017.
4. See, for example: 'The 9 charts that show the 'left-wing' policies of Jeremy Corbyn the public actually agrees with', *Independent*, 23 July 2015; Chris Curtis, 'Corbyn's policies really are popular with centrist voters. But he still isn't', *The Guardian*, 28 September 2017.
5. I address this argument in Lorna Finlayson, 'Don't elect him, he's unelectable!', LSE Forum for European Philosophy Blog, 11 January 2016. Versions of the 'unelectability' argument have been made by Alastair Campbell (Ned Simons & Graeme Demianyk, 'Jeremy Corbyn is unelectable and will cause "chaos" if he wins Labour leadership, says Alastair Campbell', *Huffington Post*, 10 August 2015), David Miliband (BBC News, 'Corbyn's Labour "unelectable and undesirable" – David Miliband',

22 September 2016), and David Blunkett ('Labour is unelectable under Corbyn says Blunkett', *Daily Express*, 26 September 2016), among many others.

6. Andrew Hindmoor, *What's Left*, Oxford University Press: Oxford, 2018, p.43.

7. Alex Nunns, *The Candidate: Jeremy Corbyn's Improbable Path to Power*, OR Books: New York, 2018, pp.10, 57.

8. *Ibid.*, p.99.

9. *Ibid.*, p.101.

10. *Ibid.*, p.80.

11. *Ibid.*, p.31.

12. *Ibid.*, p.74.

13. *Ibid.*, p.74.

14. *Ibid.*, pp. 227-34.

15. Sir Michael Lyons, quoted by Des Freedman in Mark Perryman (ed.), *The Corbyn Effect*, Lawrence & Wishart: London, 2017, p.99.

16. Justin Schlosberg, 'Should he stay or should he go? Television and online news coverage of the Labour Party in crisis', Media Reform Coalition in association with Birkbeck, University of London, 2016.

17. See for example Alan Johnson, 'Labour is now institutionally antisemitic – it has one last chance to save itself', *Telegraph*, 20 February 2019.

18. Philip Stephens, 'Jeremy Corbyn feeds the nasty populism of the left', *Financial Times*, 6 September 2018. See also *The Guardian*'s series of think pieces on 'The new populism'.

19. See for example Andrew S. Crines, 'Shallow, hostile, toxic: Corbynism's social media problem', LSE British Politics and Policy Blog, 11 September 2018.

20. See for example Leo McKinstry, 'Jeremy Corbyn's Left is one of poison and intolerance', *Daily Express*, 5 February 2018.

21. Malia Bouattia, 'A more equal society', in Mike Phipps (ed.), *For the many: Preparing Labour for Power*, OR Books: New York, 2017, p.199.

The Left v. Authoritarian Populism

Andrew Gamble

The decade since the financial crash in 2008 has not been an easy one for progressive politics. The fortunes of liberal centrist politics have been declining in many Western democracies, while new illiberal democracies and authoritarian regimes have been on the rise across the world. Examples include the administrations of Donald Trump in the USA, Jair Bolsonaro in Brazil, Matteo Salvini in Italy, Viktor Orbán in Hungary, and Recep Tayyip Erdoğan in Turkey. After the end of the Cold War the number of democracies rose steadily, but since 2008, it has begun to fall.[1]

One of the most detailed assessments of the health of liberal democracies is conducted by the Economist Intelligence Unit. Their 2018 Democracy Index[2] uses sixty indices and five categories to assess the strength of democracy in 165 states. The five categories are: the electoral process and pluralism, civil liberties, political participation, political culture and the functioning of government. Using these measures, states are classified as full democracies, flawed democracies, hybrid states, and authoritarian regimes. Only eighteen states qualified as full liberal democracies in 2018. Both the United States and France were classed as flawed democracies, mainly because of perceived deficiencies in their democratic political culture, in particular trust in political elites and levels of political participation.

At the beginning of the 1990s, there had been high hopes of a new era of democratic advance following the collapse of the Soviet Union and the end of apartheid. Hegel's idea of an end to history because there were no more fundamental ideological conflicts left to resolve was resurrected. Liberal democratic capitalism became the widely perceived horizon of political possibility.[3] A 'new world order' was proclaimed by US President George H. Bush in his speech to Congress on 6 March 1991. This order was to be based on a liberal peace, secured by the expansion of trade and democracy to all the world.

Since 2008, however, we have entered a period of democratic retreat. What is especially alarming, as Edmund Fawcett has made plain,[4] are not just the declining fortunes of democracy and fears about the stability of existing democracies in the face of the severe challenges they face, but also the growing support for new parties and movements of the nationalist right. These see themselves as insurgents against the established order, and are explicitly against liberalism, the rule of law, a rules-based multilateral international order, and science and rationalism. Many questions, therefore, which were thought to have been settled, have been reopened.

POPULISTS, AUTHORITARIANS AND NATIONALISTS

There is much dispute about what the new insurgent movements should be called. Although they share some of the same roots, they are not fascist parties in the classic sense. This is not a re-run of the 1930s. There are few street militias in these new movements of the right, no dictatorships as such, and their ideologies are very different. The new insurgents bring together instead a number of contradictory strands – economic libertarianism and national protectionism, social conservatism and social liberalism. In the case of the Tea Party movement in the US, for example, economic libertarianism was reflected in their demands for less government intervention and lower taxes, and social conservatism in their stances on abortion, LGBT rights, gender roles, and gun control. Some of the earliest insurgents, such as Pim Fortuyn in the Netherlands, combined social liberalism with economic protectionism. Fortuyn defended LGBT rights and women's rights as manifestations of Western values and Christian European identity against what he decried as the 'alien' values of Islam.[5] Protecting Western values and Western communities required strict immigration controls and the rejection of multiculturalism. There are still echoes of this position in some of the European movements today, celebrating Western freedoms against Eastern restrictions, but social conservatism and economic protectionism are now dominant as the core of the movement.

Several different terms have been used to describe these new movements. Roger Eatwell and Matthew Goodwin label them national populists,[6] while Pippa Norris and Ron Adelman call them authoritarian populists.[7] What these approaches share is an emphasis on populism and cultural attitudes and values, rather than economic interests, as defining features of the new movements. These terms need disentangling. The movements are best understood as simultaneously nationalist, authoritarian *and* populist.

Firstly, they are movements of the nationalist right, counterposing nationalism to globalism, expressing the intention to 'take back control' of their countries with slogans such as 'America first' and 'Make America great again'[8] (Brazil's Bolsonaro, for instance, has copied these exact slogans); reversing decades, as they see it, of national decline and humiliation. They are against multilateralism of all kinds, and seek to tear down the institutions of the liberal world order and reverse the trend towards ever-greater interdependence. Some of their strategists, such as chief executive of Trump's 2016 presidential campaign and White House adviser until August 2017 Steve Bannon, describe themselves as economic nationalists; they oppose globalisation and want to break up global production chains, advocate withdrawing from multilateral trade agreements, and seek a halt to immigration.[9]

Secondly, they are authoritarian in their values and attitudes. They oppose pluralism, diversity, and multiculturalism. They favour a national community which is homogeneous both ethnically and culturally. They are ethnic and cultural nationalists, and this makes them hostile to institutions of liberal democracy, such as an independent judiciary and a free press, which provide checks and balances on power, and protection for minorities. They are in favour of democracy, but an illiberal rather than a liberal democracy, in which power is centralised in the hands of a powerful executive leader who can directly implement the 'will of the people'. They incline to forms of plebiscitary democracy, such as referendums, rather than representative democracy.

Thirdly, they are populist because their leaders use the rhetoric of populism; pitching 'the people' against 'the elites', claiming that they, rather than supposed remote liberal cosmopolitan elites, represent the people. These elites include all the mainstream parties of the centre right and the centre left that have governed Western democracies for the past seventy years. Such populism has a long history. Margaret Canovan has argued there has always been a potential for it in Western liberal democracies because of the structural conflict between the legal and constitutional order favoured by liberalism to curb arbitrary power, and the popular sovereignty celebrated by democracy, which is intolerant of opposition.[10] Similarly, Ernesto Laclau and Chantal Mouffe have pointed out that all forms of popular-democratic politics are constructed around counterposing the people to the interests that control the state.[11]

In the 1980s, Stuart Hall used the term 'authoritarian populism' to describe Thatcherism.[12] He was influenced by both Laclau's work on ideology and Nicos Poulantzas's work on authoritarian statism. By authoritarian statism Poulantzas meant the intensification of state control over economic life, combined with a radical decline of the institutions of political democracy and the curtailment of formal liberties.[13] Hall argued that what the idea of authoritarian statism left out was 'the steady and unremitting set of operations designed to bind or construct a popular consent to these new forms of statist authoritarianism'.[14] This is what Thatcherism supplied. Thatcher placed herself with the people against the state, claiming she would fight to liberate them from the vested interests (which Poulantzas called 'the power bloc') that controlled the state. In their populist discourse, Thatcher and her allies counterposed bureaucracy, social democracy and creeping collectivism to possessive individualism, personal initiative and freedom. Thatcher saw her mission as wielding the authority of the state to wrest control of government from those interests, in order to protect the freedoms of the people. The state had to be strong to break the resistance of collectivism and the labour movement, and liberate the economy. This was the free economy and the strong state. Just as Stuart Hall recognised that the authoritarian populism of Thatcherism was a new kind of Toryism in the UK, so we need to understand the new authoritarian populism of the present era as a new form of politics of the nationalist right, which has the capacity to create new parties and new coalitions, and reshape existing ones.

The leaders of these new movements are an elite contesting established elites. They are now a presence in almost every major Western democracy, and their most recent successes include the election of Donald Trump in 2016, the Brexit victory in the UK's referendum of the same year, the formation in Italy of a governing coalition between the Five Star Movement and the League in 2018, the entry of the Alternative für Deutschland (AfD) into the German Bundestag in 2017, the 34 per cent of the vote achieved by Marine Le Pen in the 2017 French presidential elections, and the reappearance of the Spanish far right in the shape of Vox.

Who is responsible for the global rise of this new hard-right insurgency? Part of the blame lies with the failure of progressive politics and the parties that have dominated for so long. Trump's success, for example, came from his ability to tap a wellspring of anxieties, frustrations and legitimate grievances to which the leaders of the mainstream parties, both Republican and Democrat, had no compelling answers. The centre left has gradually embraced a technocratic liberalism which does little to challenge the assumptions of the reshaped international market order that emerged from the ideological battles of the 1970s and 1980s, and whose emergence led to a sharp rise in inequality and the internal fracturing of societies into winners and losers from globalisation. Francesco Ronchi has argued that what we now face is not primarily an attack on liberal democracy from without, but the implosion of liberal democracy from within.[15] Liberals became so entranced by technocratic administration that they readily embraced the depoliticisation and marketisation of huge swathes of public policy. Democracy was hollowed out, and progressives forgot how to articulate a vision of community. Labour MP Jon Cruddas describes this as a loss of ethical grip,[16] while Michael Sandel points to the unwillingness of progressives to engage in substantive moral argument.[17]

FINANCIAL CRASH

All these criticisms have some validity, but we also need to consider the wider context. Most, although not all, of these nationalist right insurgencies were also active in the 1990s and early 2000s. What has given them such traction more recently are the events that followed the financial crash of 2008. This puncturing of the boom ushered in a period without parallel in the Western capitalist economy since 1945. The failure of the economy to bounce back as it had done after every earlier recession meant a period of very slow recovery and grinding austerity, accompanied by exceptional economic policy interventions, including quantitative easing and zero interest rates. Quantitative easing involves central banks injecting money directly into the economy to stimulate demand and investment. It supports asset prices and redistributes wealth to asset-holders. Zero interest rates also stimulate the economy, and protect corporate balance sheets by keeping the cost of borrowing low. In 2018, the Western economies began to show some signs at last of a real recovery, but it remains too early to be certain that this will last. There are already ominous warnings from many credible sources, including the Bank of International Settlements, the Organisation for Economic Cooperation and Development and the International Monetary Fund, that with a continuing savings glut, high levels of unsecured debt, and continuing reckless behaviour by some market traders, the possibilities of another major financial crisis and even a global depression are very real. As a minimum, the continuing uncertainties, not least those provoked by trade tensions between the US and China and the EU in particular, make the present pronounced slowdown in the world economy likely to continue.

This is one of the main reasons why liberal democracy appears to be imploding. The liberal international capitalist order on which it has been based for the entire post-war period is under huge strain. No parties of the liberal centre, whether centre left or centre right, have yet developed policies that can resist the storm which is engulfing them. These parties were once successful at delivering prosperity and security. Their failure to do so since the 2008 crash has created the opportunity for new insurgencies, of the left as well as the right. Another major financial crisis would be devastating for the stability of many liberal democracies. The new nationalist right is well aware of this. It thrives on chaos and collapse.

Most of the new populism that has emerged has been on the nationalist right, and authoritarian. But not all – examples of left populism include Syriza in Greece, Podemos in Spain, Bernie Sanders in the US and Corbynism in the UK. Recovering the radicalism of the progressive project requires the left to create its own version of the popular-democratic, as Mouffe has argued.[18] There is a risk, however, that a left populism might itself become a form of authoritarian populism seeking to reshape the state in illiberal ways to consolidate its hold on power, as has already happened in parts of Latin America. Nevertheless, populist rhetoric, counterposing the people to the powerful, is an essential means of constructing any new form of progressive coalition. A political movement seeking radical change must define its friends and its enemies; what it is for, but also what – and who – it is against. Leaders of successful progressive coalitions have always done this.

A PLURAL LEFT

We certainly need a new moral vision and a new readiness to engage in moral argument and political persuasion. But we also need a new political economy which can empower local communities, and most important of all, we need to find a new way of doing politics, one which is both pluralist and inclusive. Such a project may be advanced by collaboration among many different political parties and movements – liberal, green, social democratic and socialist. Such coalitions are much easier to build under a proportional representation electoral system, but in the UK we do not have such a system. Here, a progressive coalition can only be achieved by changing the tribal and sectarian culture of the Labour Party. This is a huge task, but a necessary one. We need to abandon the idea that one tradition of progressive thought has all the answers.[19] Were we to successfully shift this paradigm, electoral competition between parties would remain, but alongside a willingness to cooperate in pursuit of common ends.

We need both an openness to new policy ideas such as universal basic income and shortening the working week, and an openness to recognising past mistakes, for example the centralised administration of public-sector industries and services. We need to be confident enough in our own ideas to be able to draw on a variety of different intellectual traditions, including, when they have something useful to contribute, the work of serious thinkers of the right. We must engage with people from a wider range of communities and backgrounds and from many different countries, learning from their experience of putting progressive ideas into action. We need to reject false polarisations between nativists and cosmopolitans; we can be citizens of the world and at the same time citizens of particular nations, cities and communities. Many on the left find it easy enough to see Scottish nationalism as a broadly progressive civic-nationalist force, but harder to feel the same about English nationalism. But there is a long progressive tradition in English nationalism too, as John Denham and Michael Kenny have reminded us.[20] We need to be concerned with issues of place and identity, as well as with international cooperation and global networks, and this means giving greater priority to communities, families and households than to the profit and loss calculations of faceless state and corporate bureaucracies.

We live in complex post-industrial economies and multicultural societies. Many old certainties and landmarks have already disappeared, and others are doing so at an increasing pace. We have to live with wide disparities in opinion, interests, and knowledge. In these circumstances, to be 'open' is necessary, but this should not be at the expense of the core principles that any progressive politics must uphold. Fawcett puts it well when he cites the period after 1945 as an era when a frame of politics was established in which the gap between avowed aims and actual achievements became measurable, discussable in practical terms, and to a degree closeable.[21] It is that frame that the insurgents of the right most want to tear down.

A FOUR-POINT PLAN

In these circumstances, there are four clear policy priorities for the beginnings of any such plural left.

The first is an open multilateral international order. The creation of such an order under US leadership following the devastation wrought by the Second World War was assisted by the British Labour government after 1945. This order had many shortcomings, but it provided a framework for post-war prosperity and international co-operation. It ran into severe difficulties in the 1970s, following the demise of the Bretton Woods system, and was reconstructed in the 1980s and the 1990s after the collapse of communism. Now it is under challenge again, especially since the 2008 financial crash, and urgently needs a major reconstruction. Authoritarian populists want to see the international order and its institutions abolished, and the world revert to the rule of great powers and regional blocs. If that is to be avoided a new international order must be built, which goes beyond the Western-centric order of the past and fully involves the rising powers of Asia, Africa and South America in determining the rules that should govern this order. If we fail to maintain multilateral institutions, imperfect although all of them are, we risk a return to economic nationalism and military adventurism.

The second priority is an inclusive and sustainable economy. We must abandon the pursuit of economic growth at any cost and the single-minded maximisation of shareholder value. Instead, we need a political economy which safeguards the biosphere as its top priority and maximises value for all stakeholders, particularly domestic households and local economies, and rebalances the economy in their favour. We cannot do any of this without strengthening the state's capacity to make possible a more decentralised, egalitarian and – genuinely – sharing economy.

The third priority is a remodelled welfare state, founded on policies that can provide both security and autonomy for all citizens. There are many creative ideas for how to revive and reformulate the idea of democratic citizenship that lay at the heart of the universal welfare states that were among the great progressive achievements of the last century. We need to draw liberally upon these ideas.[22]

The fourth priority is a renewed democracy. Much was achieved in the hundred years since women won the vote, but much still remains to be done. The quest for equal citizenship targeting the many forms of discrimination, disadvantage and abuse that exist remains a central progressive aim. We need to find ways to decentralise power to achieve local accountability and participation. And to be constantly vigilant about the many threats, some old, some new, to the rule of law, media plurality, and our freedoms of association and speech.

A POLITICS FROM BELOW

Both liberals and progressives need to recover their voice and their moral compass; to formulate a politics based once again on ethical principles and a conception of the common good. There are different ways of doing this. As a candidate, French President Emmanuel Macron promised to be a politician who would challenge the tide of authoritarian populism with an 'offensive liberalism'.[23] Initially he succeeded in mobilising many French voters against the Front National and boasted he would take the fight to authoritarian populists across Europe. But as president, Macron quickly became aloof, remote and out of touch, part of the very elite he had promised to overthrow. This sparked a renewed populist revolt, this time against him, and uniting elements of right and left, in the form of the *gilets jaunes* protests.

Macron's instinct that progressives needed to go on the offensive was right, but he failed to understand that we no longer live in a time when technocracy suffices. There needs to be a new politics of passion and commitment and belief, and it must come from below. There can be no certainty this will succeed. But to refuse to engage in the debate and the struggle against the nationalist right would be to guarantee the failure of the progressive project. One immediate, and achievable, objective is to develop common sense public-good policies, improving the lives of citizens in our localities. Giving priority to the foundational or everyday economy,[24] as has been done in Preston,[25] for example, can involve citizens once again in their local communities and the decisions which shape them. Progressives have huge historical resources on which to draw, but we need to rediscover the energy that comes from a politics from below. The greatest strength of the authoritarian populists is that they connect directly with popular feelings and concerns. It is why there is so much energy in some of these movements. Progressives need to become insurgents too.

As democracy campaigner Anthony Barnett has argued, the old order is broken and cannot simply be patched up.[26] The Brexit morass is the surest sign of this. We do not all have to unite under the same banner, but we do need to co-operate and learn from one another. A plural left is not an impossible dream. It is something we urgently need, to combat the dangers we face. Corbynism is an insurgency from below that was unexpected, but which brought back new life and purpose to Labour, in particular through the trebling in size of the party's membership. It has created spaces for new and old radical ideas to reshape the Labour mainstream. A symbol of this creative energy at its best has become The World Transformed festival, which now runs alongside the main Labour Party conference each year.

Since 2015, Corbynism has been in the ascendancy ideologically and organisationally in the British labour movement, and it registered a significant electoral advance at the 2017 general election. But Jeremy Corbyn's Labour Party is not yet ready for power; it still has much to do to construct the kind of broad-based national coalition and progressive platform that swept Labour to power in 1945, 1966 and 1997. The manifesto the party adopted in 2017 was a very good start. It contained policies and pledges which commanded support across the Labour Party and among voters. It aimed at addressing the many imbalances of power in British economy and society. Labour under Corbyn is steadily building a platform for domestic reform which has the potential to tap into a broader consensus on the progressive left that supports this kind of ambition, inside and outside of Labour. The 2018 report from the Commission on Economic Justice of the Institute for Public Policy Research (IPPR) titled 'Prosperity and justice: A plan for the new economy' is an example of the breadth of this consensus.[27] Left economic ideas and politics are once again in the ascendant, despite the quagmire of Brexit. Where Corbyn's Labour Party has been much weaker is in developing the idea of a plural and open left. The inability to deal effectively with antisemitism within Labour, the failure to end the civil war in Labour's ranks, the tendency to suppress differences over Brexit – all this means that Labour is currently perceived by many voters as a divided party.

Part of the reason for this lies in the continuing strength of sectarian politics on the British left, and the desire of many on both sides of Labour's civil war to fight it to a finish, driving one wing or the other out of the Labour Party permanently. Angela Rayner's call for a party with 'all shades of red' received volleys of abuse,[28] yet a party that does not contain every shade of red and which cannot unite behind an inclusive and hegemonic leadership will not be able to project the kind of confidence and purpose to the electorate that are necessary to win elections. The Corbyn turn in Labour politics contains the possibility of a left populism, and has created the opportunity for a watershed moment in British politics: the election of a radical Labour government that might rank with Attlee's. But for this to become a reality, Corbyn's Labour must build the kind of progressive coalition that the movement under Attlee, Wilson and Blair succeeded in doing. It needs political imagination and political courage to achieve this. The Corbyn leadership has set the party in a new direction, but it urgently needs both a strategy and the political will to build this plural left that can carry Labour into power, and defeat the challenge of the nationalist right.

NOTES

1. Economist Intelligence Unit, 'Democracy Index 2018', www.eiu.com.
2. *Ibid.*
3. Francis Fukuyama, 'The end of history', *The National Interest*, Vol. 16, 1989, pp3-18.
4. Edmund Fawcett, 'The hard right and its threats to democratic liberalism', Open Democracy, 7 April 2018.
5. Tjiotske Akkerman, 'Anti-immigration parties and the defence of liberal values: The exceptional case of the List Pim Fortuyn', *Journal of Political Ideologies,* Vol. 10, No. 3, 2005, pp337-54.
6. Roger Eatwell and Matthew Goodwin, *National Populism: The Revolt Against Liberal Democracy*, Penguin: London, 2018.
7. Pippa Norris and Ron Adelman, *Cultural Backlash: Trump, Brexit, and Authoritarian Populism*, Cambridge University Press: Cambridge, 2019.
8. 'America first' has been used by US politicians from Woodrow Wilson to Pat Buchanan. In the 1930s, the America First Committee campaigned against US involvement in the Second World War.
9. For an analysis of Trump's economic views, see Charlie Laderman and Brendan Simms, *Donald Trump: The Making of a World View*, Endeavour Press: London, 2017.
10. Margaret Canovan, *The People*, Polity: Cambridge, 2005.
11. Ernesto Laclau and Chantal Mouffe, *Hegemony and Socialist Strategy*, Verso: London, 1985.
12. Stuart Hall, *The Hard Road to Renewal: Thatcherism and the Crisis of the Left*, Verso: London, 1988.
13. *Ibid*, p.126.
14. *Ibid*, p.127.

15. Francesco Ronchi, 'Liberals, Year Zero', Open Democracy, 22 May 2018.

16. Jon Cruddas, 'Response to Michael Sandel', Open Democracy, 17 May 2018.

17. Michael Sandel, 'Populism, Trump and the future of democracy', Open Democracy, 9 April 2018.

18. Mouffe, *For a Left Populism*, Verso: London, 2018.

19. See for example Neal Lawson, 'Beyond monopoly socialism', Compass, Thinkpiece 94, March 2018.

20. Michael Kenny, *The Politics of English Nationhood*, Oxford University Press: Oxford, 2014; John Denham, 'A New Progressive Patriotism', *Political Quarterly*, Vol. 88, No. 1, January 2017, pp97-105.

21. Fawcett 2018.

22. See, for example, Lawson, '45° Change: Transforming society from below and above', Compass, February 2019.

23. Benjamin Tallis, 'Offensive liberalism: Emmanuel Macron and the new European politics', Open Democracy, 25 May 2018.

24. Rachel Reeves, 'The everyday economy', www.scribd.com, 2018.

25. Aditya Chakrabortty, 'In 2011 Preston hit rock bottom. Then it took back control', *The Guardian*, 31 January 2018.

26. Anthony Barnett, 'I am not a liberal, but if I have to get into bed with them I will', Open Democracy, 10 May 2018.

27. IPPR, *Prosperity and Justice: A Plan for the New Economy*, Polity: Cambridge, 2018.

28. @AngelaRayner, 3 March 2019.

A Tale of Two Crises

Phil Burton-Cartledge

The Labour Party is in crisis. There are people shaking their heads at the party's antisemitism war,[1] with some regarding it as irrefutable proof of an institutional culture of anti-Jewish racism. Such claims are far from uncontested, as the issue now doubles as a factional marker, with views on the matter tending to line up along pro- and anti-Corbyn lines. Nevertheless, the matter is a serious one, with the party's deputy leader, Tom Watson, having branded it a symptom of 'a crisis of the party's soul'.[2] He is right. There is a struggle going on for the party, but it is expressing itself in two parallel and intertwined crises: a crisis of recomposition for one of its wings, and a crisis of decomposition for the other. Each has different roots, involves different forces, networks and patterns of class fractions within Labour, and both have their cumulative effects.

This is a tale of not one crisis, but two.

THREE WAVES OF CORBYNISM

There have been three waves of Corbynism. The first broke over the Labour Party with the 2015 leadership election. Up until the entry of Jeremy Corbyn into the race, it was all set to be a rather staid affair. Six candidates initially presented themselves to the selectorate but this quickly fell to three, as Mary Creagh, Tristram Hunt and Chuka Umunna had all dropped out by early June, leaving the field to Andy Burnham, Yvette Cooper, and Liz Kendall. Politically there were differences of nuance, but all offered a similar diagnosis of why Labour under Ed Miliband had lost the 2015 election: there was not enough hope, there was disconnect, there was no appeal to aspiration.[3] The solutions offered tended toward the technocratic, and involved conceding the argument around the deficit to the Conservatives. That is, either agreeing that Labour had spent too much money prior to the 2008 crash, and/or accepting the 'necessity' of David Cameron's and George Osborne's austerity programme – an acceptance that had been implicit in Miliband's criticism of the coalition government for cutting 'too far and too fast'.[4] When Corbyn announced his candidacy and secured his place on the leadership ballot, his anti-austerity message resonated with a membership accustomed to, but resentful of, sacrificing values for perceived electoral expediency; and with people outside Labour who saw his pitch as an opportunity to reassert the primacy of a left-wing anti-austerity politics free of the compromises of previous Labour leaders – and their would-be successors. As Seumas Milne, now Corbyn's chief adviser, noted at the time,[5] the party's membership and registered supporters tripled in number over the course of campaign – mostly to vote for Corbyn and against this existing fiscal conservatism.

The second wave of Corbynism took place in the aftermath of the EU referendum in June 2016. There was a real risk of a split in the Labour Party when virtually the entire front bench resigned in protest against Corbyn's leadership. Corbyn was held to have failed to mobilise enough Labour supporters behind the Remain campaign, which, it was argued by those resigning and others, demonstrated his unsuitability to lead the party into a general election.[6] This episode culminated in a vote of no confidence in Corbyn being overwhelmingly passed by the Parliamentary Labour Party on 28 June, but even this failed to dislodge him. Instead, for the second successive summer, there was a leadership election, and Labour's divisions dominated the political headlines as anti-Corbyn forces in the party cohered around the leadership challenge of Owen Smith. All that this achieved, from the standpoint of the party's internal balance of forces, was a second surge of new members – who joined mainly to vote in defence of Corbyn's leadership – and a weakening of the authority of the Parliamentary Labour Party, coupled with an assertion of the sovereignty of the party membership.

The new members from the 2015 and 2016 campaigns, who now constitute the largest bloc of Labour's membership, may be grouped into two types. First, as described by Alex Nunns in his 2018 book about Corbyn's rise, *The Candidate*,[7] there were the networks of existing activists around the labour movement and other traditional left-wing campaigns and causes. The second grouping was equally as important: those who were interested in but otherwise new to party politics, and those who had previously supported Labour but had felt pushed away by the Blair-Brown years. These members tended to be atomised socially but linked up digitally, and effectively entered the party as a mass of individuals inspired by the politics of the leadership campaign. The arrival of this second type was connected to a wider process of political recomposition that had taken place in British politics over the course of the previous decade, which had seen the rise and fall of the Liberal Democrats, the British National Party, the UK Independence Party (UKIP), the Green Party and, from summer 2014 onwards, a surge in support for the Scottish National Party (SNP).[8] In the case of the SNP and Labour, the growth in their support was related to the working-through of significant changes to the political economy of class in the UK. Drawing on the work of Michael Hardt and Antonio Negri,[9] we can say that this transformation was driven by a growing dominance of networked, socialised, affective and immaterial labour and culture among the working class.[10] Labour, via Corbynism, was speaking to this class fraction in the language of anti-austerity, housing, jobs, and hope. Despite its roots in the statist Alternative Economic Strategy of 1970s and 1980s Bennism,[11] Corbynism proved resonant in intersecting with and appealing to contemporary subaltern class positions. Corbynism thus provided an entry point into party politics for a new mass of people.

The third wave of Corbynism accompanied the 2017 general election. While Labour did not win, partly because of the preceding eighteen months of sharp internal struggle in the full media glare, the party polled better than expected precisely because it had a programme that spoke to the concerns of affective and immaterial labour, and it was able to mobilise its mass strength through digital networks and the social weight of the party itself. Having a party member in practically every social circle, every friendship group, every workplace in England and Wales proved the most effective way of countering the fear-mongering and divide-and-rule politics of the Conservative Party's campaign and the Tory-supporting editorial offices of the right-wing press. The Labour vote materialised to a far lesser extent in Scotland because the SNP had managed to speak to and politically monopolise a similar constituency in the lead-up to the 2014 independence referendum, and retain it afterwards. In response, Labour in Scotland's 2017 general election campaign placed little emphasis on contesting for this rising constituency and focused instead on capturing unionist votes[12] – which tend to come from social layers that lie outside networked/socialised workers.

The 2017 general election enabled Corbynism to expand and draw behind it thirteen million voters – 1997 aside, the highest number of absolute votes Labour has polled since 1966. For a time, this closed down questions about Corbyn's leadership and electoral viability to make his position unassailable.

IT'S MY PARTY

The influx of large numbers of new members brought with it its own challenges for Labour; what might be called a crisis of political recomposition. The structure of the party is unwelcoming and bewildering to the uninitiated, with a tendency for MPs and local government party cliques to actively block and hinder the participation of new members.[13] Partly as a result of this, most Corbyn supporters remain inactive – at least when it comes to participating in the party's official structures. In my own constituency Labour Party, Stoke Central, there are 500 members, but only a small fraction attend constituency meetings or branch meetings, or are involved in regular campaigning. Far less than half turned up to Labour's selection meeting[14] for the February 2017 Stoke Central by-election. Had more new members done so, it is quite possible that Allison Gardner, the overtly pro-Corbyn candidate on the shortlist, would have won the selection over the eventual victor and (at the time of writing) sitting MP, Gareth Snell. Labour's effort during this crucial by-election had to rely heavily on activists travelling in from outside the constituency to carry out the bulk of the campaigning. Of course, some new members have become more involved, and for a number of them, tramping the streets and steep driveways of Stoke Central's by-election canvassing was a dress rehearsal for the general election campaign to come a few months later, but, as an overall proportion of the Corbyn surge, 'activist Corbynism' is small. Where newer members tend to contribute most is as advocates for Labour outside formalised activism and – much to the disappointment of the Labour right – as reliable voters for Corbyn-supporting candidates in the party's internal elections.

The question, then, for anyone sympathetic to the Corbyn project is how to move the project's supporters from the status of 'inactive activists' to becoming more of an active, participating presence. In the 2017 election, Momentum proved useful in getting mainly new, and often young, members to target seats and campaign. This was a crucial factor in overwhelming the meagre forces that local Conservative Associations mobilised in response. But the promise of Momentum as a vehicle for a different way of doing politics – what the political scientists patronisingly term 'unconventional politics' – or for the community politics of re-engagement, is yet to be fulfilled. An obvious way forward would be if Momentum were to get more involved in (but not take over, unlike the past practice of sundry Trotskyist groups) existing local campaigns. In Stoke, for example, Momentum activists, alongside other Labour members, have actively participated in a community campaign against council plans to build 1,300 houses on one of the city's large green spaces.[15]

LEARNING TO LABOUR

Labour Party political education is appalling, for a number of historic reasons. At the time of the party's foundation in the early twentieth century, 'intellectuals' were much more privileged than many of their equivalents are today. Standing above the mass, they could – and did – participate in polite, bourgeois society. They were thus in a position to form close relationships with business, as the purveyors of (financial, legal) professional services; and they tended to see their role as 'improving' the working-class comrades with whom they occasionally rubbed shoulders in the labour movement.

The eyes of these early Labourite intellectuals were fixed on the pragmatic goal of seeking piecemeal improvement, of socialising with and persuading the powers that be to temper the capricious nature of business, and its tendency to drive wages downward. These were Labourism's Establishment insiders, seeking to manage the aspirations that the party drew together, without exploding the system. Their gradualist philosophy left open only narrow spaces for approved intellectual activity, a narrowness that persists today. Thus, contemporary policymaking from Labour-supporting think tanks and similar groups is mainly focused on what Labour should do in government. There is nothing wrong with this, but it can be stultifying, and comes packaged with a lot of assumptions. First and foremost among these is the idea of the essential neutrality of the state: in this view, the state is an apparatus that may be reliably wielded for whatever ends the executive sees fit, and that thus ensures the smooth implementation of the aims of policymakers. Past history has shown on more than one occasion how civil service departments can water down legislation, and the Corbynist movement must think seriously about how to manage this.[16] The other permissible intellectual activity is punditry. Pundits write newspaper articles in support of Labour; popularising party policies and attacking and condemning the Tories, and they may occasionally publish books highlighting a particular injustice.

Labourism as it is performed in these ways is thus simultaneously technical and moral, without these elements being fused into a coherent whole. Inequality is episodically condemned, and technical solutions are proposed for complex problems. Nowhere is the question asked why the injustices and problems keep occurring, and nowhere is there a recognition that Labourism itself is a collective response to the systemic conflict at the heart of British capitalism. This distance between the twin poles of the technical and the moral is no accidental happenstance: it is a product of an outlook conditioned by the lived realities of Labourist intellectuals, wedged in and borne along by the weight of the party's investment in the day-to-day battles of constitutional democracy. Any political-intellectual project that is not immediately tangible and requires a degree of abstract thought, for example understanding neoliberalism as a set of economic policies, a technology of governmentality, and the practice of class rule,[17] is dismissed and disparaged.

The poverty of Labour's political education cannot be understood apart from this studied absence of systemic critique, and the hiving off of intellectual culture into the province of specialists, and away from the practical political work of vote-catching. This segregation has exacerbated Labour's antisemitism crisis because the party lacks an embedded critical and intellectual culture that can resist the blandishments of a so-called 'radical' critique that shares more with conspiracy theory than with anything else. This problem then tends to be reinforced by the 'alt-left' media, which offers hyper-partisan commentary as an alternative to mainstream sources.[18] Too often what it produces is a treatment of power and inequality in terms of shadowy goings-ons, which serves to reinforce a two-dimensional view of the world. Instead of politics being presented as a multi-faceted struggle of a variety of interests pitted against one another, it is reduced to the machinations of bad people determined to get Corbyn and Labour. This feeds into the view that antisemitism is solely a product of anti-Corbyn manoeuvring, which is not helpful when there are obvious and appalling cases of Labour Party members wittingly or unwittingly promoting antisemitic memes, statements and tropes.[19]

Addressing party education could certainly help with this, but the leadership ought to be taking a more active role. There is a growing range of resources that seek to develop the tools of socialist analysis, including the ideas website New Socialist, the films, live radio and podcasts that Novara Media produce, the relaunched *Tribune* magazine and The World Transformed Festival, including its local versions. These and similar projects draw on a shared consciousness that socialist theory and critique are part of a movement that must develop an imagination and capacity to address the difficult problems of the early twenty-first century.[20] But, unfortunately, developments such as these tend to happen outside of the Labour Party's own structures; party activists participate in spite of the party, not because of it.

These are difficult challenges, and they present issues that, unless addressed, could sink Labour in the long term. We cannot be content with a situation in which the majority of Corbyn supporters are mere spectators who will donate a fiver here, or share a social media post there. We cannot leave people's political participation to chance, and we cannot let utter bullshit, conspiracy thinking and antisemitism dressed up as radical chic rule the roost. All these are consequences of Labour ballooning in size, and the left of the party repeatedly defeating the right through sheer weight of numbers. The left's crisis, overall, is one of coping with a mass following that more or less appeared overnight. It is a crisis of getting swamped by new adherents. It is a crisis of recomposition.

NOT ALL RIGHT NOW

Since the summer of 2015, what had been the Labour mainstream – and the Blairist and Brownite right in particular – have not put a single foot 'right'. Disorientated by a left challenge that appeared to come from nowhere, their rearguard actions ever since have consisted of Project Fear-style warnings, sniping at and undermining the leadership, an attempted coup and the failed Owen Smith leadership challenge of 2016, and threats of splits (and a small actual one, in early 2019). They have seized on any difficulty – above all, the ongoing antisemitism scandal, and divisions over a second Brexit referendum – as a means of making factional hay. Theirs has been an entirely negative programme of sabotage, characterised above all by an absence of political critique. MPs and activists on the right of the party had a choice: their opposition could have taken a more constructive character, but it has not. The Labour right has collectively chosen to be entirely oppositional – something more usually associated with the left – and the result has been their decline, decomposition and disintegration.

The problem is that their social base, both in the party and wider society, is disappearing. From its inception, the Labour Party was an alliance between the trade-union movement and elements of the professional and middle classes. This not only shaped Labour's intellectual culture, it also provided a base for the party machinery in the trade unions. For instance, while workplace organisation was stronger and consequently more militant before 1979 than it was after, it was accompanied by a quiescent trade union bureaucracy uninterested in rocking the boat in the wider party. The trade unions did not intervene too overtly or consistently in 'high politics', provided Labour delivered the policies. In return they were expected to pacify and discipline their memberships at the party's behest. The relationship gave trade union leaders and senior officials direct access to ministers and Number Ten, and an input into policy, but led to combustible politics, as the record of the 1974-79 Labour government shows.[21]

Margaret Thatcher's election in 1979 was both a response to this, and a promise to address the problems arising. We know what happened next. In a series of set pieces,[22] the Tories planned and carried out assaults on key sectors of the trade union movement and trussed up what remained afterwards in the restraints of the anti-trade union laws. With effective resistance removed, they were more or less free to demolish Britain's manufacturing base, privatise and fragment nationalised industries, and introduce markets into the public services.

The cultural consequence of this was a dieback of class consciousness, and with it the virtual erasure of collectivist and socialist ideas from popular and media cultures. Fewer organised workplaces meant that fewer workers from the shop and office floor made their way into Labour politics at the local and national levels. The trade unions were still able to make their presence felt bureaucratically within the party, via the conference block vote and patronage, but politically their voice was diminished. As elements of the rising Blairist right made the case for moving away from 'class issues' and the language of old Labour, those not prepared to go along with this were hamstrung by diminishing support for an alternative, and so the party was able to move to the right and become New Labour precisely because of the weakness of the labour movement itself. Upon Tony Blair's election as Labour leader in 1994, the relationship between the party and the unions became increasingly one-sided. The trade unions were expected to rein in industrial action, and in return, the Tories would be defeated.

This was an unsustainable situation. From the late 1990s, the trade unions slowly turned left. General secretaries preaching the virtues of 'partnership' and collaboration with the employers were replaced by a clutch of elected officials collectively dubbed the 'awkward squad' by the press.[23] Politically speaking, they were within the envelope of big-tent trade unionism, but, to greater and lesser degrees, they took more uncompromising stances than their predecessors with regard to members' interests. This firmed up further after Gordon Brown's election defeat and the formation of the Tory-Lib Dem coalition government in 2010. Most affiliated trade unions voted for Ed Miliband in the 2010 Labour leadership contest and later, under pressure from their activists, supported Jeremy Corbyn in 2015 too. Meanwhile, trade union officialdom had been almost entirely replaced by a layer of organisers who were lay members during the New Labour years and who, in some cases, had participated in disputes when Blair and Brown were in office, on some occasions against New Labour's own policies. The overall result was a shift in the sympathies of trade union bureaucracies and their powerful lay committees, making them more sympathetic, first to the soft left, and then to Corbynism. Only the USDAW and Community unions remained largely unaffected.

In class terms, New Labour should be understood as not only the unparalleled dominance of the right within the party, but also its middle-class wing over its labour-movement wing. In the New Labour years, the parliamentary party was the pre-eminent institution whose supremacy was unchallenged, and within that, the diktat of the leader's office was unchallengeable. In that era, elections were the be all and end all, and the role for affiliated unions was less one of taking up members' concerns and more one of trying to dampen them down so as not to inconvenience the government. Office was everything, the movement nothing. Unsurprisingly, many of the party's remaining left did not stick around as, in some important respects, New Labour was indistinguishable from the Tories.

New Labour's renovation of public services and building of new hospitals came with hefty helpings of corporate welfare via the previous Tory government's private finance initiative (PFI) schemes. A combination of targets and internal markets disorganised and bureaucratised the public sector further, while conditionality and 'workfare' were extended in social security. The hated Work Capability Assessment was introduced. Tuition fees and loans replaced the student grant that had previously been the bedrock of the universities' funding. And then there was the aggressively enthusiastic support for, and participation in, George W. Bush's Iraq war. While there were positives from this time, including the Building Schools for the Future programme, new hospitals, Sure

Start centres – the minimum we would surely expect from any Labour government, as distinct from a Conservative one – their value was seriously compromised by their delivery through PFI vehicles. Overall, New Labour reinforced prevailing class relationships by undermining the security and economic power of the very people who put them into government.

New Labour was a symptom of and response to the labour movement's weakness as a result of the defeats suffered under Thatcherism. It used its period in office to disorganise and weaken the labour movement still further, with the ironic consequence that it eventually eroded the right's (and therefore its own) base within the party, as the trade unions became more and more unhappy with the way they were being treated, turning to the left in consequence. New Labour showed nothing less than an open contempt for trade unions, through its attacks on the Fire Brigades' Union's right to organise, its failure to support UNISON and others in their fight to protect public-sector pensions, its undermining of the Communication Workers' Union's opposition to Royal Mail privatisation,[24] and its reneging on the Warwick Agreement between Labour and the trade unions, which had promised unions more money in return for increased policy input. Combined with its suspicion of and animosity towards the bulk of the party membership, this tendency of New Labour gave it many of the characteristics of an elite party-without-a-party that predated the outright break with Labour by a small number of MPs in 2019.

NOT ONE CRISIS BUT TWO

Two leadership elections, multiple internal elections, conference votes, parliamentary selections, control of the party apparatus: all of these, in recent years, have been won by the left. In part, this is because the Labour right have fought the left through administrative means, and they have taken to the media to attack their own party and Jeremy Corbyn in highly personalised terms, fanning the flames of internal difficulties, while studiously avoiding the presentation of an alternative politics. At the same time, Labour MPs resigning the whip, as those who went on to form Change UK did in early 2019, along with a handful of others since June 2017, demoralises and weakens the Labour right that remains. The more the Labour right talks up the party's problems with antisemitism (while remaining more or less silent about anti-black racism and Islamophobia), the more its own supporters quit. Deputy Leader Tom Watson has accompanied his warning[25] of splits in the party with a demand for the 'calling off' of deselections and no-confidence votes. Watson is committed to undoing the present method of electing a leader, and wants instead to see the return of the electoral college – which gave MPs' votes more weight than those of hundreds of ordinary members. He is, of course, well aware that in the absence of a mass membership of 'moderates', the only way the Labour right can come back is by reasserting the parliamentary party's supremacy, and insulating it from the rest of the party. In other words, even now, as the Labour right is the weakest it has been since the party's foundation, all this wing of the party has to offer is another quick organisational fix to avoid the hard job of convincing members and potential members that their way is the best way. And, as a result, it is a fix with no chance of being implemented, because the right is so heavily outnumbered by the left among the current membership.

The Labour Party, then, faces twin crises. These are the problems of recomposition, of building something new; and a crisis of decomposition, of the right in all its variants fraying, dissipating. In other parts of Europe, what has happened to social democratic and labour parties where the right has remained in charge? Electoral defeat, and the party's destruction and disintegration. This process has been called 'Pasokification',[26] after the collapse of Pasok, the main party of the Greek centre left, following its implementation of austerity measures during its 2011-15 coalition with the conservative New Democracy party. The French Socialist Party imploded in office between 2012 and 2017 and has yet to recover, while centre-left parties in the Netherlands, Italy, and Ireland have in recent years suffered the worst electoral collapses in their history. Even the German Social Democrats, once a model for the European left, are now a study in what not to do, as their poll ratings plunge beneath those of the far-right Alternative für Deutschland and the German Greens. The common theme across these European examples is centre-left parties' participation in policies against the interests of their own base – sometimes while in alliance with the centre right. The eruption of Corbynism has meant that the British Labour Party has avoided this fate for now, meanwhile, the Labour right's position is compromised by its history, in the Blair-Brown years and since, of justifying and indeed advocating politics that have patently failed to arrest the precipitous decline of centre-left parties everywhere else in Europe. Why would it be any different for Labour in Britain?

Because the Labour right have not looked to the continent and drawn the appropriate conclusions, their comeback is difficult to conceive. But if, by hook or by crook, they do rally, their behaviour and tin ear to contemporary political developments imperils the continued viability of the Labour Party. More factionalising and besmirching the party's name undermines the unity necessary to win an election and begin addressing the sorts of problems the Labour right would presumably also like to see dealt with – poverty, insecure work, economic regeneration in the regions, to name three. Active sabotage could cost the party an election, or, if Labour forms the next government, block the implementation of a transformative policy agenda. Such folly would simply occasion a third, possibly terminal, crisis for Labour, one everything possible must be done to avoid.

NOTES

1. Phil Burton-Cartledge, 'Institutional antisemitism and factional struggle', www.averypublicsociologist.blogspot.com, 3 March 2019; David Hirsch, *Contemporary Left Antisemitism*, Routledge: Abingdon, 2017; Dave Rich, *The Left's Jewish Problem*, Biteback: London, 2016.
2. Nigel Morris, 'Tom Watson's warning to Jeremy Corbyn: Labour faces a "crisis of the soul"', *iNews*, 24 February 2019.
3. Patrick Wintour, 'Andy Burnham looks back to 1997 as he launches bid to be next Labour leader', *The Guardian*, 13 May 2015.
4. Nigel Morris, 'Miliband turns his fire on the Chancellor for cutting "too far and too fast"', *Independent*, 24 March 2011.
5. Seumas Milne, 'Jeremy Corbyn's surge can be at the heart of a winning coalition', *The Guardian*, 20 August 2015.

6. Daniel Boffey, Claire Phipps and Anushka Asthana, 'Labour in crisis: Shadow ministers resign in protests against Corbyn', *The Guardian*, 26 June 2016.

7. Alex Nunns, *The Candidate: Jeremy Corbyn's Improbable Path to Power*, OR Books: New York, 2018.

8. Burton-Cartledge, 'What is happening to the Labour Party?', www.averypublicsociologist.blogspot.com, 17 July 2016.

9. Michael Hardt and Antonio Negri, *Empire*, Harvard University Press: London, 2000.

10. Burton-Cartledge, 'Class politics and the revenge of the future', in Mark Perryman (ed.), *The Corbyn Effect*, Lawrence and Wishart: London, 2017.

11. Matt Bolton and Frederick Henry Pitts, *Corbynism: A Critical Approach*, Emerald: Bingley, 2018.

12. Atul Hatwal, 'New poll analysis: Watson, Skinner and Flint facing defeat. Cooper, Miliband, Reeves and Rayner on the edge', Labour Uncut, 20 May 2017.

13. For an example, see Joseph Watts, 'Corbynites attack "stitch-up" as Streatham Labour party backs Owen Smith', *Evening Standard*, 29 July 2016.

14. Burton-Cartledge, 'Inside Stoke Central's selection meeting', www.averypublicsociologist.blogspot.com, 27 January 2017.

15. 'Residents holding public meeting over housing development concerns', www.signal80s.co.uk, 8 March 2018.

16. See Christine Berry and Joe Guinan, *People Get Ready!: Preparing for a Corbyn Government*, OR Books: New York, 2019.

17. Pierre Dardot and Christian Laval, *The New Way of the World: On Neoliberal Society*, Verso: London, 2013.

18. Jim Waterson, 'The rise of the alt-left British media', BuzzFeed, 6 May 2017.

19. See the work undertaken by Socialists Against Antisemitism: www.saasuk.org.

20. James Meadway, 'After the cataclysm: Why we must build a new economics from the ground up', Open Democracy, 15 March 2019.

21. Alexander Gallas, *The Thatcherite Offensive: A Neo-Poulantzasian Analysis*, Haymarket: Chicago, 2017.

22. *Ibid.*

23. Andrew Murray, *A New Labour Nightmare: Return of the Awkward Squad*, Verso: London, 2003.

24. For an overview, see William Brown, 'Industrial relations in Britain under New Labour, 1997-2010: A post mortem', *Journal of Industrial Relations*, Vol. 53, No. 3, 2011, pp402-13.

25. Nicola Bartlett and Dan Bloom, 'Tom Watson unleashes savage attack on Labour's direction in Andrew Marr interview', *Daily Mirror*, 24 February 2019.

26. James Doran, 'An antidote to Pasokification', in Mark Perryman (ed.), *The Corbyn Effect*, Lawrence & Wishart: London, 2017.

Acid Corbynism for Beginners

Jeremy Gilbert

The term 'acid Corbynism' emerged in the optimistic afterglow of the 2017 general election. The phrase was coined that summer by my friend, Labour activist Matt Phull,[1] at a festival somewhere in central England. At the time, it was a light-hearted way of describing the particular form of social and cultural 'Corbynism from below' that he felt the Labour left needed to develop.

The term was partly an allusion to Mark Fisher's 'acid communism', the title of the book Mark had been working on when he died in January 2017. Mark's unfinished introduction has recently been published,[2] in which he uses this phrase to denote a broad structure of feeling — utopian, libertarian, egalitarian, anti-capitalist — that seemed to be shared by many different constituencies in the late 1960s and early 1970s, from aristocratic hippies to militant trade unionists. But Matt wasn't particularly familiar with Fisher's work when he came up with 'acid Corbynism'; intrigued as much by the resonant possibilities of 'acid' as a political adjective as by any part of Mark's substantial arguments. So 'acid Corbynism' quickly took on a life of its own that included some engagement with Mark's ideas, but also took in many other sets of related interests and themes: dance culture, radical democracy, non-individualist philosophy.

At that time, the summer of 2017, excited plans were being made for the second The World Transformed[3] event. This is an annual 'festival of ideas' for the pro-Corbyn left, held to coincide with Labour's official annual conference, that has since developed into a growing national movement for radical political education. The 'acid Corbynism' idea was picked up enthusiastically by the organisers, who invited me to convene a discussion of its possible implications.

The first person I contacted to take part was Keir Milburn,[4] an active member of libertarian communist group Plan C.[5] Plan C's recent experiments in convening radical 'consciousness-raising' groups had constituted an attempt to learn directly from the women's liberation movement of the 1960s and early 1970s, and had been a direct inspiration for Mark Fisher to re-evaluate his previously dismissive attitude to the radicalism of that period. Keir had in turn been organising 'acid communism'-themed discussions and workshops with his Plan C comrade, Nadia Idle,[6] an experience that he brought to the panel discussion at The World Transformed in Brighton that September. Adding great historical and intellectual depth to that conversation, we recruited Lynne Segal,[7] a veteran of the 1960s women's liberation movement, and the London libertarian socialist milieu in which Jeremy Corbyn had begun his political career. Adam Harper prepared a suitably psychedelic soundtrack for the post-panel party.

The central theme of that conference session was the idea that the counterculture of the late 1960s and early 1970s had not been, as most mainstream commentary (including on the left) generally assumes, an embarrassing diversion from serious politics. Rather, the hippies, commune-dwellers and psychedelic experimentalists had been asking fundamental questions about how we should live together in a technologically advanced society. Those questions have only become more pressing as the decades have passed. Their contemporaries in the Black Power, women's liberation and gay liberation movements may have focused on different issues, but they all shared a commitment to a politics that was radically libertarian, while rejecting the alienating individualism of advanced consumer capitalism in favour of the belief that social life can be simultaneously joyful, empowering and just. The question posed by the idea of 'acid Corbynism' is: what would it mean to take seriously this observation, while attempting to connect it with Corbyn Labour's electoral politics? Many answers were suggested, among the most popular being: it would mean pursuing a cultural policy that supported creativity in all citizens by making everyone less dependent upon waged work in the corporate sector, through universal provision of services and Basic Income. This would stand in marked contrast to the idea that the only aim of cultural policy is to turn our creativity into profits for the 'creative industries'.

The core question addressed by that first panel seems to have intrigued and engaged a fair few people on the emergent pro-Corbyn left. The subsequent series of talks, articles, panels, workshops and interviews that have been held on this subject in different parts of the UK have involved discussion of a huge range of subjects,[8] and a small group of dedicated acid Corbynists has been putting a together podcast series: #ACFM, hosted by Novara Media.[9] Whether the idea will have any serious effects or implications beyond this, we don't yet know. But even to have been able to have these conversations is a remarkable development in itself. Following the great defeats of the 1980s and throughout the Blair-Brown years, the leadership of the Labour Party was explicitly and unequivocally hostile (or at best indifferent) to anything like radical culture: in return, radical culture was largely unimpressed by Labour during the same period. Despite the name, we can't claim any enthusiastic support for acid Corbynism' from the office of the Leader of the Opposition. But the fact that 'acid Corbynism' was launched, and continues to be discussed at events explicitly supported and participated in by both Jeremy and all the key figures in the Labour leadership, marks a remarkable historical shift.

HIGHER CONSCIOUSNESS AND TECHNOLOGIES OF THE SELF

During the 1960s and 1970s, a political sensibility was shared by the psychedelic experimentalists of the counterculture and a number of political radicals. This utopian orientation rejected both the conformism and authoritarianism that characterised much of post-war society, and the crass individualism of consumer culture. It sought to change and raise the consciousness of singular people and the whole society, be that through the creative use of psychedelic chemicals, aesthetic experiments in music and other arts, social and political revolution, or all of the above.

Mark Fisher himself had never had any personal interest in psychedelics or psychedelic culture (like mine, his interest was aesthetic, political, historical and theoretical), but he liked the idea of 'acid' as an adjective, describing an attitude of improvisatory creativity and belief in the possibility of seeing the world differently, in order to improve it, deliberately 'expanding' consciousness through resolutely materialist means.

From this perspective, techniques of self-transformation like yoga and meditation (or even psychedelics, in theory) might have some kind of radical potential if they are connected to a wider culture of questioning capitalist culture and organising politically against it. By the same token, of course, they can just as easily become banal distractions, ways of enabling individuals to cope with ever-intensifying levels of exploitation and alienation, without ever challenging the sources of those problems. These 'technologies of the self',[10] to use Michel Foucault's term, have no inherent political meaning. The question from a political perspective is if and how they can be used to raise political consciousness, challenging entrenched assumptions of capitalist culture, and enable us to overcome our individualism in order to create potent and creative collectivities.

For the women's liberation movement of the early 1970s, the most important 'technology of the self' was probably the 'consciousness-raising group': small groups of women who would meet to discuss all kinds of personal and social issues from a feminist perspective, seeking to liberate themselves from sexist and patriarchal assumptions. This was also the moment when Black Power and the gay liberation movement reached their most intense levels of politicisation, and when the politics of the 'New Left' was at its most influential. What linked together all of their political positions was a rejection both of traditional hierarchies and of any simple individualism. These movements were libertarian, promoting an ideal of freedom, but they understood freedom as something that could only be achieved or experienced collectively.[11]

Mark was interested in reviving the idea of 'consciousness raising', and in theorising the effects of capitalist ideology in terms of a 'depletion of consciousness'. This is a particular way of thinking about the effects of ideology on groups and individuals. 'Ideology' is sometimes understood simply as a form of propaganda, giving us a false impression of the world in order to protect the interests of the powerful elite. Certainly, when we look at the kind of flagrant misrepresentation of the world engaged in by the right-wing press it can seem that this is exactly what happens. But many thinkers have also explored the idea that ideology, and various apparatuses of power (from the state to the church), function not just by feeding us lies, but by affecting our emotional responses[12] in order to make us feel less able to act[13] in the world, less able to think creatively or dynamically.[14] From this perspective, 'raising' consciousness is not just a matter of giving people information about the sources of their oppression, but also one of enabling them to feel personally and collectively powerful enough to challenge it.

There's a fascinating confluence between the idea of 'higher' consciousness that emerges in some of the mystical, yogic and philosophical literature of the twentieth century, and the idea of politically 'raised' consciousness that became so central to 1970s radicalism. Both of these ideas had older antecedents. The idea of raised political consciousness had its roots in the Marxist idea of 'class consciousness', whereby workers come to realise that their shared interests as workers are more significant than their private interests as individuals,[15] or the cultural differences they may have with other workers. The mystical idea of 'higher' ('elevated', 'universal', or 'cosmic') consciousness has its roots in Vedic and Buddhist ideas that the individual self is an illusion. Escape from that illusion – realisation that the self is only an incidental element of a wider cosmos – is sometimes referred to as 'enlightenment', but the original Sanskrit and Pali terms might be better translated as 'awoken'. Maybe it's not such a coincidence that 'woke' has become a popular radical slang term for raised political consciousness.

PSYCHEDELIC SOCIALISM

Many writers thinking along similar lines have argued that radical politics can take strength and inspiration from cultural forms that promote feelings of collective joy (festivals, disco, etc.), overcoming the alienating individualism of capitalist culture.[16] 'Acid Corbynism' (or if we want to be less politically specific, 'psychedelic socialism') is a useful term on which to hang a wider discussion of the issues. The key question that such phrases invite us to consider is how we might link the politics of the mainstream left to this tradition of utopian experimentalism.

In fact, there are already historical links between them. A crucial feature of the politics of the 1960s New Left was its critique of bureaucratic authoritarianism.[17] The huge corporations of the post-war industrial boom, the paternalistic welfare state of countries like the UK, and the authoritarian institutions of Soviet state socialism were all seen as requiring radical democratic reform or revolutionary overthrow. All of them were criticised for imposing order and uniformity on populations, persuading and compelling citizens to accept a single vision of the good life, be it the 'American Dream' of suburban consumer capitalism, or the Soviet vision of socialism in one country.

To broadly endorse such critiques is not to deny the fantastic achievements of social democracy during this period, including the American 'New Deal' and the foundation of the National Health Service in the UK. But while these institutions offered security to the citizens of the industrialised countries, they provided very little autonomy for those they sought to serve. Women in particular were offered highly restricted roles. For example, the British welfare system was organised on the assumption that every household would be headed by a single bread-winning male, to whom all supplementary benefits would be paid, leaving married women fully dependent on their husbands. In response, the radicals of the New Left called for the democratisation of households, workplaces and public institutions, from schools to the BBC.

It remains to be seen whether the modern version of this critical tradition – which is certainly an important component of the pro-Corbyn movement – can be developed into a much broader project to democratise British institutions, including the Labour Party itself. But history suggests that political and social change on the scale that all Corbyn's supporters seek must be accompanied by extensive cultural innovation. The shape of the new forms of expression that may emerge in the years ahead, nobody can predict. What seems certain, however, is that the struggle against neoliberalism and authoritarian conservatism will require forms of culture and political organisation that are collectivist without being conformist, liberating without simply breaking social ties.[18] What is less certain, for all that it remains a tantalising proposition, is whether somehow techniques of 'consciousness expansion' derived from the mystical and psychedelic traditions might be put to work in the service of progressive politics and radical consciousness-raising.

At the level of concrete political policy, acid Corbynism would favour a twenty-first-century socialism based on principles of co-operation, collaboration and experimentation.[19] A key feature of the 1960s counterculture, psychedelic culture and the 1968 New Left was always the attempt to find new forms of non-hierarchical, experimental, creative collectivity. There is no reason why such principles could not be applied to the design and implementation of public services today.[20] In fact, some very mainstream ideas in social policy have developed around a very similar idea of recognising social-service outcomes as 'co-produced' by both service users and professionals, rather than seeing them as simply retail services sold to customers by 'providers'.[21]

At the same time, the experimentally technophilic aspects of much of the 1960s and 1970s counterculture, and its proximity to the emergent culture of Silicon Valley, have become increasingly prominent in contemporary radical thinking.[22] The desire to escape the routinised cycle of work and consumption that Fordist capitalism had installed was always the driving force behind the counterculture. Today, utopian hopes[23] of a future in which technology is socially deployed, in order to vastly reduce the time most people have to spend at work, and in which the 'sharing economy' might be genuinely shared, have been widely revived. The aspiration is nothing less than a society in which human life is not dictated by the demands of toil. Recently, this desire has begun to crystallise into specific calls for Labour to commit itself to the implementation of a four-day working week as standard across the British economy. If you want a good example of an 'acid Corbynist' political demand, with a sound basis in objective economics, that is it.[24]

FAULTLINES AHEAD

However, it must be said that such aspirations, and the general spirit and mood of the movements associated with them, has had only a limited impact on the Labour Party so far. During the 2017 general election, the innovative apps and platforms deployed by Momentum directly enabled the revolution in grassroots campaigning and social-media political messaging[25] that appealed particularly to new, mostly younger, campaigners and first-time voters. However, to date that experience of grassroots horizontal self-organising has had almost no impact on the formal decision-making processes of the Labour Party. This is despite one of Corbyn's first promises as leader being to renew the democratic systems of the party. Disappointingly, the Labour Party's 2018 Democracy Review[26] focused entirely on procedural issues of the sort that the Bennite left of the late 1970s focused on – the composition of the party's National Executive Committee, mechanisms for electing the party leader, etc. The question of how to encourage, extend, intensify and institutionalise the spirit of self-organised enthusiasm that emerged among so many party members during that historic 2017 election campaign should have been the Review's central question. Instead, it was ignored.

A fear is growing among otherwise Corbyn-supporting Labour members that the leadership is unwilling to reform the centralised culture that we had hoped to leave behind. Having decisively seen off all challenges from the Labour right, the 'leader's office' is already acquiring a reputation for secrecy, authoritarianism and narrow-mindedness that may well be an inevitable product of seeking success within the Westminster system, but which threatens to demoralise the membership base. The Leninist background of some of Corbyn's closest advisers does little to reassure, but it is the apparent desire of the Unite trade union to exercise absolute authority over the party that poses the greatest danger.

In 2018, Parliament voted to allow Heathrow airport to build a third runway: a catastrophic decision from an environmental perspective. It was pressure from Unite that prevented the party leadership from instructing MPs to oppose this measure. Environmentalism still seems to be regarded by trade union leaders, including Unite's general secretary Len McCluskey, as a marginal issue. To them, all that is important is protecting and creating jobs for their members in the same industrial sectors in which they have traditionally been strong. Environmentalism may once have appeared marginal to Labour and the wider trade union movement, but it is hard science that now tells us that every single warning issued by the countercultural green movement since the 1950s has turned out to be correct. And, as one response to Unite's support for Heathrow's expansion put it, there will be 'no jobs on a dead planet'.

Given the centrality of climate change to the concerns of young people today, this situation does not bode well for the future of a united left. There is every chance of Corbyn's coalition fracturing along such lines within the foreseeable future. If this is to be avoided, a measure of good faith and patience will be certainly be required on both sides of the argument.

On the one hand, those of us in the 'acid Corbynist' camp would do well to practise a bit of mindfulness, a bit of appropriately Taoistic relativism. We know we're right. But if we were the leadership of a trade union with over a million members, that had done more than any other institution to enable Labour's leftward turn, including funding the training scheme from which almost every pro-Corbyn MP has been drawn, would we be willing to concede any authority to a bunch of hipsters who mostly only joined the party since 2015? No. 'Corbynism from below' will have to be built from below, patiently, by campaigning, debating and theorising together for longer than a couple of years, before we can expect the empowered membership really to become equal partners with the century-old trade-union bureaucracy. On the other hand, sooner or later both the trade-union bureaucracy and the party leadership will have to accept, if any real progress is to be made, that real resources and real autonomy must be conceded to the membership. Otherwise, any talk of Labour as a 'social movement' will always ring utterly hollow.

RAISING CONSCIOUSNESS

The final element of praxis to consider here is one that can only be discussed speculatively, but which has enormous potential implications for the future of left politics. Mark Fisher's interest in the idea of a politics of consciousness was directly inspired by his engagement with the libertarian communist group Plan C: in particular, Plan C's experiments with the idea of consciousness-raising groups as a useful form of radical politics.[27] Historically, within the women's movement and then within strands of gay liberation and Black Power, such groups served a number of purposes. Primarily, they acted as vehicles for collective political education, theorisation and analysis, generally raising the levels of understanding of gendered power relations, within the movement and beyond it. At the same time, they served a kind of therapeutic and what we might call a 'super-therapeutic' function, enabling participants both to overcome their sense of personal alienation and disenfranchisement, and to feel increasingly empowered to engage with a patriarchal society on their own terms – by which I mean terms set by the movement and its demands, not simply the personal 'terms' of each individual woman.

This latter point is crucial, and it indicates something about what any form of progressive 'consciousness-raising' would have to involve today. Consciousness-raising has always meant coming to an understanding that one's 'personal' problems are in fact not individual, discrete, private elements of experience at all. Rather, such problems come to be understood as the result of large-scale social and historical processes; and individuals come to recognise that the solution to them cannot be found through individual actions of any kind, but only through solidarity and creative collaboration with others with whom one shares material interests. It is always, on some level, the effects of individualism that consciousness-raising seeks to overcome. By 'individualism', I mean not just casual selfishness, but rather a whole ideology and worldview that assumes experience to be fundamentally individual in nature: private before it is public, personal before it is social. This is a demonstrably mistaken assumption, even though it remains fundamental to Anglo-Saxon capitalist culture.[28]

The contradiction in which almost all of us find ourselves living, in this over-developed capitalist world, in the early twenty-first century, is this: many of us are quite aware that the classical bourgeois liberal idea of the 'individual subject' is nonsense. We know that we are all products of social relations; that nobody comes into the world alone; that we are dependent upon a vast network of social relations to meet every one of our material needs; that our bodies are teeming with symbiotes;[29] that our brains are not individual computers isolated behind the firewall of our skulls, but networked galaxies of neurones dependent upon interaction with the rest of the ecosystems we inhabit in order to function; that even our dreams are not merely our own.

But, at the same time, we inhabit a culture whose institutions, laws, economies and social practices have for centuries been organised around the opposite idea, attributing individual responsibility to every action, treating private property as the foundation on which society is built, teaching us that private emotion is the seat of authentic experience. Under these circumstances, learning to function in such a way that the knowledge that nobody is really an in-dividual (i.e., indivisible, independent of social relations) becomes more than just abstract theory is immensely challenging. It is one thing to understand all this in theory. It's another thing entirely to undo all of our individualist conditioning and negotiate a wholly individualist set of social institutions, without finding ourselves being forced to behave like competitive individualists despite ourselves, or simply going crazy. Ultimately, if consciousness-raising has a purpose, it must be to assist us with this work, both at the level of singular subjectivities and in groups on every scale.

TECHNOLOGIES OF NON-SELF

And here is where the whole countercultural panoply of raves, psychedelia, yoga, chi kung, Zen etc. might come back into the picture. Because, in fact, this is precisely what most of these techniques were designed to do. The early scriptures of the Buddhist canon are very clear – the fundamental 'fetter' from which the practice of meditation is supposed to free us is 'self-view': the mistaken belief in the permanence and consistency of our 'individual' selves.[30] Modern yoga derives from tantric practices aimed (like all theistic mysticisms) at seeking unity with the divine, which is different from the Buddhist nirvana of non-existence, but which nonetheless involves an equivalent abolition of the subject's individuality. If the discovery of psychedelic drugs – which can induce experiences comparable to classical mystical experiences,[31] both regularly and repeatedly – has made one major contribution to scientific thought, it is to demonstrate conclusively that such experiences are not supernatural or fictitious, but inherently corporeal, material, and physical.

If the words 'acid' or 'psychedelic' designate anything in phrases like 'acid communism' and 'psychedelic socialism', then it is a set of practices and ideas that are at one and the same time mystical and materialist – a materialist mysticism that acknowledges the complex potentialities of human embodied existence, without tying that recognition to any set of supernatural or theistic beliefs.

SUPER-THERAPEUTIC PRACTICE

Could such technologies of non-self be put to work in the service of radical collectivist politics? This isn't a new question or a new idea, although concrete examples of such ends being achieved in recent years are few and far between. What could such projects even be imagined to involve? Here perhaps we have to distinguish between the therapeutic and super-therapeutic uses of such practices. By 'super-therapeutic' I mean something more than just fixing people up, repairing some of the damage done by daily life under advanced capitalism, such that individuals can get on with their lives. I mean something that might have those effects, but also go beyond them, enabling people to become extraordinarily empowered precisely by enhancing their capacity for productive relationships with others (which capacity is what John Protevi names, following Deleuze and Spinoza, 'joyous affect'[32]).

We can already point to countless examples of yoga or meditation classes being offered cheaply by community facilities, and accessed by hard-working citizens and activists who would find it much more difficult to function productively without them.[33] In general, however, the normal expectation is that the effects of such practices will rarely exceed the merely therapeutic – except in the case of very rare practitioners who can dedicate themselves almost full time to those practices. And such full-time devotion is likely to preclude them from any serious involvement in wider struggles, political work or social innovation.

Of course, we must not dismiss the value to individuals of having forms of therapy that are not more harmful than the problems whose effects they seek to remedy (as many types of therapy, such as relying heavily on anti-depressant drugs, almost certainly are). If people can use yoga or something similar to feel better, instead of getting themselves hooked on tranquillisers, then that's something good. But it is also kind of a waste of a technology as powerful as yoga only to use it in this remedial way, when its purpose is a complete re-engineering of the psycho-physical system that is a person.

One mundane material issue here is time. In a capitalist society, most people survive by selling their time for currency that they can exchange for consumer goods. This is one of Marx's most basic and most perspicacious observations. And Marx is specific that it is not our labour as such that we sell, but our capacity for it: in other words, mainly, our time. (This is why is it always an issue for capitalists to figure out how to extract the most possible actual labour from the labour power that they have purchased – do you whip the workers on the chain gang, or let them play arcade games until they feel like writing some code? At the end of the day, these options are both answers to the same question that the capitalist must ask herself: 'how do I extract actual labour from the labour power that I paid for?'). As long as too many people have to sell too much of their labour power for too little money, simply in order to survive, then they will have to spend too much time at work. Under these circumstances, only specialised professionals will ever have time for a really transformative practice.

At the same time, a related key issue is that of what kinds of social or political practices, configurations, institutions or habits might help to enable these technologies of the non-self to become progressive, rather than regressive, forces. This is a fundamental point. Like almost any technology, these practices might have certain tendential properties, based on their actual measurable physical effects on bodies. But what the wider social or cultural significance of those effects might be will depend entirely on the ways they are used, by whom, to what ends, in what contexts. This applies in more or less the same way whether we are talking about, say, the Linux operating system, or mescaline, or the mindfulness-of-breathing meditation. They can all be used in many different ways, depending on context and intention.

This isn't a new observation: in the US in particular, there are well-established Buddhist communities[34] that explicitly place a radical political project at the core of their understanding of the practice and its social role. To a lesser extent, communities also exist that practise yoga, tantra and Taoism with that perspective.

HEARTS AND SOULS

When efforts are made to bring these technologies of non-self into direct contact with explicit radical politics, there is rarely any real attempt to consider how theoretical insights from one domain might inform the other. There are isolated examples of attempts to bring insights from feminist and postcolonial theory into the practice of yoga,[35] for example, but could we imagine a situation in which a feminist and historical materialist account of exploitation and alienation is brought into conversation with, say, a tantric understanding of energetic flows in the 'subtle' body, in order to develop new forms of physical and/or political practice?

An interesting, rare example of just such a project is Ann Weinstone's 2004 book *Avatar Bodies: A Tantra for Posthumanism*.[36] Weinstone's basic point is that tantra's embrace of radical anti-individualism, corporeal materialism/non-dualism (the belief that body and spirit are the same thing on some level, if not all levels), and the positive affects of pleasure and desire as potential vectors of liberation, gives it a strong affinity with strands of post-humanism, radical politics and critical theory.

One direction in which such thinking could lead might be to use ideas like Weinstone's as a way of illuminating what possibilities might exist for imagining how good human life could be, and on what terms. After all, Margaret Thatcher had a notoriously clear vision of what kind of people her legislation was intended to produce (and what kind it was intended to punish). 'Economics are the method: the object is to change the heart and soul', she famously declared.[37] Her objective in privatising public services, cutting public spending, reducing taxes on the rich and undermining the trade unions was to produce a nation of hard-working, aspirational, yet sober and self-disciplined Protestant entrepreneurs.

In contrast, what kind of persons might Corbynism want to help produce? Would it not be people equipped to both navigate and, when required, overcome the complexities of everyday life and be joyful in the fact of their infinite relationality,[38] and to do this as part of local, national, global communities? Wouldn't that be a better guiding principle for our politics than the relentless pursuit of ever-increasing rates of economic growth? Wouldn't this be a good way of orienting debates over whether, and when, and how, to pursue growth at all? And isn't the fact that talking like this makes me sound like a crazy hippy merely a symptom of the political success of Thatcher and her kind? Doesn't overturning her legacy mean, in part, re-admitting such ideas and preoccupations into public discourse?

AGAINST HIPPYPHOBIA

This was the argument I made to Mark Fisher, years ago, when I suggested to him that the 'hippyphobia' that still characterised his attitudes at that time was itself a symptom of 'capitalist realism', the term he had originated to describe the belief that neoliberal capitalism could never really be truly escaped, transcended or defeated.[39] Such hippyphobia has long been a strong element in left attitudes. There are plenty of good reasons for it. The quantity of bullshit – for want of a better term – that is associated with every spiritual and meditative tradition, not to mention psychedelic culture, is more than enough to put off any self-respecting, intellectually alert radical intellectual. But the same might be said of Marxism, if you were only to respond to the worst that has been written, said and done within that tradition. A prudent fear of what Edward Said calls 'orientalism'[40] should certainly inform every encounter between white Westerners and ideas from other places. But the notion that such fear should prevent any form of intense engagement is itself tantamount to ethnic purism. In the end, hippyphobia is a lazy habit, exhibiting none of the critical objectivity that it claims to be defending.

Dismissing out of hand the possibility that practices such as yoga and meditation might have any genuinely transformatory effects on either singular persons or wider groups is a weak gesture. We do not know much about how these technologies work – they have their own models to explain their efficacy, such as Indian and Chinese models of internal energy currents in the physical or 'subtle' body, but these do not map onto anything much that current biophysics is able to identify, verify or quantify. What is evident is that these collections of physical and psychological techniques have a certain potency, the social effects of which depend on their specific modes of usage. So, from a radical political perspective, we might as well try to figure out what we can do with them. They clearly provide useful techniques for treating the debilitating psycho-physical effects of capitalism, including alienation, depression, and anxiety, without resort to dangerous drugs or to forms of psychotherapy that are more deeply intertwined with liberal bourgeois ideology, such as Cognitive Behavioural Therapy and mainstream psychoanalysis. At their best, they may prove genuinely useful in the creation and cultivation of forms of politically effective group behaviour, what I would call 'potent collectivity'.[41]

AFROPSYCHEDELIA AND IDENTITY POLITICS

Some of this thinking can shed interesting light on a key issue in contemporary left debates: the debate over 'identity politics'. The way in which this discussion is normally presented is roughly as follows. On the one hand, there is the classical 'class politics' of the left, which focuses entirely on issues of economic power and distribution and which sees phenomena such as racism and misogyny largely as side effects of capitalism, or as ideological tools used by the capitalist class to sow divisions within the working class. On the other hand, we have 'identity politics', which recognises racism, sexism and heteronormativity as specific forms of oppression that affect people on the basis of their membership of particular identity groups, and which sees any attempt to unify people across those identity groups as tantamount to an intensification of that oppression, to the extent that it tries to marginalise the importance of their specific experiences in the name of some idea of unified class struggle.

One of the many problems with this debate is that it tends to get caught up in an imaginary argument over whether class, race or gender are more important categories than each other, while never quite focusing on the real issue that critiques of 'identity politics' first tried to engage with from the 1980s onwards. That issue was never merely about class versus other categories. It was more importantly about different *ways* of addressing forms of systematic oppression along gendered, raced or other axes. The manner in which these issues were addressed by the radical movements of the

1960s and 1970s was to see them as collective problems to be over-come through collective struggle.

An alternative way of addressing these issues, that became increas-ingly prevalent in the 1980s and 1990s, was to treat them as issues primarily affecting individuals, and to see any attempt to generate collective solutions to them at all as potentially or even inherently oppressive to those individuals. This is essentially a form of radical liberalism, that sees racism, sexism and heteronormativity as prob-lematic, not because of the way that they oppress particular groups of people systematically, but because of the ways that they limit particular individuals from participating fully and without preju-dice in the life of a competitive, market-oriented consumer society. The problem with it is that it ends up treating both oppression and empowerment as essentially things that happen to individuals. From this perspective, personal identity becomes something to be defended like private property. In this context racism, for example, is treated more or less as an intrusion on that private property – to be legislated against at various institutional levels – rather than as a social problem whose solution is the creation of more opportunities for public discussion, debate, and the construction of shared forms of social power.

The antithesis of such a liberal-individualist, privatised form of identity politics would not be a simple reversion to 'class politics',[42] but an approach that sought both to democratise all social rela-tions and to render visible, changeable and questionable the social and provisional nature of all supposed 'identities'. This is not just a hypothetical proposition. A great example of this kind of politics was the position taken by the Gay Liberation Front (GLF) in Britain during the early 1970s. This early campaigning organisation actu-ally *rejected* the UK government report, the Wolfenden Report, that recommended the decriminalisation of homosexual acts between consenting men, precisely because it predicated its arguments on the claim that sex was a private matter. Taking their lead from the women's movement's assertion that 'the personal is political', the GLF argued for a position that sought to make gender and sexuality, and the power relations in which they are always caught up, subjects for open public discussion and questioning, not simply matters of individual privacy. Intriguingly, theirs was an attitude that shares a great deal with the historic Buddhist suspicion of *all* personal identity, and with the psychedelic desire to explore sensation and perception beyond the limits of such individualised selfhood. It was a radical, experimental, collectivist sensibility.

This attitude found another expression in some of the most exciting and lastingly important cultural output of the late 1960s and early 1970s. The intersection of black and anti-colonial liberation politics with countercultural psychedelia gave rise to a range of extraordinary sonic experiments in the work of Alice Coltrane, Miles Davis, Jimi Hendrix, and others including Herbie Hancock, Santana, and Parliament-Funkadelic. This afro-psychedelic aesthetic deeply informed the emergence of disco and electronic 'dance' musics, that themselves became important elements of the culture of gay liberation (and the influence of all these currents persists today as strongly as ever, for example in the work of deep house producers such as Joe Claussell[43]). All such music is notable for the ways in which it uses improvisation, experimental studio recording and a range of other sonic effects to produce work that sounds at the same time incredibly free and incredibly collective. It rarely sounds like just a soloist with a backing band, and it is often characterised by a real democratisation of the different elements of the group (Miles Davis' *On the Corner* remains perhaps the most perfect expression of this tendency – the trumpet of Miles himself almost disappears into the multitudinous miasma which his band becomes, and the effect is astonishing). If we want to know what radical, potent, liberating collectivity feels like, then it's this afro-psychedelic tradition that offers some of the most powerful aesthetic examples.

FREEDOM IS AN ENDLESS MEETING

What is at stake in the idea of a psychedelic socialism is a radically different conception of freedom to the one we have inherited from the bourgeois liberal tradition. Within that tradition, freedom is basically equated with the capacity to own, and dispose of, private property. Freedom is a property of individuals and becomes indivisible from individual property. What's public and collective is thus depicted as inherently oppressive – a fetter on the freedom of the individual. Psychedelic socialism would be one manifestation of a quite contrary tradition, understanding freedom and agency as things that can only be exercised relationally, in the spaces between bodies, as modes of interaction. It would be the creation, constitution and cultivation of spaces of collective creativity, including schools, laboratories, dance-floors, workshops, and gymnasia, which it would seek to create while recognising how hostile capitalism will always be to them.

Of course, 'psychedelic socialism' or 'acid Corbynism' are not the only names for such a politics. We could just as well call it 'radical democracy' or 'libertarian socialism', or even just the 'twenty-first-century left'. But whatever we want to call it, the legacy of the counterculture and the various technologies of non-self that it helped to popularise in the West will need to play a significant role in it, if it is to become a viable political project in the twenty-first century.

ACID CORBYNISM

So what more might this mean in practice? Of course I am not suggesting that everyone should take psychedelic drugs (which are illegal in most countries), or take up yoga, or anything else in particular. Nor am I romanticising the counterculture of the 1960s. However, its failures have become so well-known and so well-documented that it has become easy to forget both that it had some significant positive effects, and that its failures were not only intrinsic to it, but also a result of its political defeat by the New Right and their allies.

The lessons of this history and its consequences should be learned by anyone who wants to see either a revived and successful counter-culture or a successful democratic left. Because the evidence suggests that without a strong, vibrant, popular and strategically successful political left, then any kind of counterculture will just end up being captured by capitalism.

Likewise, it is simply impossible to imagine a successful political challenge to neoliberalism that isn't allied in some ways to a broader culture that rejects neoliberal and bourgeois values more generally. And if that culture isn't going to look something like the counter-culture of the 1970s, then I don't know what it is going to look like.

What it would certainly involve would be an embrace of a number of themes that too often have been kept well outside the mainstream socialist and social-democratic traditions since the early 1980s. For example, as I have already suggested, moves to embrace the four-day week[44] as a concrete political aspiration should be accelerated; it is an easy policy to popularise, and is entirely consistent with the historic aspirations of the labour movement. A whole raft of policies aimed at asserting the public's 'right to the city' should be brought forward and celebrated. Rent controls would be a start, but support for co-operative housing, for community arts, for independent social and cultural venues, for community banking to support such ventures, for creative education for all, should all be part of the picture.

Crucially, there can be no question now about the urgency of the ecological agenda, and of the need to place it at the heart of all attempts to imagine a better society in the twenty-first century. Labour adopting a 'Green New Deal'[45] is the very minimum that we should expect. But this agenda will only move forward if the entire public can be engaged in a multi-level, democratic and open-ended conversation about how we want to manage the environmental crisis, what our priorities are as a society, how we want to live and who we want to be. Labour should aspire to lead that conversation, or at least to do everything in its power to enable it to happen: not just online but on doorsteps, in town halls and community centres, and in our party branches and constituencies.

What would all this actually look like? We're already seeing examples of best practice emerging from the most fertile grassroots of popular Corbynism. Branches and constituency parties with active and imaginative education programmes, which are still sadly too few and far between,[46] have been organising parallel series of events to those meetings dealing with ordinary business, in order to encourage members interested in ideas and debate to participate. Some have launched film screenings, others reading groups. Amongst the most ambitious have been club nights that seamlessly mix dance culture with a style of political discussion entirely different to what Labour is too used to accepting as the only way of doing it.[47]

This kind of activity is neither cosmetic nor supplementary to the 'real' business of the party: across the European left, the whole apparatus of political education – reading groups, lecture series, summer schools – is regarded as central to the very idea of members' and supporters' political participation, and to the cultural life of these parties. The annual The World Transformed (TWT) festival, which runs alongside Labour's formal annual conference, now inspires autonomous local festivals of ideas on similar lines, including in Bradford, Bristol, Derby, Durham, Lewes in East Sussex, Manchester, Southampton, and elsewhere. But such a vital initiative operates on a shoestring, with not nearly enough financial support from the party or trade unions for it to expand to its full potential. A Corbynite Labour and trade union leadership that understood anything much about the nature of social and political change would find significant funding for TWT so that it can become a pathway to a better informed, more participative, more active party, in the process paying back any investment over and over again.

Above all, the joyous, creative, democratic potency of the Labour membership and the entire Labour-supporting public must be allowed to express itself in all of its immanent complexity. Open primaries should be allowed for all candidate selections, to enable the widest plurality of voices to contribute to the relevant debates. Resources should be devoted to experiments with online democracy and deliberation, increasing the involvement of those members who will never have time or inclination to attend meetings. Online consultations over the manifesto is a good start, but unless this process comes to feel very different to members from the type of corporate 'consultations' with which we are all far too familiar, then its potential will be entirely squandered. The members themselves should be enabled and encouraged to debate not just the personalities of their politicians, not just the general shape of policy, but the very nature and purpose of the party: its philosophy, and its political strategy for realising it.

Is 'acid Corbynism' the best name for such an agenda? Maybe – maybe not, it doesn't really matter. Right now, the important thing is to have ideas in circulation and discussed as widely as possible, whatever we decide to call them. 'Corbynism' is perhaps not best understood as an ideology or even a movement at all. As Keir Milburn likes to point out, when we speak about 'acid Corbynism', the 'Corbynism' we refer to is, as much as anything, a historical phenomenon, a specific moment in time. The term designates not a clear political project, nor a sense of undying personal loyalty to Jeremy Corbyn, but a moment of new political possibility: of which Corbyn's election as Labour leader was only one early manifestation.

Can that radical possibility be realised in a creative and dynamic movement to democratise the Labour Party, the labour movement, and British society? If it can, then it's hard to see it happening without Labour expanding its collective consciousness, beyond the limits bequeathed to it by Thatcherism. Socialism in the twenty-first century will have to be at least a little psychedelic, if it is to manifest the future that we need.

NOTES

1. See Matt Phull on Twitter, 'Trade unionist, acid Corbynite, leftist dad', @maphull.
2. Mark Fisher, 'Acid communism', in Darren Ambrose (ed.), *K-Punk: The Collected and Unpublished Writings of Mark Fisher 2004-2016*, Repeater: London, 2018, pp751-73.
3. See www.theworldtransformed.org.
4. See Keir Milburn, *Generation Left*, Polity: Cambridge, 2019.
5. See www.weareplanc.org.
6. See www.notaloneintheworld.com.
7. For Lynne's account of the period, see her autobiography: Lynne Segal, *Making Trouble: Life and Politics*, Verso: London, 2017.
8. For irregular updates, see my 'Acid Corbynism: The story so far', at www.jeremygilbertwriting.wordpress.com.
9. #ACFM, on www.novaramedia.com.
10. Luther H. Martin, Huck Gutman, Patrick H. Hutton (eds), *Technologies of the Self: A Seminar with Michel Foucault*, Tavistock: London, 1988.
11. For an expanded version of this part of my argument, see Jeremy Gilbert, 'Liberalism does not imply democracy', Open Democracy, 26 September 2009.
12. For my own explanation of this, see Gilbert, 'Sharing the pain: The emotional politics of austerity', Open Democracy, 28 January 2011.
13. On this point, see Gilbert, 'Disaffected consent: That post-democratic feeling', *Soundings*, No. 60, Summer 2015, pp29-42.
14. On this point, see We Are Plan C, 'We are all very anxious', www.weareplanc.org, 4 April 2014.

15. See, for example, Georg Lukacs, *History and Class Consciousness: Studies in Marxist Dialectics*, Merlin: London, 1975.

16. For a fairly recent example, see Barbara Ehrenreich, *Dancing in the Streets: A History of Collective Joy*, Granta: London, 2008.

17. See for example Raymond Williams, *The Long Revolution*, Pelican: London, 1965; Tom Hayden, *The Port Huron Statement: The Vision Call of the 1960s Revolution,* Public Affairs: London, 2005. For a post 1960s example of thought in the same tradition, see Rowbotham et al, *Beyond the Fragments: Feminism and the Making of Socialism*, Merlin: London, 1979.

18. For a full explanation of what this might look like, see Gilbert, *Common Ground: Democracy and Collectivity in an Age of Individualism*, Pluto: London, 2013.

19. Gilbert, 'For 21st-century socialism: Two short articles', www.jeremygilbertwriting.wordpress.com, 26 August 2016.

20. Fisher and Gilbert, 'Reclaim modernity: Beyond markets, beyond machines', Compass, October 2014.

21. See, for example, Zoë Gannon and Neal Lawson, 'Co-production: The modernisation of public services by staff and users', Compass, June 2008.

22. Fred Turner, *From Counterculture to Cyberculture*, University of Chicago Press: Chicago, 2006.

23. Nick Srnicek and Alex Williams, *Inventing the Future: Postcapitalism and a World Without Work*, Verso: London, 2016; Aaron Bastani, *Fully Automated Luxury Communism*, Verso: London, 2019.

24. Will Stronge and Aidan Harper (eds), 'The shorter working week: A radical and pragmatic proposal', Autonomy, January 2019.

25. Michael Savage and Alex Hacillo, 'How Jeremy Corbyn turned a youth surge into general election votes', *The Guardian*, 10 June 2017.

26. 'Labour Party Democracy Review', September 2018.

27. See We Are Plan C, 'C is for consciousness raising', www.weareplanc.org, 31 May 2015; and Nadia Idle and Milburn, 'Building acid communism', *Transmediale*, Issue 1, 2018.

28. Gilbert 2013, pp22-49.

29. Bacteria and related organisms that live in our cells, that are not part of them, but without which they cannot fully function.

30. See Bhikkhu Bodhi (ed.), *In the Buddha's Words: An Anthology of Discourses from the Pali Canon*, Wisdom: Somerville, MA, 2005.

31. Hannah Devlin, 'Religious leaders get high on magic mushrooms – for science', *The Guardian*, 8 July 2017.

32. John Protevi, *Political Affect: Connecting the Social and the Somatic*, University of Minnesota Press: Minneapolis, MN, 2009.

33. See, for example, www.kldyoga.org.

34. See, for example, www.dharmanet.org.

35. See, for example, www.decolonizingyoga.com.

36. Ann Weinstone, *Avatar Bodies: A Tantra for Posthumanism*, University of Minnesota Press: Minneapolis, MN, 2004.

37. Quoted in Ronald Butt, 'Mrs Thatcher: The first two years', *Sunday Times*, 3 May 1981.

38. Gilbert 2013, pp111-18.

39. Fisher, *Capitalist Realism: Is There No Alternative?*, Zero: Winchester, 2009.

40. Edward Said, *Orientalism*, Penguin: London, 2003.

41. Gilbert 2013, pp143-71.

42. I am not saying that class is not central to politics – if anything, it is so universally important to all politics that the very notion of 'class politics' is simply oxymoronic. The point is that all politics involves class issues and conflicts between competing class interests, but this does not mean that the issue of class struggle covers or exhausts all political questions.

43. See and listen to www.joaquinjoeclaussell.com.

44. See and support www.4dayweek.co.uk.

45. For background on this idea, see Laurie Laybourn-Langton, 'A Green New Deal could signal a fundamental shift away from neoliberalism', *Red Pepper*, 22 March 2019. For a campaigning initiative supporting Labour to back such a deal, see www.labourgnd.uk.

46. On the necessity of this, see Tom Blackburn, 'Waking up the giant: Political education and the labour movement', New Socialist, 17 June 2018; and James Meadway, 'After the cataclysm: Why we need to build a new economics from the ground up', Open Democracy, 15 March 2019.

47. See, or better still visit, the Chorlton Socialist Club, @ChorltonSC. Read about it and similar ventures in Tom Blackburn, 'Culture and the community', *Tribune*, 5 January 2019.

Building Blocs from Below

Members Not Only

Jess Garland

Political party structures are changing, and the way in which they are highlights a fundamental tension in the nature of participatory democracy. Parties with distinct historical principles and organising ideologies are shifting to adapt to a changed political market; one in which the participants no longer behave in the way they once did. For Labour, a party founded on the idea of popular participation, and committed to bringing the voices of the many into politics, this is a challenge that must be met.

Having attained a larger membership in 2016 than at any point in the last three decades, Labour has talked of reaching a million members. It is not the first time the party has aimed for such a goal. Neil Kinnock, Tony Blair and Gordon Brown all declared the same intention as leader. In fact, the desire for numbers is so pervasive in party culture that the goal of a large membership often goes unquestioned. For what purpose, a million members? Different answers will seem obvious to different people. Are members needed so that the party can amass an army of campaign foot soldiers preparing to secure victory in the next election battle via the expenditure of shoe leather? Are members the answer to the Tories' billionaire backers, funding the party through membership dues, donations and the purchase of commemorative tea towels? Is a larger membership the route to a more diverse pool of candidates for elections? The answer might be all or none of the above. After all, parties need members for a whole range of reasons. But whilst the reasons for a mass membership may be multiple, holding on to a mass of members is increasingly difficult.

It's not just Labour seeking to raise membership numbers. Parties of all stripes are engaged in a process of matching up the reasons they think they want or need members to the reasons members might be attracted to parties. And those reasons, on both sides of that equation, have changed and continue to change. Partisans have changed in their participatory choices. For the past two decades, political participants have been increasingly drawn to individual, direct, single-issue, online and one-off forms of political action; a growing range of participatory repertoires as highlighted by Pippa Norris in her seminal work on the subject, *Democratic Phoenix*.[1] During the same period, parties have changed what they want, and expect, from their partisans. There was a period (associated with the Blair years, but beginning a long time before them) when polling, focus groups and advertising campaigns seemed to be replacing the traditional members' tasks of canvassing and other forms of public campaigning. In recent times, however, the ground campaign has taken on renewed significance: the 2015 general election campaign was launched by Ed Miliband with a plan for four million 'doorstep conversations',[2] while in 2017, Momentum initiated target-seat mass canvassing days.

Of course, over the past decade, social media has also taken an increasingly central role in political campaigns. Though there is significant debate about the influence of digital political advertising, there is no doubt that parties have been waking up to the potential.[3] Reported spend on digital advertising by campaigns rose from 23.9 per cent of all advertising spend in 2015, to 42.8 per cent in 2017, according to the Electoral Commission.[4] And the reported spend on the well-known platforms, to which these figures refer, is only part of the picture – as several investigations have revealed, there is a lot more going on.[5] There is not much doubt that while social media offers a new range of campaigning opportunities, the online campaigning sphere is also heavily overshadowed by murky practices of data harvesting, dark ads and disinformation, which raises questions about the role of online campaigning in democratic contests.

Alongside these various shifts, one of the most significant developments in political parties recently is the recognition of the role of supporters, who do many of the same activities for the party as members, but are not formally signed up. Supporters, that is, non-members who support or identify with the party, are often actively and heavily involved in campaigning. They contribute funds and engage in a range of activity for the party, from delivering leaflets to retweeting. Though party members are far more likely to be engaged in the 'high-intensity' activities like canvassing, supporters, being larger in number, contribute a significant quantity of volunteer labour to party activities.[6] It is a contribution that has been recognised by parties across the board, who are now creating more opportunities to pull these supporters in.

In seeking to attract greater support, many parties across a range of democracies are also extending leadership selection and policy rights to members. The trend towards this democratisation within parties, in particular the expansion of leader and candidate selection, is 'one of the most remarkable and widespread organisational changes in the past two decades'.[7] Some 43 per cent of parties[8] now give party members a direct vote on the election of their leader. Some parties – including Labour – are even using these rights to attract wider support, extending such rights to non-members.

Parties that offer a range of affiliation options beyond traditional membership have been labelled 'multi-speed membership parties'.[9] Multi-speed parties differ from traditional membership parties in creating new affiliation options for supporters whilst also attempting to maintain a traditional membership base. Such parties sometimes also extend traditionally member-only intra-party democratic rights to supporters. The multi-speed way of organising is particularly popular in the UK (perhaps in reaction to steeply declining membership numbers over the last four decades) and most notably in the recent changes within the Labour Party. But Labour has not just dipped a toe in multi-speed organising, it has gone further than most parties, extending significant democratic opportunities beyond the membership to non-member supporters. In doing so, the party has made itself a rare case of 'open plebiscitary intra-party democracy'[10] – involving supporters in intra-party democracy in a way that departs from the idea of the party as a closed organisation with a clear boundary. To date very few of the 'old' parties have made such a change.

Of course, this process of attracting new support and changing the opportunities attached to it is not without difficulties. We might imagine that the reasons parties want to recruit members would bear some correspondence to the tools with which they seek to attract them. For instance, democratic opportunities, leader selections and policy influence are all incentives to attract participants who are interested in democratic opportunities. However, as past experience shows, using plebiscitary opportunities to attract more members does not necessarily lead to an increase in highly active members outside of those particular moments.[11]

CREATING A MULTI-SPEED PARTY

There were two key moments in Labour's move towards more open intra-party democracy. The first began with the initiation of the 'Refounding Labour' review in 2010, which led to the inclusion of party 'supporters' within Clause One of the party rule book.[12] With this change, the clause formalised the role of non-members in helping the party achieve its goals. Clause One changed from simply committing the party to winning elections, to a broader definition of its primary goal, which included a commitment to 'bring together members and supporters who share its values to develop policies', and to 'make communities stronger through collective action'.[13] These changes began the process towards supporters having a vote in leader elections. The second key moment was the ratification in 2014 of the Collins reforms, which replaced the electoral college for leader selections with a One Member One Vote (OMOV) system, which for the first time also included these registered supporters.[14] The new leader election rules gave supporters a vote in the leadership election if they paid three pounds and agreed to a statement in support of the party's aims and values. The new OMOV+ system was used in the election of Jeremy Corbyn as leader and Tom Watson as deputy in 2015 and again to re-elect Corbyn in 2016; OMOV+ has also been used for Scottish Labour leadership elections since 2015, the London mayoral selection from 2015, and the Welsh leadership election in autumn 2018. The continuation of the scheme was set out at the beginning of the party's 2018 Democracy Review publication, and this included a commitment to continuing to give supporters a vote in leadership elections. The pathway to membership of the party that the supporter route has created appears to be a factor in the decision to continue its use.

This open plebiscitary intra-party democracy that Labour has adopted seems to be staying for now. Yet there appears to be little appetite to go further, towards a more multi-speed model. Despite suggestion of further changes to selection in the 2018 Democracy Review, there have been no further steps towards open selections or primaries, and the questions to ask now are: how permanent is the change that has been made, and will it last?

GOING BACK TO SINGLE-SPEED

As formerly exclusive rights have become inclusive and the party has opened up, it might appear that the distinction between members and supporters has blurred. And yet, it seems that membership has not lost its distinctive status.

To understand why this might be, it is important to understand the organising ideology of the Labour Party and the role of the membership in its history. There are natural tensions here. The Labour Party is, after all, a party based on the idea of representing the collective, and of representing the interests of a defined group, and which, ostensibly at least, makes its decisions through an assembly-based conference. The process of opening up to a wider constituency of support, of becoming a party which responds to political participation in an individualised form, thereby adopting a wider notion of the collective, is a difficult move. Some of these tensions can be seen in the 2018 Democracy Review, which considered the internal organisation of the party and put forward proposals to change, once again, the rules for leadership elections.

The 2018 Democracy Review clearly put membership at the centre, with proposals for a 'member-led' annual conference; for ways to maximise member involvement in policy, including direct and digital democracy pilot schemes; and for making sure that members' rights are clearly set out in the party rule book, including rights in leadership elections. But for a party that has introduced open democracy, specifically going beyond members, in a recognition that the party needs to look outwards and appeal to supporters too, this exclusive focus on members appears to be a step backwards.

This move back towards a more member-focused model highlights the tensions inherent in the model of organising that Labour has been moving towards. These tensions have been felt ever since the £3 supporter option was first introduced, sending the party into a frenzy of vetting procedures. Moving beyond the membership has always been difficult for Labour because of the structures, culture and traditional role of members in the organisation.

It has been argued that a party's organisational choices are linked to its values, which have an impact on decisions about membership. Susan Scarrow's analysis of political-party membership changes[15] highlights the importance of norms and values within a party, which can work as a filter on membership decisions. Scarrow argues that the decisions that party elites make are shaped by implicit or explicit 'narratives of legitimacy'.[16] These narratives are used to identify the party's credibility and they may also shape how parties develop organisationally. Different narratives of legitimacy imply different roles for members. In 'cleavage representation' parties, which represent group interests, members are the ties to the groups represented.[17] Cleavage representation parties are therefore likely to view mass participation as central to the party's legitimacy, and have rules that expect members to commit to party aims. Changing this model necessarily pulls against the party's 'narrative of legitimacy', and for cleavage representation parties, the move to multi-speed organising is particularly difficult. The widening of affiliation seen in multi-speed organising challenges a cleavage representation concept of political legitimacy: it represents a shift in who the party represents, who the leadership is accountable to, and who should define the party's values.

Scarrow argues that because of the link between a party's ideology and its organisational model, as much as ideology might influence the direction of organisational change, changes in party organisation, such as the expansion of political rights, may also signal a change in the organising ideology of the party.[18] For instance, a move to open leader elections may shift the notion of leadership support and legitimacy. What this does is to subtly change the party from one that represents one fixed collective, to one that is more responsive to a political marketplace, responding in this way to citizens' new ways of doing politics.

Labour, traditionally, is a party in the cleavage representation-type; formed to represent the interests of a defined group. In this type of party, members are not fans or adherents, they are not supporters of one particular leader, they are not followers of a single cause or issue, they are instead part of the party's collective. Seeing the role of members in this light helps explain why the shift to multi-speed membership has been at times controversial, and why a shift back to a more exclusive member-focused model might be attractive to the party.

MOVING AWAY FROM MASS MEMBERSHIP

It might be tempting to fall back on the notion of absolute, unwavering collective loyalty, but it would mistake the way that politics and partisans are changing. People do politics differently now – and the party that can respond and harness those new ways is the one that will survive. Moving towards a multi-speed membership model of organising is a recognition of the more fluid nature of partisanship. Lifelong commitment and loyalty are no longer the norm. Memberships are fluid – more like a revolving door than a party for life. Though some members do develop a long-term commitment, others move with the political tides.

Membership of other parties over recent years reflects this fluctuation. The Scottish National Party (SNP) and Liberal Democrats saw a broadly linear increase in membership 2015 to 2019, while the Greens and the UK Independence Party (UKIP) have lost members. It is quite easy to see the drivers of these changes. SNP membership started growing in 2014 after the Scottish independence referendum. For UKIP, membership dropped dramatically following the Leave vote in the 2016 EU referendum. The Liberal Democrats lost a lot of members after the 2010 election, but gained members in 2015 and 2017. Political events drive membership changes, and there is no reason to suppose this would be different for Labour. It is therefore important to recognise this fluidity and create party structures that can deal with it.

Multi-speed membership is not a strategy for holding on to a large and stable membership base, but it is one that can respond to the more fluid and less stable membership environment. In other

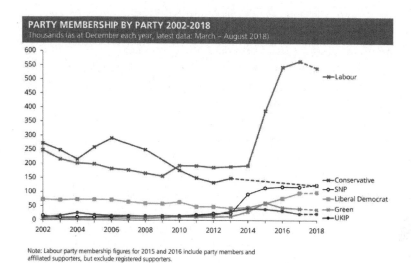

PARTY MEMBERSHIP BY PARTY 2002-2018
Thousands (as at December each year, latest data: March – August 2018)

Note: Labour party membership figures for 2015 and 2016 include party members and affiliated supporters, but exclude registered supporters.

Graph from House of Commons Library Briefing Paper, 'Membership of UK political parties', 3 September 2018.

words, membership losses and gains are to be expected, and these are likely to occur around leadership contests, general elections and other major political events. There is a risk in going back to a single-speed model, a risk in refocusing on members alone, rather than on the wider landscape of support that can be harnessed around key events. Adaptation to the current situation requires a certain level of openness and flexibility in party structures, which has, as we saw in the first Labour leadership election in 2015 using new 'multi-speed' rules, proved uncomfortable for many in the party. This is a natural tension, a consequence of the challenge of opening up party structures that have traditionally drawn a boundary around membership, and of having to deal with those few who have sought to exploit this openness.

But, at its core, what the idea of multi-speed membership highlights is that the familiar model of an enduring lifelong commitment, underpinning 'high-intensity' activism, isn't the only form of party membership. Members and supporters drop in and out of both activism and membership, and they engage in a range of different activities at different times. Building and maintaining a stable and highly active membership base is an attractive idea, but one that is highly unlikely to be sustained over the long term. Yet, maintaining some form of base is also a strength.

Though there is a range of different types of organising structure, most political parties are modelled on the subscriber type, with local branches, an annual congress and, crucially, paid membership. Parties that have adopted less traditional structures – more common in new left, green and populist parties – have often found that their more fluid structures are difficult to sustain over the long term, or when their representatives enter the legislature. 2019 saw two new parties, the Brexit Party and Change UK contesting UK elections. Unlike the more established parties, these newer parties did not have time to build up the traditional infrastructure, but starting from scratch opens up a range of possibilities. Like French President Emmanuel Macron's La République En Marche, formed in 2016, these new parties did not develop from an existing party or movement. En Marche adopted a follower-type model, with 'adherents' instead of members. This model enabled Macron's campaign for the presidency to attract a large number of volunteers and 'crowdfunded' donations, without any formal party structures, but since the 2017 election, they have moved towards more local organisation.

THE VALUE OF NUMBERS

Despite a rise in political movements outside of parties, the democratic institutional reality is a partisan one: parties structure democracy. And because parties dominate our political institutions, they have a responsibility to draw people in, to build a bridge between the governing institutions – in which there is growing distrust and disillusionment – and the role that people, as citizens, might play within them.

Members and supporters form part of that bridge. Parties derive legitimacy from the linkage they provide between citizen and state – giving legitimacy to the system of party-based democracy. Mass parties that emphasise getting people involved in politics provide a 'participatory linkage', making party membership strength an important indicator of linkage strength.[19] This participatory linkage can be representational (selecting candidates for public office) or policy based (transmitting citizens' policy preferences into political programmes), or it can be realised in creating spaces for wider political participation.

Membership decline can impact on these linkages by creating a smaller pool of candidates to draw from (and therefore a potentially less representative one), weakening the party's connection to citizens' views, and drawing fewer people into political activity. Membership decline can therefore affect party strength by decreasing different types of linkage, and this can have an impact electorally. The extent to which a party has reach in a community helps to demonstrate that it is connected to the concerns of the electorate, which not only presents a picture of the party that can be electorally beneficial, but also provides a connection to the community it serves. Participatory linkage is key for parties, like Labour, that were created to give a voice to groups hitherto not represented in Parliament. This is why members are important, but also why membership alone is not enough.

It is worth remembering that the UK is well below average for party membership as a percentage of the electorate. At less than 2 per cent of the electorate, party membership in the UK is one of the lowest across Europe. So, whilst Labour's membership has grown, it still represents a very small slice of the voting public (just 1.1 per cent). And it's not a very representative slice, either, with members being on average much older, whiter, more male and better off than the UK population average.[20]

This is also why the trade union link has been so important and continues to be. Labour has drawn its authority, its participatory and representational linkage, not just from party members, but from its affiliated trade unions' members. Labour was a party of mass affiliation before it was a party of individual membership, only introducing individual membership in 1918 when the franchise was expanded.[21] That new constituency of newly enfranchised and potential Labour supporters drove the move to include individual members in the party. Likewise, the recent registered supporter proposals were conceived looking outwards to new potential support. These wider constituencies of support provide the party with linkage.

Whilst maintaining a large and active supporter base may be a fool's errand, numbers matter for these linkage reasons – reasons that might not always be at the forefront of the minds involved in recruitment campaigns, which often owe more to the pressing demands of party funding and canvassing teams. However, it remains important to think beyond the 1 per cent, and not just for financial or electoral reasons. These linkage connections are not merely symbolic; the connection to individuals is crucial for sustaining a healthy democracy.

A NEW COLLECTIVE POLITICS?

Since Jeremy Corbyn's election as Labour leader, there have been some troubling developments in the nature of political participation. Social media platforms are becoming a more frequently used source of political information and debate. Whilst social media presents a great opportunity for democratic mobilisation, the positives must be balanced by the threats posed by disinformation, foreign interference and damaging levels of online abuse. These developments in political campaigning have brought into question the very integrity of the electoral arena.

The extent to which our democracy is open to exploitation is troubling, but the solution must lie in bringing people into a participative politics. And political parties are uniquely placed to do this. Yet it is also individuals (as distinct from party or other institutions) who have created an atmosphere of hate in online political debate. Whether it is deliberate attempts to disrupt from abroad, or a coarsening of democratic debate within political parties and their support bases, it is clear that responsible and open debate is under threat.

This tendency is not only a product of the new online channels of discourse, but also a reflection of the move away from collective ways of doing politics. There has been a long-running shift away from assembly-based democratic decision-making, where debate and decision occur at the same time, to plebiscitary-based forms of engagement, which separate the vote from the discussion of the choices: individual ballots rather than conference or group decisions[22] – not just in the Labour Party, but in a whole range of parties across different democracies. This is a significant development because it shifts the role of individuals within the process – their role becomes more individualistic, independent, atomised – a position that may lend itself to more polarised debate. This same direct and individualised form of participation can be seen in the enhanced role for members in Labour's 2018 Democracy Review – showing a party turning to direct and online engagement, instead of more deliberative forms of participation. Involving members is positive, but care must be taken as to how.

The potential for reaching out and engaging in real conversations and activism is something that parties can exploit to create a better form of democratic participation. At the beginning of 2018, Labour announced that it would fund a Community Organising Unit, which would help to work on community campaigns on local issues in areas where Labour needs to win. This was a welcome return of the community organising practices that Ed Miliband championed, and demonstrates how politics can be effective at a time when Westminster feels very remote. The commitment to community organising reflects the party that Labour should be – connected to people, looking outward – but there is a need to be more ambitious for democracy, and consider how to make Westminster less remote too.

In the era of Brexit, now more than ever, we need to bring people into real processes of decision making. Our democratic institutions do not allow for the type of participatory and movement politics that Labour favours. So alongside creating democratic spaces and movements outside of state institutions, it is also important to consider how these institutions themselves might be reformed to become more complementary and responsive to, and eventually transformed by, a more inclusive way of doing politics.

An inertia has settled over politics in the shadow of Brexit, and our focus for democratic change has become too limited to thinking about how we can change the Labour Party, rather than how we can reshape how politics works. It is quite wrong to ignore the problems in our democratic system outside of the party that prevent the social policy changes that are devised within it. The disconnect that people feel will not be resolved by giving them a greater say in the reselection of their Labour MP or selection of their party candidate – a more fundamental change to politics is needed.

Labour will struggle to bring more people into the party if

they feel that politics at large has little interest in what they have to say. Creating an inclusive and responsive party means creating a more widely inclusive and responsive democracy at the broader institutional level. The question for a genuine movement-based politics is less about internal party rules, than about how the party can begin to reshape the entire democratic process. This means being bold enough to challenge the Westminster system, to reimagine how democracy could function, and to move away from the paralysis created by our creaking and outdated electoral model.

Meanwhile, for Labour, going back to a single-speed model of party participation won't work: the task of developing new ways to engage an ever-widening and changing constituency of support is more necessary than ever. A more open and stronger Labour Party and a broader vision of democratic change are needed. One without the other is doomed to failure. We need them both, and urgently.

NOTES

1. Pippa Norris, *Democratic Phoenix: Reinventing Political Activism*, Cambridge University Press: Cambridge, 2002.
2. Patrick Wintour, 'Miliband launches Labour election campaign with promise of four million chats', *The Guardian*, 5 January 2015.
3. BBC News, 'Election 2017: Was it Facebook wot swung it?', 10 June 2017.
4. 'Digital campaigning: Increasing transparency for voters', Electoral Commission, June 2018.
5. See, for example, the Digital, Culture, Media and Sport Committee report on 'Dis-information and "Fake News"', House of Commons, 18 February 2019.
6. Paul Webb, Monica Poletti and Tim Bale, 'So who really does the donkey work in "multi-speed membership parties"? Comparing the election campaign activity of party members and party supporters', *Electoral Studies*, No. 46, pp64-74, 2017.
7. Susan Scarrow, *Beyond Party Members: Changing Approaches to Partisan Mobilization*, Oxford University Press: Oxford, 2015.
8. Of a sample of fifty-seven parties across ten countries drawn from the Political Party Database project. Susan Achury, Susan Scarrow, Karina Kosiara-Pedersen and Emilie van Haute, 'The consequences of membership incentives', *Party Politics*, Online First, 2018.
9. Scarrow 2015.

10. Benjamin Von dem Berge and Thomas Poguntke, 'Varieties of intra-party democracy: Conceptualization and index construction', in Susan Scarrow, Paul Webb and Thomas Poguntke (eds), *Organizing Political Parties: Representation, Participation, and Power*, Oxford University Press: Oxford, 2017.

11. Patrick Seyd and Paul Whiteley, *Labour's Grass Roots: The Politics of Party Membership*, Clarendon Press: Oxford, 1992.

12. Labour Party, 'Refounding Labour: A party for the new generation', 2011.

13. Labour Party, Rule Book, 2013.

14. Labour Party, 'Building a one-nation Labour Party: The Collins Review into Labour Party reform', 2014.

15. Scarrow 2015.

16. *Ibid.*, p.20.

17. *Ibid.*, p.22.

18. *Ibid.*, p.26.

19. Kay Lawson, *Political Parties and Linkage: A Comparative Perspective*, Yale University Press: New Haven, CT, 1980.

20. Bale, Webb and Poletti, 'Grassroots: Britain's party members: Who they are, what they think, and what they do', Mile End Institute, Queen Mary University of London, January 2018.

21. Duncan Tanner, Pat Thane and Nick Tiratsoo, *Labour's First Century*, Cambridge University Press: Cambridge, 2000.

22. Von dem Berge and Poguntke 2017.

How Big Organising Works

Adam Klug and Emma Rees

In March 2019, an estimated 1.4 million children walked out of schools in 2,233 cities and towns in 128 countries from India to Australia, all demanding action on climate change.[1] What better illustration of the utter failings of our political system that schoolchildren across the world appear to understand the need for urgent, systemic change when adult political leaders plainly do not?

In this time of political upheaval, the vast majority of social democratic parties in Europe and North America are in woeful decline; unable to offer solutions to the needs of the moment and suffering 'Pasokification', as it is sometimes called, referring to the near-collapse of Greece's erstwhile main centre-left party, Pasok. In recent years, the failings of social democratic parties in European democracies that have proportional representation (PR) have given rise to alternative left parties, from Syriza to Podemos. In the UK, a similar dynamic of discontent emerged after Ed Miliband's 'austerity-lite' Labour Party lost the 2015 general election. However, mainly because of our first-past-the-post electoral system (FPTP), this dynamic manifested itself within the existing party, not outside it, leading directly to both Jeremy Corbyn's election as party leader and the emergence of Momentum, a grassroots organisation campaigning for a transformative Labour government. Similarly, in the US, which broadly shares a FPTP system, there has been the increasingly successful insurgency within the Democrats represented by figures including Bernie Sanders, Alexandria Ocasio-Cortez (AOC) and Ilhan Omar, as well as the creation and expansion of movement organisations such as Justice Democrats, Democratic Socialists of America and others.

These insurgencies within both the UK Labour Party and the US Democratic Party mark a shift in political ideas and orientation, not just personality and personnel. At the first Labour Party conference after Corbyn became leader in 2015, the new leader declared that the Labour Party would now challenge and reject austerity.[2] In the US, Medicare for All and a Green New Deal – policies championed by Bernie Sanders, AOC, and other democratic socialist insurgents – have become litmus-test issues to which Democratic frontrunners are at least paying lip service in the run-up to the 2020 presidential races.

Having previously been primary-school teachers, the authors of this chapter volunteered on the campaign to elect Corbyn as Labour leader, and then found ourselves, in the weeks that followed his victory, part of the small group who established Momentum, seeking to build on the energy and enthusiasm sparked by the campaign. In the early days, Momentum had very few resources: borrowed office space, three low-paid organisers (of whom we were two), and mountains of volunteer energy and goodwill from people all around the country who wanted to build a new politics. Now, Momentum has grown into a network of tens of thousands of members and more than 150 local activist groups. Its aims are to elect a Labour government with a transformative, socialist programme; to extend democracy within Labour to ensure that the politics and culture of the party are directed by members and trade unionists; and to link up with and strengthen relationships with the wider movement for economic, racial and social justice. Since its launch in October 2015, Momentum has supported left candidates to significant gains in internal Labour Party elections. The organisation was central to Jeremy Corbyn's second leadership election campaign when hostile Labour MPs tried to drive him out in 2016. It played a decisive role in Labour's historic 2017 general election comeback, using a mixture of viral social media content and innovative mobilisation techniques. Since 2016, The World Transformed, which grew out of Momentum, has attracted thousands of people to its festival of politics and culture alongside the Labour Party conference, and is now helping to initiate similar events, organised by grassroots activists, around the country throughout the year. While there undoubtedly is a great deal more that could have been, and still needs to be, done, Momentum has played a significant role in a process of revitalisation that has seen Labour Party membership treble to over 500,000 members and the party's share of the vote between 2015 and 2017 increase by the largest margin since the Second World War.[3]

In contrast, support for social democratic parties across Europe has declined further. Nobody is suggesting that the British left has all the answers; huge challenges loom ahead, not least whatever aftermath follows the eventual conclusion of the Brexit impasse. Yet, with its recent relative gains, the British labour movement is well placed to foster stronger international networks of mutual solidarity and support. For the left to win, we must notice trends, learn from each other and offer practical help and support in each other's struggles. This new internationalism has the potential to link both party leaders and policy programmes, as well as forging mutually supportive networks of solidarity among grassroots organisers and activists.

This cannot happen soon enough. What campaigning journalist Owen Jones dubs the 'Far-Right International' is also on the rise.[4] In 2018, the 'Free Tommy' movement associated with anti-Islam activist and rabble-rouser Stephen Yaxley-Lennon, who styles himself as 'Tommy Robinson', became a growing, populist-racist force on British streets. Thankfully, Yaxley-Lennon failed to get elected in the 2019 European Parliament elections. However, Nigel Farage's Brexit Party topped those polls, just weeks after launching, which will undoubtedly embolden the hard right in the Tory Party and send further shockwaves across the British political terrain. Meanwhile, parties led by openly racist politicians are on the rise across Europe. Among such figures are Viktor Orbán in Hungary, Marine Le Pen in France, Heinz-Christian Strache in Austria, Jarosław Kaczyński in Poland and Matteo Salvini in Italy. It is the failings of the status quo that have created the conditions for the – very different – anti-elite populisms of both left and right.

In this climate, the left must work together, within and across national borders, to combat the threat of the far right, and build a politics of hope capable of offering solutions to the needs of the moment. Of course, each national-political context is unique; not least in the impact the voting system has on the expression of left-populist ideas, with the general tendency being for these ideas to manifest within an existing social democratic party under FPTP, and outside it under PR. But there are enough common trends for lessons to be learned.

We argue that progressives must recognise the need for two inter-related approaches. The first is a bold political vision that offers solutions every bit as big as the huge problems we face.[5] The second is a 'big' approach to organising – one that brings together social movements and electoral politics, and builds systems to empower volunteers to drive campaigns at scale.

A BIG POLITICAL VISION

As we stand in an increasingly polarised world, teetering on the edge of climate catastrophe, it is clear that progressives need to articulate a big, bold, alternative vision of the future. This must start from a recognition of the very real pain and indignity that the status quo inflicts on vast swathes of the population. According to the Child Poverty Action Group, 'more than one in four children grow up in poverty in the UK'.[6] As primary-school teachers, it was common-place for us to see children come to school hungry, for parents and carers to lack the income or facilities to wash their children's school clothes, for families to live with the immense anxiety of insecure housing and precarious work. For those living in such circumstances, technical-sounding policy announcements that appear to tinker at the edges of systemic problems aren't going to cut it. The solutions offered must be as big as the problems they seek to address, or why should anyone believe that voting this way or that is going to make any material difference to their life? This isn't just about 'talking left'. It is about socialist and social-democratic parties viewing their role as serving human need over profit, and putting forward aspi-rational political programmes to rebalance wealth and power in the interests of the many. We require a positive, creative, inclusive vision of the future for generations to come.

Labour's 2017 general election manifesto 'For the many, not the few'[7] began to sketch out what this vision might look like in prac-tice. The pledge to build a million affordable new homes, half of which would be owned by local councils; tax rises for the wealthiest five per cent; the abolition of university tuition fees; the creation of a national education service providing free, lifelong education for all – each policy was an indicator of the alternative society we would live in under a left Labour government. Work now must be done within the Labour Party to build on the 2017 manifesto, to expand beyond social-democratic promises and ensure that Labour's transformational offer comprises what are known as 'non-reformist reforms', that is, changes that effect shifts in wealth and power that cannot easily be undone.

There is a huge, and so far under-tapped, opportunity to involve the party's mass membership in the development of Labour's big political vision through participatory policymaking. The rationale for a more democratic approach to policy development was articulated by Corbyn in his first leadership campaign: 'Shadow ministers and policy advisers do not have a monopoly on wisdom, so they must interact with party members and supporters. By making policy together, we make better policy.'[8] It is reasonable to speculate that had Corbyn not won the 2015 leadership campaign, Labour's political offer would have been significantly less bold, and Labour would likely be suffering a similar fate to its social-democratic sister parties across Europe.

But for this change in political direction within the party to be sustainable in the long term, significant reforms are needed to the way that policy is developed. As National Executive Committee (NEC) member Rachel Garnham argues:

> Our 2017 manifesto was great. Now we need to put serious efforts into developing a democratic policymaking process to match…Giving members and trade unions a greater say in policy is not a luxury, but essential to our movement, developing the policies we need to win elections and form administrations that put Labour values into action. Members and trade unionists involved in meaningful processes acquire knowledge and confidence, strengthening the party overall.[9]

Meanwhile, the need to turn ideas into action exists alongside a fast-deteriorating political situation throughout Europe and North America. When the German populist-racist right, in the form of the Alternative für Deutschland (AfD) Party, made their electoral breakthrough in September 2017, political commentator Paul Mason was one of those who recognised that the far-right threat was present everywhere, and he was equally clear what the left's response should be:

> The neoliberal economic model, which social democracy sought to soften and humanise, no longer works. It is on a global life-support system consisting of $12tn of central bank money ... Until the centre-left learns to break with the logic of neoliberalism, and to construct an economic model that subordinates market forces to human needs, it will continue failing. The task is not to remedy or tweak the neoliberal economic model but replace it – just as fundamentally as Thatcher, Reagan and Berlusconi did in the economic counter-revolutions of the 80s and 90s.[10]

Particularly at a time of rising racism, bigotry and xenophobia, there is an urgent need for our big political vision to have anti-racism and liberation at its core. Journalist and lecturer Ash Sarkar explains: 'It's important to recognise that opposing racism isn't just about presenting an alternative set of values; it's about looking at how the far right play on people's hardships in order to nurture a sense of enmity between white people and those racialised as migrants.'[11] As Dalia Gebrial,[12] Gary Younge[13] and others have argued, tackling income inequality is key, but our political vision must at the same time recognise and address both endemic racism and bigotry within society, and our colonial legacy abroad.

One example of what a big political vision might look like is The Leap manifesto.[14] The manifesto aims to tackle the inter-secting crises of our time: climate change, racism and inequality, and it was co-created by participants in Canada's indigenous rights, social and food justice, environmental, anti-racist, faith-based and labour movements.[15] Unlike the insurgencies represented by Corbyn or Sanders, in the case of The Leap, there is no political figure-head leading the charge for political transformation. Instead, it is an example of social movements and progressives coming together to set out a big political vision and beginning to organise around it.

In her 2017 book *No is Not Enough*, Naomi Klein articulates The Leap's approach as the politics of a positive vision for an alternative society; a society that is not some faraway utopia but that is, given the political will, within our collective and immediate reach:

> We could live in a country powered entirely by renewable energy, woven together by accessible public transit, in which the jobs and opportunities of this transition are designed to systematically eliminate racial and gender inequality.[16]

This approach to climate change, which situates the vast-scale change required as part of the fight for class and racial justice, can also be seen in the US, in AOC's recent call for a Green New Deal, and in the 2017 creation of climate campaign the Sunrise Movement. Following this lead, in the UK in March 2019, a group called Labour for a Green New Deal was established to 'build grassroots support for a Green New Deal within the Labour Party'.[17] Like their US counterparts, the organisers of Labour for a Green New Deal set out a bold and positive vision for the future:

> As Alexandria Ocasio-Cortez and the Sunrise Movement have argued in the US, a Green New Deal shouldn't just be about decarbonising our economy; it should be a radical vision for a healthier, happier and more prosperous society. According to the IPCC [Intergovernmental Panel on Climate Change], we may only have eleven years left to limit the worst of the climate crisis. But that's eleven years in which we could change everything.[18]

The group was clear from the outset that it was breaking with the depoliticised environmental rhetoric of the past, which has tended to focus on encouraging lifestyle changes on the part of individuals, rather than on structural changes to society and the economy. Announcing the group's formation, a spokesperson declared: 'Climate change is fundamentally about class, because it means chaos for the many while the few profit'.[19] However, Dalia Gebrial has warned against the left falling into the trap of 'green colonialism', meaning that it must '[understand] that any "Green New

Deal" or "green industrial revolution" cannot be bound within our nation's borders, or prioritise the wellbeing of Westerners over black and brown lives in the rest of the world.'[20] This highlights the need for anti-racism and internationalism to be at the core of our big political vision for an alternative future.

But as schoolchildren the world over call for people of all ages to join their global strike,[21] it is clear that the younger generations are agitating for wholesale systems changes – and it is the adults who need to catch up.

In tandem with setting out a big political vision, we argue that a 'big organising' approach is also needed for the left to win. In fact, it is the other side of the same coin. 'Big organising' is the term used to describe a mobilisation approach pioneered by the 2016 Bernie Sanders presidential campaign. There is significant overlap with the 'people-powered' approach of Momentum, and increasingly the Labour Party itself. We'll explore some of the specific principles and tactics in the next section, but at its core, 'big organising' denotes an attempt to transform the philosophy and culture of politics by harnessing the energy of the grassroots and embracing the mass participation of people and movements. It is an approach that departs from elitist and 'professionalised' politics, seeking instead to connect social movements with electoral politics.

BIG ORGANISING

In recent years, campaign tactics and strategies have been developed that enable people to participate in political campaigns at an unprecedented scale. This is good news, given the size of the challenges we are up against. For the left to win, it is just as important for activists to share nuts-and-bolts organising lessons internationally, as it is to exchange political ideas.

In their 2016 book *Rules for Revolutionaries*, Becky Bond and Zack Exley tell the story of a breakthrough experiment conducted on the fringes of the Sanders campaign of the same year. A technology-driven team empowered volunteers to build and manage the infrastructure to make seventy-five million calls, launch eight million text messages, and hold more than 100,000 public meetings.[22] The fact that Sanders didn't win the Democratic nomination in 2016 does not diminish the sheer scale of the achievement. And activists from the Sanders campaign were instrumental in making significant breakthroughs for democratic socialists in the 2018 midterm elections.[23]

Bond and Exley list 'rules' that challenge conventional campaign orthodoxy, and the idea of big organising is at the book's core. On the 2016 Sanders campaign, big organising was all about setting up systems that enabled volunteers to participate in campaigning on an unprecedented scale. The authors point to the hundreds of thousands of people who volunteered for Bernie Sanders as proof of the appetite for greater levels of participation in politics when a big political vision is being put forward. They also argue that the role of paid staff should be to develop and refine systems to facilitate volunteer participation, noting that in traditionally run campaigns, this is not always the case. For example, if a potential volunteer needs to have contact with a staff member before they can get stuck in – be it a phone call, a one-to-one meeting or a training session – then the number of volunteers is inevitably limited by the ratio of volunteers to staff. But in the 2016 Sanders campaign, a web-based system was built and managed by a handful of staff that enabled those eight million text messages to be sent, and seventy-five million phonecalls to be made using the 'Bernie dialler', in an example of tech being employed to reduce the need for volunteer-to-staff training contact. The number of staff required to operate this system would not have varied greatly if there were half or double the number of volunteers.[24]

During the 2016 Labour leadership election, the Jeremy for Labour campaign initiated 'campaign call-outs' based on Bond and Exley's 'barnstorm' model of mass organising rallies.[25] Across the country, we brought people together in mass meetings, demonstrated how to use the 'Call for Corbyn' phone-canvassing app (built by volunteers from Momentum Bristol), and encouraged volunteers to host 'pop-up phone parties' in their own homes.

In the course of the 2017 general election, 100,000 individual users visited Momentum's marginals map mynearestmarginal.com to find out where to canvass. The map was built by volunteer web developers, and teams of volunteers across the country kept it up to date with canvassing information throughout the election campaign. The map is an example of a 'big', or 'distributed', organising platform because it is a system that allows huge volumes of people to participate in a campaign in a meaningful way – in this instance, to go canvassing in key marginals – by distributing knowledge or resources across a network.

Whilst exploring different organising tactics or the role of technology in campaigning is useful, we suggest that there is also something more fundamental at play. 'Big organising' and the people-powered approach that has been central to the rise of Corbyn recognises that 'the people', not politicians or elites, are the agents of political transformation. The various tactics and tools are derived from a theory of change which views a mass movement of ordinary people as vital.

A key example of this approach is demonstrated by the victory of AOC.[26] AOC overcame all the odds to unseat the ten-term incumbent, Congressman Joe Crowley, in a primary election to become the Democratic candidate for New York's Fourteenth Congressional District in 2018, and went on to be successfully elected to the House of Representatives in the 2018 midterms. She ran on a bold, democratic socialist platform and was powered by an army of volunteers knocking on doors and talking to voters.

Following her stunning win in the primary, writers Matt Stone and Jeremy Gong noted both the victory's antecedents, and its significance:

> Like Bernie Sanders and Jeremy Corbyn, Ocasio-Cortez… used her campaign to invite ordinary people into a movement, raising their 'consciousness of this vast potential power'. This could be called the Sanders playbook, and her campaign might have done it even better than Sanders' did.[27]

Stone and Gong ascribe a political commonality to Corbyn, Sanders, and Ocasio-Cortez, arguing that each has 'proven that elections can play a crucial role [in] politicising the working class and inspiring them to organise'.[28]

The relationship between movements and electoral campaigning here is symbiotic. Reflecting on the 2018 US midterm elections, which saw a record number of women, ethnic minorities and ethnic-minority women elected to Congress, journalist and writer Gary Younge draws out the interplay between movements, protests and electoral politics. He highlights that some of the largest demonstrations in US history had taken place in the two years since the previous midterms, including the women's marches and the youth-led protest for gun control. 'There is an intimate connection between those years of protest and the nature of this election victory that has national significance in the US. It provides a lesson about the connection between movements and parties, elections and politics, that the Democrats would do well to learn...'[29]

Momentum's flagship 'persuasive conversations' canvassing model, now adopted and delivered by Labour Party staff, has drawn inspiration from these US examples. During the 2017 general election, Momentum ran training sessions in every major metropolitan area and key marginal.[30] Following the election, it established a training network using a 'train the trainer' model to roll out 'persuasive conversations' more widely. Consistently more than half of the people attending had never canvassed before; following the training session, all the attendees would go out on the doorstep together. Not only did this increase 'boots on the ground', but it also shifted the view of the Labour activist's role in the political process – helping activists to understand themselves as people who could use their own experience and position within their community to win hearts and minds, as well as to collect election data. When Labour closed the Conservatives' twenty-point lead and won seats that hadn't been held by Labour for generations, the activists who had knocked on doors will, no doubt, have had a politicising taste of the change that they, as part of a mass-movement party, can bring about.

We have, however, noticed a tendency among some to try to depoliticise this movement-based, 'big organising' approach. In place of politics, these voices offer 'magic-bullet' solutions – *if we focus more on social media or introduce a digital tool, young people will miraculously start voting for us, we'll get more members and active canvassers*, and so on. But the 'big organising' approach requires a mass of people to be prepared to give up their time for free. There is no reason to believe that people will be mobilised on anything like the scale the Labour Party requires if all that is offered in return is a remodelled version of the status quo. People will not put in the time and effort if they are not inspired by the vision on offer. Volunteers need to believe in the worth of what they are doing, and sense the importance of the role they are playing within the movement. If people are being asked to campaign for a small change, rather than a big one, most, quite rightly, won't view this as a worthwhile use of their unpaid time and political energy. Nothing other than the ambition of the political vision on offer comes close to explaining Jeremy Corbyn's appeal, a point the paid commentariat spectacularly failed to grasp when Jeremy first stood for, and won, the Labour leadership.

THE SHAPE OF BIG THINGS TO COME

Labour's 2017 general election performance greatly boosted confidence in the power of these ideas to refashion how the party campaigns. Those within the party who had previously been at best mildly suspicious, at worst actively and politically opposed, were at least in part won over. In seats like Battersea that had been regarded as 'no hopers', the results spoke for themselves. Labour stands to benefit electorally from all of this, in addition to expanding its relationships with individuals, campaigns and parties around the world, from whom we can continue to learn so much. We will need, not just to stay ahead of the curve in how we organise and campaign, but also to develop policy ideas, as the programme for a transformative Labour government evolves. But opposition and caution remain, and arguably both have increased as the memory of the heady days of the 2017 election become more distant, and detached from the chaos current British politics finds itself in.

In the US context, Bond and Exley describe the need to put radical trust in volunteers. However, they argue that this is not about letting volunteers do whatever they like. Indeed, the 'big organising' approach they describe requires a clear, centralised plan to win — *we need to speak to X people, in X seats* — to ensure that volunteers' time is being spent in the most effective way possible.[31] A difference between this and more traditional electoral campaigns is that they advocate for the campaign plan to be made available to volunteers, as well as to the staffed campaign. This challenges campaign orthodoxy, in which the idea is that only a small number of senior people know what the campaign plan is and what progress is being made, so as to prevent information ending up in the hands of the opponents. However, we argue that this is a price worth paying. None of the campaigns we are seeking to win, whether electoral (a Labour government) or policy-based (a Green New Deal), are going to be winnable by a staff team alone. We need systemic change, and we can only change the system with a people-powered, mass movement. In order to motivate and engage volunteers at the scale needed to win, and to ensure that every volunteer hour is spent doing work that contributes directly to the campaign strategy, volunteers need to know what the plan is, and what progress is being made.

A small-c conservative organisational culture in which information is held by a handful of people at the top will struggle to fully unleash the power of volunteers. If we believe that change will only be possible with a mass membership or wider movement, then campaign staff must embrace the cultural shift, and embrace techniques that recast the base as a core part of the campaign team, not as mere foot soldiers or campaign fodder.

One core change to the party that has developed under Corbyn, following an earlier, but in the end abandoned, effort when Ed Miliband was leader,[32] is the establishment of a Community Organising Unit (COU).[33] By March 2019, the COU had thirty organisers working in marginal seats that Labour needs to defend or win back, typically in Scotland, post-industrial areas of the North and Midlands, and seaside towns. While this is clearly part of a longer-term electoral strategy to rebuild trust in areas that were let down by New Labour, the work of the COU sits outside immediate electoral cycles. Community organisers are forging relationships with people inside and outside of the party, building teams, facilitating listening campaigns, and using these to develop community campaigns that can win change in the here and now, not just at election time. Writer and activist Richard Power Sayeed explains the significance of this effort: 'If Corbyn gets his way, when you think of Labour, you won't imagine rows of MPs on green leather benches, or a smartly suited minister chatting to a reporter. Instead, you'll think of activists reinvigorating their estate's tenants association, while others organise their co-workers and stand with them on picket lines.'[34]

The COU is an extremely welcome development, and we believe it will play a core role in Labour's process of renewal. However, our view is that it needs to be supplemented by a big organising strategy, to ensure that the hundreds of thousands of members and supporters outside the seats that the COU are working in can play an active role in securing a Labour government able to deliver a transformative agenda.

We vigorously reject any suggestion that moves towards a big political vision and 'big organising' should be jettisoned, or that the idea has had its moment, or is no longer applicable. There is no going back, instead we need to lean into our strength by ensuring that Labour puts members at the heart of the party's politics, culture and strategy. We need to embed internationalism at the core of our activism – a move that is more, not less, urgent in the era of Brexit. We should maximise the use of the internet and social media to share our experiences and learn from others, and build a Labour Party and movement that facilitates skill-sharing, training and network-building within and across borders.

We are living in a time of great uncertainty and upheaval. The challenges we face – including climate change, inequality and bigotry – will never be solved within one locality or country. To be in with a fighting chance, Labour must work together as a party with members learning from each other. We must think and act Big.

NOTES

1. Damian Carrington, 'School climate strikes: 1.4 million people took part, say campaigners', *The Guardian*, 19 March 2019.
2. 'Jeremy Corbyn's Labour Party conference speech in full', *New Statesman,* 29 September 2015.
3. Harriet Agerholm, 'Jeremy Corbyn increased Labour's vote share more than any of the party's leaders since 1945', *Independent,* 9 June 2017.
4. Owen Jones, 'The hard right can only be defeated from the left, not from the centre', *The Guardian*, 18 July 2018.
5. See Becky Bond and Zack Exley, *Rules for Revolutionaries: How Big Organizing can Change Everything*, Chelsea Green Publishing: White River Junction, VT, 2016.
6. Child Poverty Action Group, 'Child poverty facts and figures', July 2018.

7. Labour Party 2017, 'For the many, not the few: The Labour Party Manifesto 2017'.

8. Jeremy Corbyn, 'Jeremy Corbyn: As Labour leader, how I will unify MPs, rebuild the party and win in 2020', *New Statesman*, 19 August 2015.

9. Rachel Garnham, 'Labour's policies are great: Now our policymaking process must improve', Labour List, 20 December 2018.

10. Paul Mason, 'The AfD's breakthrough shows that parties of the left must get radical', *The Guardian*, 25 September 2017.

11. Ash Sarkar, 'This isn't just a culture war – we need a radical anti-fascist movement right now', *The Guardian*, 21 August 2018.

12. Dalia Gebrial, 'As the left wakes up to climate injustice, we must not fall into "green colonialism"', *The Guardian*, 8 May 2019.

13. Gary Younge, 'Shocked by the rise of the right? Then you weren't paying attention', *The Guardian*, 24 May 2019.

14. See www.theleap.org. For a broad explanation of the kind of 'big' politics that framed The Leap's manifesto, see Naomi Klein, *No is Not Enough: Defeating the New Shock Politics*, Allen Lane: London, 2017.

15. See 'FAQs', www.theleap.org.

16. Klein 2017, p.267.

17. Matthew Taylor, 'Labour members launch Green New Deal inspired by activists in the US', *The Guardian*, 22 March 2019. See also www.labourgnd.uk.

18. Labour for a Green New Deal spokesperson, quoted in Taylor 2019.

19. Quoted in *ibid*.

20. Gebrial 2019.

21. Greta Thunberg, 'Young people have led the climate strikes: Now we need adults to join us too', *The Guardian*, 23 May 2019.

22. www.rulesforrevolutionaries.org.

23. Ryan Grim, 'How Bernie Sanders accidentally built a ground-breaking organizing movement', The Intercept, 28 May 2019.

24. Bond and Exley 2016, pp25-36.

25. *Ibid*, pp72-83.

26. See www.Ocasio2018.com.

27. Matt Stone and Jeremy Gong, 'Alexandria Ocasio-Cortez's transformational vision', *Jacobin*, 7 March 2018.

28. *Ibid*.

29. Gary Younge, 'The new wave of Democrats owes a huge debt to people power', *The Guardian*, 29 November 2018.

30. See Nadia Khomani, 'The US Bernie Sanders campaigners lending Jeremy Corbyn a hand', *The Guardian*, 30 May 2017.

31. Bond and Exley 2016, p.49.

32. For an introduction to the initiative, see Rowenna Davis, 'Arnie Graf: The man Ed Miliband asked to rebuild Labour', *The Guardian*, 21 November 2012. For Arnie Graf's explanation of why he believed it failed, see Arnie Graf, 'Labour's failure had little to do with organisers in the field', Labour List, 4 August 2015.

33. Labour Party, 'Introducing Community Organising', www.labour.org.uk.

34. Richard Power Sayeed, 'Jeremy Corbyn is about to transform the Labour party – again', *Independent*, 9 January 2018.

A Workplace to Win

Heather Wakefield

Lewis Minkin has called it 'the contentious alliance'.[1] For Keir Hardie it was the 'great' one. Feminist chroniclers of the relationship between the trade unions and the Labour Party have meanwhile noted the occasional reluctance of both to support women's demands. Describing the ongoing battle for equal pay by trade union women following the 1968 Ford women machinists' strike, Sheila Lewenhak says:

> Yet the unions were still not wholly committed to women's equality. Along with the Labour government and employers, they were concerned in an attempt to frustrate the women's demands. This was over whether women should yield restrictions on their hours of work...in return for equal pay.[2]

Whether contentious or great, supportive of women or not, the relationship between the trade unions and the Labour Party has persisted since the formation of the Labour Representation Committee in 1900, despite its collapse being 'prophesied as often as the demise of English cricket'.[3] With over six million members, the unions – and the link between them and the Labour Party – are of critical importance for the success of Jeremy Corbyn's radical Labour project – and for the future of unions themselves. But to make it work, both they and the party will need to change.

Support for Corbyn amongst trade union affiliates of the party is clearly evident. 58 per cent of members of affiliated unions who 'opted in' to the ballot as individuals voted for him in the 2015 leadership election – compared to 26 per cent for Andy Burnham, his nearest rival – and 60 per cent again in 2016.[4] But not all Labour-linked unions nominated Corbyn in 2016. UNISON, Unite, ASLEF (the train drivers' union), the Bakers, Food and Allied Workers Union (BFAWU), the Communication Workers' Union (CWU), the Fire Brigades Union (FBU), and the Transport Salaried Staffs' Association (TSSA) did – along with RMT (the union for transport workers) and the POA (prison officers' union), which are not Labour affiliates. 42 per cent of UNISON's members opted for his opponent, Owen Smith – who was also nominated by Labour affiliates Community, GMB, the Musicians' Union, and the Union of Shop, Distributive and Allied Workers (USDAW).[5]

Despite fluctuating levels of enthusiasm for Corbyn among some general secretaries and full-time officials – and by no means universal support among grassroots members – there are others such as Dave Ward, general secretary of the CWU, who speaks positively and power-fully about why some trade unions, including his own, and many tens of thousands of the unions' activists on the left, do support him:

> We need a fundamental change in Labour politics and Jeremy Corbyn recognises this. He is the candidate to drive through the change that ordinary people are crying out for – opposing damaging austerity measures and tackling the housing crisis which is causing misery for so many.[6]

THE UNION LINK

'For the many, not the few'[7] would make no sense at all without the active engagement of organised workers. Corbyn and Shadow Chancellor John McDonnell have consistently distinguished 'Corbynism' from the passive attitude towards trade unions and narrow parliamentary focus of most previous Labour leaderships. Indeed, Corbyn has regularly voiced his pride in the link, and the need for Labour to be more 'in touch with' working people:

> As leader I am proud of the link between trade unions and the Labour Party – it is not just a historic link, it's what makes Labour succeed. We win when we're in touch with the needs and concerns of millions of working people and their families – the people trade unions represent.

Before being elected to Parliament I worked as a trade union official, with garment workers who were owed back pay by unscrupulous employers and with public sector workers fighting to protect their jobs and services, and low paid women fighting for equal pay. I know how much harder it is now today for the trade union representatives – with the most restrictive anti-union laws in Europe, which are about to get even more restrictive.[8]

He also emphasises the need to both expand Labour's community organising and form 'a coalition of social movements' to create, develop and sustain Labour's new political project and radical manifesto. McDonnell too emphasises the importance of being 'in touch with' the unions, but he also suggests a more dynamic 'active engagement on a daily basis between government and civil society and the real experts on the shop floor'.[9] Momentum, which presents itself as a people-powered movement aiming to transform not only the Labour Party but entire communities too, has the potential to be a key player in this project, but immersed as it is in winning internal party elections and target seats this aim, as yet, remains unfulfilled.

Left writer and activist Paul Mason, who is sceptical of Labour's ability to simultaneously hold office, run for power *and* lead a broad social movement, identifies the hollow space that could undoubtedly appear between a passive population and a left-wing government.[10] For him, the 'shop-floor movement' has been replaced by 'the social factory' of the fragmented, privatised, digitalised economy, and he calls on Labour to shift its focus to 'building left-wing social capital on the ground', rather than rely on old labour movement institutions.[11]

Journalist and activist Owen Jones takes a slightly more traditional left view, arguing for the need to 'bridge the chasm between the views of Labour members and the general public', and suggests that 'Labour needs to adopt a strategy – led by trade unions – to recruit and give leadership positions to under-represented working-class people, particularly in the north'.[12] Whoever is right, and the two viewpoints are not necessarily mutually exclusive, a heavy responsibility lies with trade unions to be – and to amplify – the voice of working-class people and to empower them within and outside of the party as part of a new, concerted social movement for real, sustained, socialist change.

TAKE NOTHING FOR GRANTED

This is not a role that will come easily to what are often bureaucratic, culturally – and sometimes politically – conservative unions. Only 28,000 of the 1.3 million members of the largest union – UNISON, the public services union – were Labour Party members in their own right in 2015. 15,000 signed up as supporters before the leadership election and 430,000 were opted into UNISON's affiliated political fund, which supports the Labour Party. While they comprised 30 per cent of the electorate, just 17 per cent of all trade union votes returned in that election came from members of affiliated unions who were not party members or supporters.[13] The relationship between the labour movement's 'shop floor' and its newly radicalised political wing cannot be taken for granted, and it will require mutual co-operation, imagination and commitment to navigate the tensions and evolve a trade-union movement for change.

Just twelve of the thirty-seven trade unions certified by the government's Certification Officer are affiliated to the Labour Party – the FBU having rejoined in 2015. Non-affiliated trade unions include large teaching and health unions such as the National Education Union and Royal College of Nursing, with almost half a million – mostly women – members each, PCS in the civil service, and the university and college union UCU. Militant and politically aligned with Corbynism, the railway and transport workers' RMT nevertheless remains for its own reasons unaffiliated.

Of the affiliated unions, it's all about numbers. The two largest unions, UNISON, with its membership of 1.3 million, and Unite, with its over a million members, are both broadly supportive of Corbyn's Labour leadership. Of the two, Unite has generally proved to be the stronger, more consistent supporter. Neither the GMB nor USDAW, the next-largest unions, with half a million members each, supported Corbyn in the two leadership elections, nor have they shown much enthusiasm for the radical change in the party's direction. While CWU and TSSA – operating in the privatised postal and railways services – have shown steady and vocal support, their numbers and influence are not as great as those of the 'big four'. With this balance of forces, Corbyn's Labour cannot take trade union support and co-operation for granted.

Three small, independent unions – the United Voices of the World (UVW), the Independent Workers Union of Great Britain (IWGB) and the Industrial Workers of the World (IWW) – have had notable recent success in mobilising and winning litigation, the Living Wage and other workplace rights for groups of outsourced and precarious workers, mainly in the cleaning and food industries. They are also supporting housing campaigns and other community struggles in what Callum Cant, a former Deliveroo rider, activist and commentator on these 'gig unions', calls 'community syndicalism', an approach which he describes as 'building the base for a mass socialist movement'.[14] BFAWU – an affiliated union which supports Corbyn – has worked closely with them in the recent wave of high-profile 'McStrikes', and GMB has also turned its attention to precarious workers.

The gig unions are not affiliated to Labour, priding themselves on their political independence and new ways of mobilising, starting with workers' own issues and self-organisation. Despite their independence and challenging approach to Labour, their aims chime with Corbyn and McDonnell's desire for daily engagement with civil society and the shop floor, and the Shadow Chancellor has actively supported their campaigns. As Cant writes: 'Self-organisation via direct action that builds power in the workplace and community is the only viable methodology to win the coming struggle on [a] warming planet', but he also highlights their independence and differences from Labour: 'The programme of the Labour Party needs to be systematically challenged from below: instead of share schemes, we can pose the slogan expropriation under workers' control. There's a lot to be getting on with!'[15]

However, the numbers involved in such unions are not large, and their organising faces suspicion and resistance from some parts of the traditional trade union movement. While there is a campaigning imperative for the Labour Party to both listen to and work with these self-organised grassroots workplace initiatives, it would be naïve to assume that on their own they will be sufficient for the scale of transformation of working conditions and workplace democracy that Corbynism requires.

Meanwhile, mainstream trade unions are facing their own problems as a result of the 2008 financial crash, and the resultant onslaught of austerity, deregulation and privatisation. All three are exacerbated by continuing attacks on the right of trade unions to organise, enabled by the 2016 Trade Union Act. While Labour's membership numbers have soared, trade union membership has plummeted – from a peak of thirteen million members in 1979 to 6.2 million in 2017.[16] The proportion of employees in unions has continued to fall too – from 32 per cent in 1995 to 23 per cent in 2017 – despite the fact that more than 25 per cent of women are now unionised, compared to 21 per cent of men. Younger workers are less likely to be union members now than they were in 1997,[17] while Black British workers are slightly more likely than white employees to be in a union – although only 9 per cent of trade union members are black or minority ethnic, compared to almost 12 per cent of the population overall.[18]

THIS IS WHAT A TRADE UNIONIST LOOKS LIKE

Central to Labour's new approach to the workplace, the economy and building social networks must be the fact that women are now 50 per cent of all trade union members. Gill Kirton and Geraldine Healy have written of the need for unions to recognise the connections 'between communities and unions, women and unions, minority ethnic and migrant workers and unions and the gendered character of employment relations' as part of a more effective, intersectional approach to organising and leadership at every level of union life.[19]

Engaging women trade unionists in campaigning for Labour's vision will mean listening much more closely to them than ever before, prioritising the issues they face, and paying attention to where they work and how they are organised. 53 per cent of women in all professional occupations are unionised, compared to just 29 per cent of men in the same group – reflecting the relative strength of trade unionism among teachers, nurses, social workers and others in public services. However, unionisation levels in female-dominated service occupations including care – largely privatised – are just 25 per cent, while in retail they fall to 14 per cent, and to 12 per cent in so-called 'elementary occupations' such as cleaning and catering.[20]

Social care is a sector that demands particularly close attention. Employing more workers than the NHS – 1.47 million[21] – in England alone, 78 per cent of social care is outsourced to the private sector, throwing away public money on rising procurement costs and profits. It is a sector dogged by low pay, zero-hours working, poor conditions, little access to training and high turnover. It is also a key area of women's employment, and one which must be a key focus of Labour's social-movement programme for change, engaging workers, users and their families in policymaking and mobilisation. To initiate this, however, means tackling low levels of unionisation in the sector through the Labour Party, Momentum, women's groups and anti-poverty campaigners working with UNISON and the other local government unions to rebuild workplace organisation.

A primary focus on an apparently homogeneous 'working class' or 'shop floor' – in reality code for blue-collar men – is unlikely to produce an organising strategy capable of generating a coalition of support for Labour across very different sections of the population or workforce. Labour and the unions together need to find ways of bringing coalitions together – including anti-poverty groups, tenants, LGBTQ, women's and anti-racist campaigns – to support local community struggles, unionisation campaigns and workers' demands for a fair deal.

The establishment of Unite Community – a new wing of Unite, open to the unemployed and community activists – is one such interesting development which offers the possibility of joint local organising and campaigning between workers, users and community groups. Its aims are clear – though arguably yet to be realised:

> Organising and activism are at the centre of strong communities, which is why Unite's community membership provides a way people can find and use their political voice. Whether it is taking a stand against a service closure or coming together to improve your living environment, as a Community member, Unite will be on your side.[22]

COALITIONS OF CHANGE

Much more than the usual resources, funding and election campaigners supplied by the unions throughout Labour's history will be needed to build this kind of coalition of change. To argue for, experiment with and sustain Corbynism's policies of redistribution, insourcing, anti-discrimination and workplace democracy demands a clear and well-articulated political commitment by the

unions, which in turn must provide greater democracy and respon-
siveness for members *within* the unions themselves. Membership
density needs to grow significantly. New leadership at all levels to
replace the current older, white male profile from the shop floor to
the general secretary's office must happen. Unions need to reori-
entate themselves – not just towards unorganised workers crying
out for voice and power, but towards those in their unions facing
discrimination, those members whose voices are rarely heard and,
indeed, towards entire communities suffering all the dire consequences of neoliberalism in our precarious times.

To achieve this, the Labour Party needs to look beyond the national
and develop a much stronger politics of the local. Arguably Labour
councils are where Labour politics come closest to communities, local
trade unions and social movements, and could effect some change
while Labour is out of office at Westminster. But few Labour council
leaders actively support Corbynism. The last few years have also seen
a number of clashes between Labour councils and their workforces –
not to mention service users facing library closures, cuts in social care
and youth services, potholes in roads and closures of women's refuges.
Of course, all of this has been created by the Tories undermining the
powers of local government and decimating their finances by 50 per
cent and, in some cases, even more.[23] But is it not the role of Labour
councils to resist, to campaign for their communities, to offer at least
some kind of alternative? More than three quarters of local government's 1.6 million employees are women.[24] They should be central
to support for Labour's industrial relations and employment-rights
agenda, and wider supporters for Corbynism as a consequence.

But school support workers in Durham and Derby have found
themselves at odds with their own Labour councils over cuts to pay and
working conditions, as have home care workers across the north west,
and refuse collectors in Birmingham, Brighton and elsewhere.[25] Most
Labour councils have engaged in deep cuts to the working conditions
of their workforces in recent years; not so different from Conservative
councils. It is no wonder, then, that members in UNISON and the
other local government unions are asking why Labour councils are
not speaking out or taking action against the Tories' devastating cuts,
and asking why their day-to-day reality is so different to the new politics Jeremy Corbyn has promised Labour will stand for.

In 2018, the local government unions – UNISON, GMB and Unite – drew up an agreement with the Labour Group of the Local Government Association; 'Labour local government trade union principles',[26] which declared the principle that 'Trade unions and Labour councillors are part of the same labour movement and share the same values of equality, social justice and solidarity.' The agreement promotes good industrial relations, exemplary employment practice, equality and in-house services, and is a strong statement of Labour's 2017 manifesto commitments. Yet despite the fine words, to date there has been little evidence that it has led to any greater resistance to cuts by most Labour councils or support and solidarity with their overwhelmingly female workforce.

Nowhere has the dismay and anger this causes been more sharply displayed than in Birmingham, where women employed by the largest Labour council in England as highly experienced, long-serving re-ablement workers, providing care and support in the home for those recovering from an illness or injury, faced the threat of massive cuts to their hours. This came just a few years after their enhanced unsocial hours payments were removed. In response, these women were out on strike for more than a year from early 2018, in contrast to the industrial action of the council's mainly male refuse collectors, whose dispute was settled much more quickly. While some local Labour councillors showed support, too many stay silent and only one of Birmingham's nine Labour MPs – Jack Dromey – actively intervened with the council on behalf of the strikers.

This led the strikers and their union UNISON to adopt an overtly political strategy, leafletting and lobbying in support of their cause across the wards of the council leader and cabinet member for social care. During their strike, when I interviewed Sue, Jenny and Margaret,[27] who have a combined eighty years of service to Birmingham City Council between them, and have been Labour voters all their lives, they had this to say about their feelings towards their party:

'How can a Labour council that is supposed to be for the working class do this?'

'We're all Labour supporters…my parents were always working class, so I've carried on…the thing is, if not Labour, where do you go?'

'The Labour values are still Labour values ... but are they acting for Labour, you know? They don't seem to be for the working-class people who use our services.'

The dispute was finally resolved in May 2019. Those women remaining in their jobs (some left because they wouldn't have been able to live on the money from the reduced hours) have had their hours protected, but they have been moved into the NHS, with the council no longer running the re-ablement service provided for decades by my interviewees. The concerns of the Birmingham strikers were reinforced for me when I spoke to a number of other women UNISON activists.[28] Sonya Howard is UNISON Branch Secretary in the London Borough of Kensington and Chelsea – now known as the 'Grenfell' council – and was, at the time of my interview with her in February 2019, UNISON National Executive Committee member:

It's low-paid women leading the way in strikes. We shouldn't have to be striking against Labour councils. Labour isn't hitting the spot for women and I say that from the gut. [Labour] appeals to me because of what I believe – but not as a woman, not really.

At the time of interview, Claire Ransom was a young UNISON local government branch activist in Southampton, and a strong Corbyn supporter:

I always paid into UNISON's Affiliated Political Fund (APF), but I had no idea what was going between the union and the party. It's only since I joined the party as an individual member that I've got any idea about Labour politics. If someone is paying into the APF, UNISON should be saying "this is what we're doing", so we can see the impact of where our money is going. Our branch Labour Link Officer doesn't attend any meetings and there are no report-backs from the Regional Labour Link Committee.

Laney Walsh is a UNISON branch secretary in Redditch Borough Council, where Labour lost control to the Tories in 2018. A long-time, highly successful community activist with huge credibility in the town, she envisages the union playing a key role in creating a broader social movement for Labour and feels that the majority of her members would welcome that:

> Our branch can play a part in connecting those who want social change to like-minded activities. As a branch we can also deliver campaigns that support Labour policies, not just for our activists but for the wider workforce, our towns. As a union we need to be integral to this movement. I will challenge anyone in UNISON that doesn't get behind transforming our labour movement into a social movement because by involving ourselves in our communities we'll be rebuilding [not only] them, but unions as well.

These are the marginalised – yet experienced – voices that Labour must listen to if it wants to embed its aims and values in a genuine grassroots social movement for change. Personal experience as an activist and UNISON official for thirty years tells me that neither the 'far left' nor the right within UNISON – or any other union – understands the critical need for authentic, socialist, black and white feminist women leaders who can make the links between women's activism in their workplaces, their communities and the home – and then the Labour Party.

The Labour Party under Corbyn also needs to urgently address the political problems it faces in local government, and think hard about how it can harness the energy of Labour councils and their overwhelmingly female workforce in promoting its radical policies and strategy for developing grassroots support. Social care would be a good place to start. UNISON North West Region's 'Care Workers for Change' campaign[29] is doing both, by seeking political support from Labour councils for its organising drive to unionise and improve pay and conditions of care workers across the region working for employers commissioned by the council, and supporting radical action by care workers. It is a model that Labour would do well to emulate elsewhere.

THE MISSING LINK IS STILL MISSING

In 2017 the Labour manifesto 'For the many, not the few' undoubtedly moved the party back onto more appealing terrain for trade union activists and full-time officials tired of the blight of Blairism and years of lukewarm support from their party. It promised to empower both workers and the trade unions, and streamline recognition and access to workplaces in order to boost union membership and strengthen workers' rights from the first day of employment, in an economy boosted by public investment.[30]

But activating such good Labour policies in collaboration with trade unions requires some sober reflection, alongside a much-needed revival of campaigning energy and imagination within the party, from Constituency Labour Parties upwards. Most trade union members do not belong to the Labour Party, many that do are in the higher income brackets, the only overall recent membership growth has been amongst over-60s,[31] and for some time the signs have been that fewer trade unionists are opting to pay into the political funds that support the Labour 'link'. Most frontline members join a union to help ensure protection should a problem arise at work, not to engage in party politics. Some are hostile to a close relationship with Labour, while others do not see politics as the core business of their union. And they certainly don't want to pay extra subs for the privilege.

There needs to be a realism that these are the political conditions in which we operate within our unions, while at the same time scaling the ambition of creating a new, dynamic relationship between them and the party at every level. We need both, in a process that should be shaped by those groups of workers that too often feel marginalised by the unions' practices and Labour's traditional shop floor focus, despite their growing significance in the economy, whether or not they are members with a direct relationship with the Labour Party. For those whose employer is a Labour council, that relationship is as likely to be a negative experience as a positive one. This calls for a wholescale review of trade union democracy and new relationships with the party and local communities, which engage members from the care home to the car plant, from the supermarket shop floor to the head teacher's office. 'For the many, not the few' must also be the principle which underpins Labour's relationship with a feminised, increasingly precarious, globalised workforce.

Exasperated by the caution of mainstream trade unionism, the gig unions have found their cause through independent, bottom-up organising, led by their members. Bottom-up local campaigns by trade unionists, particularly women, show that there can be grass-roots power and effective organising, with the capacity to pressurise overly cautious national leaderships into support, and action. Many Labour members want to join them in creating a radical new movement for change, linking workplaces and communities to what the party both stands for, and does. But while 'realism' can understandably be a dirty word in trade unions and the Labour Party, that movement must start from where we are at now, not where we would like to be. Crucially, this must reflect the life of the 'whole worker', as Jane McAlevey in her book on US union organising argues:[32]

> These workers were changing their entire lives, not just their work lives, and they were doing it from the foundation of their union.... They were fundamentally building worker power, and it was an experience of community, class, race, faith, and personal liberation.

There's not just a workplace to win out there. There's just maybe a world to win too.

NOTES

1. Lewis Minkin, *The Contentious Alliance*, Edinburgh University Press: Edinburgh, 1991.
2. Sheila Lewenhak, *Women and Trade Unions*, Benn: London, 1977, p.287. See also Sarah Boston, *Women Workers and the Trade Unions*, Lawrence and Wishart: London, 2015.
3. Minkin 1991.
4. Mark Wickham-Jones, 'Trade union members did not shape the Labour leadership result as much as in past elections', LSE British Politics and Policy blog, 15 September 2015.
5. Labour List, 'Which unions have backed Corbyn or Smith in the Labour leadership context?', 11 August 2016.
6. Dave Ward, quoted in Peter Edwards, 'CWU backs Corbyn as Labour leader "for the millions, not the millionaires"', Labour List, 1 August 2016.
7. 'For the many, not the few' was the title of Labour's 2017 general election manifesto, which proved very popular.
8. Jeremy Corbyn, 'Why I am proud of the link between the Labour Party and the trade unions', www.unionstogether.org.uk, 10 February 2016.
9. Steven Fielding, 'Why Corbyn's movement has yet to gain momentum', *The New European*, 28 September 2018.

10. Paul Mason, 'Labour won the conference season but it needs a social movement to win the war', *New Statesman*, 4 October 2018.
11. *Ibid.*
12. Owen Jones, 'Mass membership alone doesn't make a social movement', *The Guardian*, 27 July 2016.
13. Wickham-Jones 2015.
14. Callum Cant, 'Taking what's ours: An ACORN inquiry', www.notesfrombelow.org, 16 August 2018.
15. Cant, 'McNetworks: Two current modes of struggle', www.notesfrombelow.org, 11 October 2018.
16. National Statistics, 'Trade union statistics 2017', 31 May 2018.
17. TUC, 'Five reasons why young workers are getting raw deal', 7 November 2017.
18. TUC, 'Section A: Labour market diversity and trade union membership', TUC Equality Audit 2018, 11 September 2018.
19. Gill Kirton and Geraldine Healy, *Gender and Leadership in Unions*, Routledge: London, 2013.
20. National Statistics, 'Trade union statistics 2018', 30 May 2019.
21. Dave Griffiths, Will Fenton et al., 'The state of the adult social care sector and workforce in England', Skills for Care, 24 September 2018.
22. 'Unite Community Membership', www.unitetheunion.org.
23. National Audit Office, 'Financial sustainability of local authorities 2018', Full Report, 8 March 2018.
24. UNISON, 'Unions call for a long overdue pay rise for hard-pressed council employees', 14 June 2017.
25. UNISON, 'AFG workers set to begin seven-day strike', 3 May 2019; Hannah Graham, 'County Durham teaching assistants celebrate "great result" as two-year pay fight ends', *Chronicle Live*, 16 October 2017; Rob Cole, 'Unite announces new strike dates for Birmingham refuse workers', *Resource*, 6 February 2019.
26. 'Labour local government trade union principles 2018', www.local.gov.uk.
27. Interview, February 2019, names changed to protect the interviewees.
28. All interviews February 2019.
29. UNISON North West, 'Care workers for change'.
30. 'For the many, not the few: The Labour Party Manifesto 2017', 'Chapter 4: A fair deal at work'.
31. Joe Dromey, 'Power to the people: How stronger unions can deliver economic justice', IPPR, 2018.
32. Jane McAlevey, *Raising Expectations (and Raising Hell): My Decade Fighting for the Labor Movement*, Verso: London, 2014, p.329.

The New Left Mediascape

Anne Coddington

Ben Sellers is in his mid forties, lives in Durham, has worked as a trade union organiser and community activist, founded a socialist bookshop, and is currently employed as the parliamentary aide to his local Labour MP, Laura Pidcock.

Sellers has been involved in two social media campaigns that have helped make the Labour left a force to be reckoned with in British politics. First, in 2015, he and other socialist activists in the Labour left grouping Red Labour drew on their digital networks to help get Jeremy Corbyn on the ballot for the Labour leadership contest, and then intensified their campaign to play a crucial part in getting him elected leader.

Two years later, Sellers coordinated Corbyn's digital media operations for the 2017 general election (the leader's own social media, as distinct from the official Labour Party sites). Jeremy became a social media phenomenon: the weekly reach of his Facebook page, for example, averaged 24 million – which meant over a third of the country was accessing campaign material via Corbyn on Facebook.[1]

'The left would be nowhere without social media', Ben explained when I interviewed him over tea at Portcullis House in Westminster. 'But what is crucial is how it is used', he added. 'Do we use it to put out information, essentially as a website does, or do we use it to genuinely engage with people?' Using social media as a PR tool is pretty limited, but when it is used as an organising tool, it can be very powerful. He explains, 'trotting out a line, whether sticking it to the Blues or cheering on the Reds, is unlikely to get much traction. It absolutely has to be interactive: asking people for their views, their ideas and ultimately their action.'

A digital campaign based around organising is the antithesis of the typical slick, tightly controlled media strategy that puts out the line and asks party members to communicate it. Sellers describes the 2015 Jeremy Corbyn for Leader campaign as 'completely organic and grassroots. We had assembled a team of activists around the left of the party: people who could design those memes, who understood Jeremy's politics, and who were in touch with the wider movement. There was deliberately no thematic line. It was creative and, at times, ad hoc, but it connected with people.'[2]

The looseness of the digital campaign, with activists creating their own media to engage with other activists and supporters, encouraged participation and contributed towards the huge numbers who attended rallies – which in itself fed back into further online stories recording the building of a grassroots movement as it happened. And it created an appetite for Corbyn's ideas, policy discussions and deeper engagement via volunteering and people sharing stories to their networks.

In his contribution to the 2016 book *Corbyn's Campaign*, Sellers offers a detailed account of how the Red Labour social media effort aided the building of Corbyn's support in the 2015 leadership contest: 'This alternative media counteracted much of the negativity... from the mainstream media, there was a real sense that this was a movement that everyone could be involved in, discuss, interact with, get answers from.' The team dealt with thousands of individual messages and enquiries to their Facebook and Twitter pages. 'If people felt like actors in this campaign, rather than "consumers" of it, a large part of that was down to our social media operation.'[3]

But the extent of mainstream media hostility towards Corbyn from the first day of the leadership campaign onwards has been enormous, and shows the continuing need for party activists on the left to develop political strategies and media tools that can circumvent this. Describing press coverage of the 2017 general election, media theorist Des Freedman writes that 'it is undeniable that whole swathes of reporting were hugely biased'. He notes the less critical coverage of the Tories – despite their appalling campaign – with Labour attracting far more negative coverage than any other party, despite running a fantastic campaign. Even the broadcasters, compelled to respect 'due impartiality', 'happily reproduced memes about Corbyn's "unelectability", his alleged links to terrorists and his reluctance to send millions of people to their death by pressing the nuclear button'.[4] Voters did access a broader range of coverage via social media, and this did have an impact, but its reach comes nowhere close to that of the legacy media.

The Labour Party, then, must be serious about adopting digital media as a counterweight to what Sellers, during my conversation with him, called 'the centrist media'. Social media changes the game, making possible deeper engagement. Media communications can no longer be top down – simply waiting for the professionals to put out a statement is not enough. But the potential remains unrealised in constituency parties, and even among some MPs. Sellers suggested to me that 'there is still a massive battle to be had around using social media in an educative way'. '[Social media] can create the most enormous consultation exercise the Labour Party and movement around it has ever seen.' But it must be used openly, and with strategic sense.

Used in this way, social media provides 'instant feedback on our ideas, our strategies and the way we do politics'. Sellers cites the suggestion of a consultation on all-female train carriages put forward in 2017 as a way to create safe spaces for women. 'We thought it was a good idea, but we shared it via social media and the feedback was negative, so it made us think again.' He explains how such consultation shapes policy: 'We would get the story out there, get feedback, identify the problems and pass it back to the policy team.' Or it can be used as a strategic tool to win the party to positions the left supports: 'if we show MPs that in the constituencies there is support for abolishing Trident, it can impact on the Parliamentary Labour Party'. He adds, 'this represents a power shift, it's an enormous democratic exercise'.

Social media also has the potential to open up dialogue between MPs and their constituents. As Sellers explained to me, 'If a constituent asks a question on social media, you can't avoid it – you can't say it's hidden in a raft of emails.' It's there on public record. Laura Pidcock uses social media to broaden the ways she engages with the local community: she recognises that not everyone is inspired by the written word, so her website, Instagram, Facebook and Twitter feeds feature videos too. And she draws on the way that these platforms are used by ordinary people to generate a closer relationship – she is an MP, but also someone who has a family, uses local services, is affected by government cuts. Hence, she talks on her social media about giving birth, or having a smear test, as well as about her role as an MP – it is a personal way into political issues. And it can build a bridge between politics as a representative mechanism and the ordinary lives of constituents – regardless of how they voted.

Sellers admits to being frustrated with those Constituency Labour Parties (CLPs) that are reluctant to embrace social media in a positive way. He says, 'many are scared of its power. It is shifting and sometimes a bit out of control and, of course, it's a threat to the way we have traditionally done things.' He explains this in terms of a broader organisational culture where those used to the traditional way of doing politics find it easier to use the formal representative mechanisms to get their views heard and can thereby exclude others from taking part in the debate.

In contrast, many of those who have joined or rejoined Labour since 2015 have done so via social media, and are expecting to enter a vibrant modern political formation. Not least because Corbyn, as the point of access, is, says Sellers, 'a dream candidate for the social media age: everything he said was clear, accessible, and without jargon'.

Sellers suggests that:

We need to concentrate on closing the gap between the 'old left', who joined pre-2015, who have less access to social media, and therefore a different experience of the changes that have taken place, but lots of expertise to pass on to younger activists, and those who have discovered their activism via social media, and have lots of ideas and energy.

So do we need political education to fill in the blanks? Ben's suggestion: 'Not lecturing, or an approach that says "we are the experts, this is what you've done wrong"', but a genuine conversation, 'where we work collectively on positions and approaches to deal with difficult issues'.

If the new members are to remain in the party, this more informal discursive culture will be very important – digital natives in particular will need to feel that they are more than simply cogs in an electoral machine and that they have the freedom to express their activism in meaningful ways. The success of social media campaigning in the 2017 election 'is already shaping the Labour Party', explains psephologist Andrew Chadwick.[5] 'The growth of digital media in citizens' political repertoire has affinities to a broader shift in youth engagement and a general scepticism towards authority.'

Indeed there are many young activists on the left who admire Corbyn and his values and want to support him, but who, as things stand, find the idea of belonging to the Labour Party too restrictive. As Michael Segalov, contributing editor at *Huck*, a magazine aimed at the millennial generation, puts it: 'Activism is a different form of politics, it's not simply about rooms where we sit and talk. It's about investing in communities. So the Labour Party is not our sole output.'[6] He explains, 'We want a Labour government, but should Labour be elected, it doesn't mean we stop pressurising the leadership to push things forward.' He adds: 'and for many of us, there is a perception that if you are in the party, you cannot criticise the leadership'.

Social media is both tool and metaphor for change. Digital communication tools can energise those who feel disenfranchised and disillusioned with the political Establishment. Corbynism was a surprise to many politicians and journalists because the people, who are expected to listen to the experts, had gone rogue. Social media has been adopted as the people's voice to bypass mainstream media coverage and lobby for social change.

Political theorist Paolo Gerbaudo summarises the phenomenon: '[Social media] has come to be understood as a platform for the voice of the people in opposition to the allegedly corrupt mainstream mass media, accused of being in cahoots with the financial and political Establishment'.[7] Gerbaudo emphasises that such media are outlets for alternative citizen journalism, where people antagonise what they call the 'mainstream media' (MSM), which is seen as not covering and representing the issues and views held by a growing portion of the population. As such, these outlets are an invitation to show certain news items that, they argue, the MSM does not want you to know about.

But digital media is not simply a progressive phenomenon. Online discussions have, Gerbaudo notes, provided gathering spaces where the 'lonely crowds produced by the hyperindividualism of neoliberal society could coalesce'.[8] These crowds can come as easily from the right, including the far right, as from the left. Hence the growth of 'alt-right' websites such as Breitbart, once run by Steve Bannon, who became Donald Trump's chief strategist, and which during the 2016 American presidential election attracted a huge following by offering an undiluted and unashamedly partisan right-wing news agenda. Or Westmonster, a pro-Brexit site edited by Nigel Heaver, a former press adviser to Nigel Farage, who describes himself as 'milk-bottle white'. Westmonster is, in Heaver's words, 'written in a way that is not politically correct,' with headlines such as 'Brits want the burka banned' and stories that blame society's ills on immigration.[9]

Digital media, from individual Twitter feeds to these well-funded alt-right news websites, is thus a technology – albeit one with a particular set of affordances that shape engagement – and, as such, it reflects the uses to which it is put.

ALT-LEFT AND VERY ANGRY

Following the financial crash in 2008, and in some cases inspired by the Occupy movement, a new generation of left-wing radicals have used digital media to air their frustrations with the neoliberal status quo using language that is both polemical and confrontational. Alt-left sites such as the Canary, Another Angry Voice, Evolve Media and the Skwawkbox have relentlessly promoted a pro-Corbyn agenda and have been quick to challenge all critical voices, in particular the perceived biases of the mainstream media. As Jim Waterson, then-political editor of BuzzFeed, put it in 2017, alt-left sites: 'positioned themselves as "Corbyn's outriders", jumping on stories without much of the nuance of outlets that remain rooted in mainstream reporting traditions'.[10]

Their distinct news agenda is, like that of their counterparts on the alt-right, unashamedly partisan. Matthew Turner of Evolve Media describes their role: 'The way we write is not without biases, but it presents an alternative point of view that is legitimate ... for us to deny that would be like the *Sun* denying they have an anti-Corbyn bias.'[11] Indeed, what unites all the prominent alt-left sites is a tone that echoes that of the *Sun* and the *Daily Mail*. Jim Waterson again: 'they are using the same tabloid tactics to reach the maximum number of people, and putting a heavy spin on quotes and statistics'. And there's a purpose to this – the sites 'are taking the view that if the right-wing tabloids are able to twist the Labour leader's words and get away with it, then there's a legitimate case for them to do the same in his defence'.[12]

It was only during the 2017 general election, when these tiny DIY websites that grew out of the blogging movement – produced by writers with little journalistic experience and even less funds – started getting shares for their stories in excess of the social media output of legacy media like *The Guardian* and the BBC, that the extent of their reach became visible. Thomas Clarke's post on his blog Another Angry Voice, 'How many of Jeremy Corbyn's ideas do you actually disagree with?', was one of the most shared stories of the election – more than 100,000 times on Facebook. Kerry-Anne Mendoza, founder of the Canary, has claimed that more than six million people visited that site during the election campaign.[13]

These sites never could have reached critical mass without the aggregating functions of social media, and Facebook in particular. Gerbaudo argues that because there is so much information online: 'algorithms tend to focus the attention of users only on those contents matching their interests'.[14] These filter bubbles can create online crowds of like-minded individuals and, indeed, support the rise of populist movements, or what Gerbaudo calls 'mobocracy'. The selection of stories to user newsfeeds tends, he says, towards 'those posts that attract a high number of reactions in the few seconds and minutes since their publication', and thus can 'favour sensational content'. Knowing how to create posts that will play well on social media is a skill, and one that the primarily millennial and younger-generation alt-bloggers well understand.

The 'echo chambers' – closed systems where people are exposed to content that reinforces their existing beliefs – that are such a feature of social media can be very effective in drawing like-minded people together. But there is, of course, a danger that they polarise debate. Where newsfeeds confirm personal opinions and values, and where a tweet that is liked or shared creates feelings of affirmation and certainty, it is easy to become disconnected from the nuance and context that are inherently part of politics. If the left is going to shift the Labour Party towards its own positions, it must engage with opposing viewpoints – the divide over Brexit couldn't make that more obvious.

The alt-left websites, while they might have the potential to be very effective organising hubs, bring a confrontational tone into politics that is not helpful. They are expressions of discontent – as names like Another Angry Voice make clear – but a tendency towards finger-pointing and hectoring language do not in the long term create change or deepen understanding of a political project. What the Corbyn project needs is a media that will support it, but also challenge it. Partisanship cannot be one dimensional. Simply shouting at detractors, or interpreting oppositional views negatively without providing fair context and giving alternative voices a hearing, is neither good journalism nor good politics. Or, as Ben Sellers puts it, 'You wouldn't sit in a pub and scream at people across the table, would you? So let's not do it on social media.'

PRINTED MATTERS

Given the ubiquity of digital communications, it is easy to forget that print-based media have always had a function of creating left-wing communities of readers. Important publications range from *Black Dwarf* and *International Times* in the 1960s, to *Marxism Today* and the Labour Party's own innovative magazine, *New Socialist*, in the 1980s, through to *Red Pepper*, which grew out of the social movements that supported the miners' strike in the 1980s, and continues to this day.

This older form of publishing has not been completely superseded by digital alternatives. Indeed, it is undergoing something of a renaissance. As David Thorburn and Henry Jenkins explain, when technological disruption occurs, it is rarely the case that older systems of cultural transmission are simply replaced, rather they 'develop new functions and find new audiences'.[15] A new generation of young digitally literate independent producers are choosing print as the medium to express their radical ambition, using the increased availability of desktop publishing software and the growth of low-cost digital printing houses.

Indie publishing is typically associated with a plethora of publications that, according to media theorist Megan Le Masurier, celebrate 'the under-represented manifestations of popular culture and creative work from independent producers of fashion, design, the visual arts, photography, music and film'.[16] In response to decades of austerity, a number of politics and current-affairs titles have entered this arena – think *Delayed Gratification*, with its focus on slow news as an antidote to throwaway media, *Weapons of Reason*, which uses infographics to communicate complex global issues, or *Good Trouble*, a beautifully designed 'newspaper' which chronicles cultures of resistance and protest. A millennial approach to politics isn't about following established news values, or speaking with authority, but looking for a fresh angle, communicating the facts in a unique voice.

Unlike more established titles such as the *New Statesman* or the *Spectator*, these titles are producer-owned – they do not have external backers or shareholders – and are often influenced by zine culture, in that they have grown out of a passion for a subject, rather than the intention to make a profit. Few start out with business plans or market-research data. They tend to grow organically, finding like-minded readers from within their own networks and subcultures, not least because, lacking huge circulations, they can't access the broader audiences that being on the newsstand can deliver. But this intimate knowledge of their readers gives them an authenticity, and the confidence to develop a more maverick attitude to journalism and an uncompromising aesthetic – many, for example, eschew cover lines and use unconventional typography.

A BLAST FROM THE PAST

Tribune, one of Britain's oldest socialist publications, was relaunched in 2018 as a bimonthly print magazine and website. With its high production values, it has the look and feel of a modern indie format. Ronan Burtenshaw, the magazine's twenty-nine-year-old editor, spoke to me about the rationale for taking this title, established by two Labour MPs in 1937 as a vehicle for the anti-Stalinist Labour left, and repositioning it for a new generation of Corbynites perhaps unfamiliar with its history, or indeed with editorial traditions of left publishing. *Tribune* is now owned by Bhaskar Sunkara, founder of the US independent left magazine *Jacobin*, which has been successful in popularising socialist ideas to post-Occupy, pro-Sanders activists in the US – who now seeks to adapt this editorial and publishing formula for the Labour left here. But wouldn't it be better to trade on the radical chic of the US brand and set up a UK edition of *Jacobin*?

Not according to Burtenshaw. He argues it is precisely *Tribune*'s heritage and historic links to the Labour movement that are valuable. 'Young people are enthused by Corbynism', he says, 'but a lot of what they hear about socialism is mocked in the mainstream media. They are described as young and naïve - and that robs them of their confidence and their pride in political activity.' Yet this tradition, founded on mass movements of working people, 'won almost every reform that makes society worth living'. Civil liberties, democratic rights, the franchise for women, trade unions' right to organise, the welfare state, were all established through collective action. Burtenshaw is keen to embrace *Tribune*'s history as a source of credibility in the here and now. Nye Bevan, a former *Tribune* editor, oversaw the construction of the NHS, Barbara Castle, a *Tribune* columnist for many years, introduced the Equal Pay Act in 1970, and Jennie Lee, regular writer for *Tribune*, founded the Open University. The new version of *Tribune* has underlined these connections by featuring full-page portrait photos of these seminal figures in its early editions.

Before Corbyn, during the New Labour years, these left traditions appeared moribund, says *Tribune*'s culture editor Owen Hatherley, 'so we have a movement that is extremely young and old. But there is a gap in the middle, and our project is to smooth that out, and create a lineage between the two.'[17] Hence the magazine has a focus on reanimating socialist history and institutions as a means to develop areas of affinity between different parts, and generations, of the left.

Tribune communicates this political project in ways that link it with indie culture. Le Masurier notes that indie publications 'stress the role of the art director'. For many, 'graphic design is as important as journalistic content, art direction as important as editing. The synergy between the two is a creative collaboration, not just the art illustrating the editorial content.'[18] *Tribune* – like *Jacobin* –

has an aestheticism that means it would not look out of place in an independent magazine bookshop, a cutting-edge art gallery 'space' or a quirky café – all of which curate their choice of publications according to the look, feel and tone of content, and their intersection with contemporary taste.

Burtenshaw is positive about the role of design in the new *Tribune*. 'We have learned a lot from *Jacobin* about the importance of design to radical ambition. It is really significant in helping people to imagine an alternative, putting things on the horizon that are not part of the mainstream. Design can inspire and illuminate ideas – it isn't just pretty packaging.' Hatherley believes that, with contemporary readers, 'you won't be taken seriously if you don't engage with design as well as content'.[19] A well-crafted format makes people take notice and builds respect. He explains: 'You can spot a left-wing publication at twenty paces and people immediately think "ah, they are from that club". But if you want to change society, it's best not to look like a club.'

Tribune's modern design is juxtaposed with subject matter rooted in the traditional social and economic concerns of the Labour left. Burtenshaw is clear about where he wants the magazine positioned: 'We want to tell the story of important industrial struggles, profile younger trade unionists, and connect what is happening in the workplace to broader social issues'. And, of course, 'create a better understanding of the concerns, and misconceptions, young people have about trade unions'.

The magazine's audience reflects the current make-up of the left. Burtenshaw, again: 'By far the biggest readership is amongst activists in the Labour Party or groups like Momentum.' Of this Labour Party readership, he identifies two particular groups: 'there is a younger, metropolitan urban audience that supported Corbyn, and then a smaller section of older, regionally disadvantaged, groups' – though he is quick to point out that more than half of *Tribune*'s 6,000-plus subscribers live outside of London.

'We can't see the two groups as blocs that are exclusive', he says.

Yes, there are differences, the younger members are aware of the 2008 crisis – that is their point of reference. And if you think of somewhere like Hull, you have older members with a different perspective. For them, the economic crisis goes back to the 1980s and the deindustrialisation that took place as a consequence of Thatcherism. That is important, they have a different understanding of society.

Burtenshaw argues that '*Tribune* is a "movement publication"'. 'We don't see ourselves as a media operation that exists outside as an external critic.' *Tribune* views itself as a participant in a political community. 'We would like to be the space where we talk about the difficult questions of the state, the economy, and the significant obstacles that would face a Labour government once in power.'

The magazine is keen to learn from *Jacobin*'s successful growth model. *Tribune*'s publisher, Bhaskar Sunkara, set up *Jacobin* in 2011, creating the first issue in his dorm room while a student at George Washington University in the US. Today it has a circulation of 40,000, and is part of an expanding enterprise including a book imprint, podcasts, an academic journal and a website with over a million monthly visitors. Sunkara has also recently launched a foreign-language edition of *Jacobin* in Italy.

'*Jacobin* has built an institution that can sustain itself, there is a business model that works', notes Burtenshaw. *Tribune*'s own financial model looks to the print format, and he argues that while this might seem outdated in the digital age, it has the advantage of being associated with a well-established revenue stream. Readers are used to paying for physical magazines, particularly through subscription, which provides regular, and much needed, income for smaller magazines. For this reason, Burtenshaw is sceptical of the conventional wisdom on the left that publishing projects need to be started online. 'It seems so easy, they are quick to set up, but it's incredibly hard to make money, so many projects go bust.'

WORDS WITH BRAINS

'It's been argued that the new Labour left lacks the type of intellectual infrastructure that provided so much support for the neoliberals' original ascent', wrote Robin Blackburn in 2018.[20] Blackburn does cite a number of intellectual resources available to the Corbyn-McDonnell project: think tanks such as the New Economics

Foundation and the Centre for Labour and Social Studies (CLASS); the opportunities for debate offered via the annual The World Transformed conference; and support from activist media outlets, such as Novara Media. Others have evolved since Blackburn wrote: in particular, a local network of The World Transformed events; Dan Hind's revival, in association with Open Democracy, of the political pamphlet; and the new Common Wealth think tank, focusing on models of public ownership. But positive though all of this is, it remains true, as Blackburn suggested, that such intellectual channels are a long way from becoming hegemonic.

This makes embedding and popularising the Corbyn revolution both urgent and challenging. A study by the Media Reform Coalition has shown a pattern of hostile media coverage of Jeremy Corbyn and his agenda.[21] And there seems to be little appetite on the part of media organisations to address this anytime soon – ironic, when the same media criticise Corbyn for dogmatism and narrow-mindedness.

Guardian journalist Gary Younge – one of the few broadly pro-Corbyn voices in the mainstream media – has noted 'a precious lack of self-awareness' within the media profession, and an inability to interrogate its own shortcomings or worldview. He cites coverage of the 2017 general election: on election night, 'the pundits were assembled, everyone knew what was going to happen – Corbyn was going to be trashed. Then there was a hung parliament. And the presenter turns to the journalists and asks "what comes next?"'. Younge continues incredulously: 'They got everything wrong for the past two years and they are the ones asked what is going to happen. And those journalists are still there, and still being asked what comes next.'[22]

The pro-Corbyn media is in its infancy. In many cases, it is produced by people with little journalistic training – not in itself a barrier, as many practitioners go into the profession without training, but they usually enter established media organisations with editorial processes in place, meaning they can learn on the job. Digital media has made setting up and finding audiences easier, but it also means that when mistakes are made – inaccurate reporting, poor fact-checking or polemical content that pushes beyond the bounds of journalistic conventions – it is also more high profile. We can debate the rights and wrongs of the reasons why alt-left websites have hectored prominent broadcasters such as the BBC's Laura Kuenssberg for biased reporting, but when this becomes the story it detracts from any other message, and all too quickly descends into plain – and unacceptable – nastiness. It is becoming clear that digital media can thrive on such confrontations to all our costs.

Journalism is a skill. Establishing news values, reporting the facts, providing space for opposing viewpoints are all beset with ethical and, indeed, philosophical problems. Ever since Stuart Hall's pioneering work in the late 1970s on media constructions of crime and the ideological news values that created them,[23] a whole academic field has developed to understand why, out of all the events happening in the world, certain subjects become news and others do not. This is a familiar area for Younge. He cites the issue of gun crime in black communities – deaths of young black teenagers that go seriously underreported. He puts this down, in part, to journalistic practice, and to the social position of many professional journalists who, Younge says, 'are more likely to be white, wealthy and educated than the population at large and less likely to live in areas where gun deaths happen, and they are less likely to know the people they happen to. For journalists this comes at a severe price, they literally don't know the people they are writing about.'[24] Rather than taking on the painstaking work of connecting gun crime to cuts in welfare spending or support for youth clubs, Younge suggests that we have a situation where 'journalists swoop into a community for the day, find the people they are looking for, gather their quotes across race, sex and class, and off they go' – doing little more than slotting people's real lives into existing stereotypes. No wonder people feel disconnected from much of what they consume in the media.

This makes it crucial that any alternative media focuses on telling its own stories and developing its own news values and agendas. Eleanor Penny, an editor at *Red Pepper* and Novara Media, describes her own experience:

Yes, getting on Sky News or a byline in *The Guardian* is important – using mainstream media to get our voices heard – but what we really need is to build an autonomous media. Our own media can reflect back our experiences, reflect the impacts of austerity and the collapse of the social – of community centres and places of local collectivity, those wellsprings of organised resistance. It is only then that our viewpoints can be validated.[25]

WRITING OUR OWN HEADLINES

The potential for this exists. The work that Ben Sellers pioneered around Corbyn's 2015 leadership campaign, creating a space for people to debate issues, draw on their own experiences and relay them to others, has begun to spread, albeit slowly. Social media initiatives have become an essential part of Labour Party campaigning. And activist-led examples of storytelling have been developing, such as Labour Voices, a series of low-budget films that tell the stories of ordinary members from across the country.[26] The first, a broadcast of Labour Party activist Guy Matthews, from Retford in Nottinghamshire, talking straight to camera with his message to working-class voters, went viral, with more than two million views in the first four days following its release in May 2019. Raw and authentic, it could be an alternative party political broadcast, and is an example of what can be achieved with a little imagination.

Michael Walker, an editor at Novara Media,[27] one of the most imaginative new left digital media outlets, outlines the difficulty of creating content that can capitalise on the hundreds of thousands of new Labour members who have reinvigorated the left. 'I'd like to see [an] LBC or *Guardian* of the radical left, but I don't know if we can.' Novara has been successful in raising funds via subscriptions from its loyal and growing audience, but becoming self-sustaining will be far more difficult. Walker sums up the problem: 'All our content is free.' Moving from being a niche outlet would have implications that Walker recognises:

It would require a certain level of professionalism. It's one thing to work on a voluntary basis, to talk about topics that will interest your friends, but if you want to make a well-produced short snappy video that talks to a mass audience, this requires a whole other level of discipline and money. Often, when you look at media products and think they are lacking, that is down to capacity.[28]

Novara, well respected for its range of original content, was founded in 2011 by then-PhD student Aaron Bastani as a weekly podcast. It has since grown into a multimedia website, and is particularly well known for its video shows that feature guests from a plurality of left positions – not always pro-Corbyn – such as *Guardian* journalist Zoe Williams, Green Party spokesperson Sian Berry, academic superstar David Harvey – even American film director Spike Lee.

Novara's appeal owes much to the confidence and irreverence of the core group of millennial editors behind it, among them Michael Walker, Ash Sarkar, James Butler and Bastani himself. Its approach is partisan, in that it does not seek to moderate between two sides of a debate – its focus is clearly the promotion of left ideas and activism – but it also offers a space for its editors to elaborate on their political interests in ways that do not always follow journalistic conventions.

For example, Bastani might open a video show with his opinions on a current topic, only to veer, seemingly unscripted, into its relationship to 'fully automated luxury communism' – the subject of his recent book[29] – or to explain 'Why Jacob Rees-Mogg is a toxic weirdo'. Sarkar might contextualise racism through an academic prism, asking 'When were white people invented?' or 'What is Islamophobia?' The treatment of politics is fun and witty, as well as informative. There is a diversity of styles, and content is newsworthy but also unapologetically theoretical, for example, in James Butler's show *Terms of Engagement*, where he explains concepts like populism or freedom of speech with clarity – offering a primer for the new generation of young left activists.

In these ways, what Novara does is more engaging and multifaceted than the outputs of much other alt-left media. Sarkar, now also a regular commentator on Sky, contributor to *The Guardian* and *Question Time* guest, notes that: 'We come from activist circles, and there is also an academic impulse in all of us.'[30] Novara recognises that large numbers of eighteen to thirty year olds voted Labour in 2017, many for the first time, and while they may need information about Labour policies, or why the Tories are wrong, they also crucially need spaces to reflect on their politics. Sarkar describes Novara's contribution thus: 'Useful, salient, accessible – they are our key words.' She adds that the question Novara always asks itself is: 'What is the most accessible and quickfire way to get complex ideas into a shareable format?'[31]

In 2016, at the height of Labour's second leadership contest involving Corbyn, Bastani took a step back from the slings and arrows of Jeremy Corbyn v. Owen Smith to write a response to Corbyn's statement that Labour would harness 'the advances of new technology so that we can organise political campaigning like we've never seen before in Britain', and take it forward to the next general election. Bastani suggested eight points for a new Labour Party media strategy.[32] His ideas are all eminently achievable, forward-thinking, and have the advantage of supporting the work many activists are already doing inside and outside the party. The creation of a 'digital leaders programme' would, for example, provide talented activist content creators with both professional media production skills and the knowledge of how to use them for political ends. It would support grassroots media activism, including at constituency party level, which is vital in a digital environment where politics and media are increasingly hybrid, one feeding off the other. Bastani also proposed that an up-skilled activist media should be supported by a 'head of new media for battleground constituencies' to implement new media-content strategies focused on target seats. And, at Labour HQ, a 'technology incubator' would create processes and technologies to enable Labour activists to communicate better amongst themselves, civil society and the electorate. To date, these ideas do not appear to have been taken up by the party. This exemplifies an enduring caution on the part of Labour to fully embrace the new mediascape.

It is at the local level that Labour's media remains especially underdeveloped. While there are examples of good practice, many CLPs, and even some MPs, have Twitter and Facebook accounts that are not updated for weeks, months, or even years and, as a result, numbers of followers and friends are a fraction of the potential. Of those who do update, the content is not always presented in a way that would maximise engagement.

If this is to change, digital media must be central, not only to

Labour's communications strategy, but also to its party organisation and culture. Taking digital media seriously would inspire and empower those, the millennials and younger generations mostly, who occupy this new media terrain as a matter of course, not choice. CLPs would be assisted to be more creative, disseminating their own media messages, and this would involve collaboration between old and new members, digital natives and techno-avoiders, between those with experience of campaigning, and those with the skills to hone these messages into a few sentences. Opportunities could be provided to share experiences between constituency parties 'horizontally', through mentoring schemes in which local parties with members who have worked on social media campaigns, or those who contribute to activist media websites, could encourage others. This would not be top-down, the imposition of the kind of technocratic modernisation so associated with New Labour, but the simple sharing of skills and knowledge. It would have an authenticity and kindness that, if Corbynism is to mean anything, must be the core characteristic of how it does politics.

NOTES

1. Mark Shepherd, 'Social media and the Corbyn breakthrough', in Einar Thorsen, Dan Jackson, Darren Lilleker (eds), 'UK election analysis 2017: Media, voters and the campaign', Centre for the Study of Journalism, Culture and Community, Bournemouth University, June 2017.
2. Ben Sellers, '#JezWeDid', in Tom Unterrainer (ed), *Corbyn's Campaign*, Spokesman: Nottingham, 2016, p.38.
3. *Ibid.*
4. Des Freedman, 'Media bias hits a wall', in Thorsen et al. 2017, p.48.
5. Andrew Chadwick, 'Corbyn, Labour, digital media and the 2017 general election', in Thorsen et al. 2017, p.89.
6. Talk by Michael Segalov at 'Activism Toolkit' Lewes Labour Party event, 27 October 2018.
7. Paolo Gerbaudo, 'Social media and populism: An elective affinity?', *Media, Culture and Society*, Vol. 40, No. 5, 2018, p.749.
8. *Ibid*, p.750.
9. Jasper Jackson, 'Arron Banks launches Breitbart-style site, Westmonster', *The Guardian*, 19 January 2017.
10. Jim Waterson, 'The rise of the alt-left British media', BuzzFeed, 1 May 2017.

11. *Ibid.*
12. *Ibid.*
13. Robert Booth, 'DIY political websites: New force shaping the general election debate', *The Guardian*, 1 June 2017.
14. Gerbaudo 2018.
15. David Thorburn and Henry Jenkins, 'Introduction: Toward an aesthetics of transition', in Thorburn and Jenkins (eds), *Rethinking Media Change: The Aesthetics of Transition*, MIT Press: Cambridge, MA, 2003, p.2.
16. Megan Le Masurier, 'Independent magazines and the rejuvenation of print', *International Journal of Cultural Studies*, Vol. 15, No. 4, 2012, p.384.
17. Owen Hatherley, speaking on 'Radicals in conversation: *Tribune*', Pluto Books podcast, 15 November 2018.
18. Le Masurier 2012, p.389.
19. Hatherley 2018.
20. Robin Blackburn, 'The Corbyn project: Public capital and Labour's New Deal', *New Left Review*, No. 111, May-June 2018.
21. Justin Schlosberg, 'Should he stay or should he go? Television and online coverage of the Labour Party in crisis', Media Reform Coalition and Birkbeck, University of London, 28 July 2016.
22. Gary Younge, 'Innovative Practices', University of the Arts London staff conference, guest lecture, 18 March 2019.
23. See for example Stuart Hall with John Clarke, Chas Critcher, Tony Jefferson and Brian Roberts, *Policing the Crisis: Mugging, the State, and Law and Order*, Macmillan: London, 1978.
24. Younge 2019.
25. Eleanor Penny, speaking at Media Democracy Festival 2019, Birkbeck, University of London, 16 March 2019.
26. See @VoicesLabour. Tragically, the project's founder, filmmaker Simon Baker, died in June 2019.
27. See https://novaramedia.com.
28. Michael Walker, speaking at Media Democracy Festival 2019, Birkbeck, University of London, 16 March 2019.
29. Aaron Bastani, *Fully Automated Luxury Communism: A Manifesto*, Verso: London, 2019.
30. Quoted in Adrian Lobb, 'Novara: "Building a social majority is about negotiating differences"', *Big Issue*, 7 July 2017.
31. *Ibid.*
32. Bastani, 'Recruit, re-tweet, re-nationalise: Eight ideas for Labour's new media strategy', Open Democracy, 31 August 2016.

Morbid Symptoms

Labouring Under Illusions

Neal Lawson

All political projects are contradictory, paradoxical and carry within them the seeds of their own destruction. They also flourish and die in a context that defines them. Corbynism is no exception. Any analysis worth the paper it is written on must examine the strengths and weaknesses of the Corbyn project in the context of its relationship to the party, wider social movements and the new emerging twenty-first-century forces of energy and vitality for change.

However, given the inevitably complex nature of this – and all – political projects, it is necessary to first locate a basic archetypal model of party-political change to help us assess Corbyn's Labour Party. Perhaps unusually, Aesop's 'Fable of the North Wind and the Sun' is my go-to source for such models. This is how it goes:

> The North Wind and the Sun disputed as to which was the most powerful, and agreed that he should be declared the victor who could first strip a wayfaring man of his clothes. The North Wind first tried his power and blew with all his might, but the keener his blasts, the closer the Traveller wrapped his cloak around him, until at last, resigning all hope of victory, the Wind called upon the Sun to see what he could do. The Sun suddenly shone out with all his warmth. The Traveller no sooner felt his genial rays than he took off one garment after another, and at last, fairly overcome with heat, undressed and bathed in a stream that lay in his path. *Moral: Persuasion is better than Force.*[1]

These two conceptions of what are, in essence, competing views of power – defined here as the ability to influence the forces that impact on our lives – help us to understand left theories of change in particular. At one end of the spectrum, we have politics done entirely to people, at the other, politics done entirely with and by people. The lesson of Aesop's fable is that kindness is more effective than severity.

Where a party or political project sits on this spectrum from control to collaboration tells us a lot about how it will govern and what type of statecraft it is going to adopt. Given that any opposition party only has dominion over how it governs and runs itself, this is likely to prefigure how it will run and govern the country. Is the predominant culture of the party to impose well-meaning change on people, or is it to negotiate new settlements through a respect and embrace of diversity and plurality – change done *with* people?

The two power traits are very different and are products of different historic and cultural moments – creatures, if you like, of their times. They sit at either end of an axis of a power culture. No party is entirely one or the other. But the direction in which a party leans is critical, and telling.

THE POWER OF THE WIND

The wind as a metaphor for change can be seen as close to the mechanistic theory of change that has been at the heart of dominant left narratives, both reformist and revolutionary, for well over a century. By class seizure or democratic vote, the left would secure power over the state, which would then be utilised to deliver social democracy or socialism from above, on behalf of the people. In both the Leninist and Fabian versions of this theory, the party acts, in essence, as a vanguard – a group of people with the skills, knowledge and higher consciousness to do good on behalf of the mass of people. The party, and especially its leadership, are the moral and mechanical arbiters of change. Thus a worthy and well-meaning elite is imagined to impose change, of varying degrees of radicalism, from the top down.

This wind-like approach was a product of its moment – the industrial and then Fordist eras (the latter named after the production-line car plants in which each worker did one specific job under orders from above). In this age, the early to mid-twentieth century, social democracy and socialism alike were shaped by this particular industrial and mechanical culture. Technocrats and managers decided and did things through order, planning and predication. The people were the cogs in the wheels, the worker ants in the factories. The same governing mentality flowed into the political realm: the government was a well-oiled machine, and the parties represented either those who owned capital, or those who laboured for the capitalists. For the left, the private good of the individual was sacrificed for the greater public good of all. This world was solid, predictable and linear. The mass party, like the mass industries, armies and classes that were also the product of this mechanical era, was based on top-down command-and-control systems.

A vanguardist or Leninist version of this approach as a blueprint for ruling an entire society has always been pretty much a minority sport in the UK, and today it is verging on extinction within the British left. Yet a version of this mindset, in which the party is the vehicle for imposing social change from above, still has a firm grip on Labour, shared to differing degrees from left to right. Arguably, it has a grip at the top of the party now. But its presence should be no surprise – this was the cultural context that gave birth, life, meaning and success to Labour, and has been the governing DNA of the party ever since.

The softer, reformist wing of social democracy has outlasted communism, but it is now going through what looks like its own, necessarily gradual, but still existential, crisis every bit as severe (if not quite as dramatic) as the fall of the Berlin Wall in 1989. This crisis – not of course confined to the UK – has many elements, including electoral failure, an outdated political narrative, and policies that have scarcely changed since the post-war foundation of the welfare state. However, there is also a wider and deeper crisis, one of an entire political culture. Social democrats and socialists everywhere still hanker after levers to pull; yearning to do good things to and for the people, who will then be satisfied with their lot and will vote for them again, or support their revolution. They want, in short, a world that has long gone.

Here in the UK this myopic hope is signified by the left's eternal fantasy that it might recreate the 'spirit of '45', in circumstances three quarters of a century and a whole new technological revolution on, circumstances that make any such repeat of history both undesirable and unfeasible.

A toxic myth hangs over the Labour Party: the idea that if only the 'right leaders' could be voted in to power, then socialism, as in 1945, could be recreated in all its glory. There are three reasons why this pervasive myth is so wrong. Firstly, because 1945 was the culmination of a rich and diverse century-long conversation, rooted in ideas and culture that spanned a political alliance much bigger than the Labour Party alone. It drew as much on the ideas of Methodists and Liberals as on those of Marxists and socialists. Secondly, because the complex problems we face today, from loneliness to Brexit, from social polarisation to climate change, require equally complex responses that, more often than not, will need to be global in their reach. Thirdly, a Labour government expected to re-enact '45 will have to do so without the agency that was Labour's historic engine, a unified and purposeful working class, while the mechanics of state delivery are now much weaker. Certainly, class still matters, and should not and must not be ignored – but there is no solid working-class base, in quantity or quality, to power a traditional left project. And while the state is still hugely important, it can no longer – if it ever could – be relied upon to deliver either socialism or social democracy from above. But even if change could still be delivered in this way, from the top down and the centre out, such an approach would struggle to deliver any kind socialism worthy of the name. A socialism for the twenty-first century can only be created by and for the people, with the party and the state playing a key facilitating role – but not the controlling role.

Fortunately, all manner of features of the twenty-first century make possible and necessary a very different form of – bottom up – change. But it won't look or feel much like 1945! The wind is not the option it once was. However, the sun has all the makings of a new, revived, model of political change.

UNDERSTANDING THE TWENTY-FIRST CENTURY

Instead of the mechanical, hierarchical and linear systems of deciding and doing that dominated the twentieth century, flatter digital networks increasingly dominate the twenty-first century. The key metaphor is no longer solid and top down, but organic and bottom up. Zygmunt Bauman has called this a 'liquid modern' culture.[2] In the twenty-first century, power is more dispersed, and identities in relation to it are more fluid. Old orientations of class, work and voting patterns are being ripped up. From the solid structures of the fixed modern world, we are moving fast to a fluid world, where we are shifting consumers before we are rooted workers, where because of our interconnectedness, anyone can know anything, connect to anyone, and organise at speed and scale. It is a very different form of agency; that of the active citizen.

The left toyed with these ideas about modernity and its successors before the current era of Corbyn. The New Times[3] project that came out of the journal *Marxism Today*[4] in the late 1980s had both radical and pragmatic variants. The more radical variant, led by cultural theorist Stuart Hall, was Gramscian and therefore still at least quasi-Marxist in its analysis of power and how to utilise it. But the more pragmatic version, championed by figures such as Charles Leadbeater, held sway within the party and was adopted by New Labour to propose the end of class antagonisms – in the words of Leadbeater's influential book, published at the turn of the century, we could all 'liv[e] on thin air'.[5] This outlook proved problematic: while its reading of the 'new times' was insightful, it was used by the politicians to adapt to a form of modernity shaped by neoliberalism. As New Labour found to its cost, the humanisation of neoliberalism inevitably proved elusive, and their attempts in this direction left us the catastrophe of the Iraq war, the 2008 financial crash, a polarised society, and now Brexit. The task we now face, therefore, is not to side-step modernity, but bend it to our socialist values.

There are many downsides to the contemporary digital world, of course: opinion echo chambers, online anonymity that enables a spiteful discourse to flourish, the monopolisation and privatisation of social goods such as public data, the rise of the surveillance state, and much else. And, of course, the technology can be used to mobilise the right as much as the left, as right-wing populists exploit both communications technology and the moment.

In spite of these problems, there is still a strong case to be made that if digital spaces are properly owned, held to account and regulated, and if we get the politics of the moment right, this flattening world holds out more hope for the left than it does for the right, precisely because, in its purest and most horizontal form, it favours more egalitarian, collaborative and democratic connections, outputs and outcomes. Modernity can now be shaped in our human collaborative and solidaristic image in ways that the hierocracies of the last century made impossible then. Like this view or not, this is the world – the only world – in which we must try to make history. The technology is not going away – it will only intensify – and so, the issue is how and to the benefit of whom: the many, or the few?

It is not an industrial society that the left must now prosecute its politics through, but the networked society.[6] And to be able to do that, the culture of our politics must change; not a little, but dramatically. A progressive networked society cannot be controlled from the centre out, or the top down. The wind, or any other external force, cannot exert its brute strength and impose change on us. Instead, change must be done *with* people – just as the sun shone and worked with the grain of Aesop's traveller. The future, if the left is to be part of it, will not be imposed by a single party, but negotiated through intense dialogue via all of us.

There has always been a more democratic and collaborative left that recognised this and rejected mechanical and state-dominated forms of change. Not least because many saw the essential truth that means always shape ends – such that the way we make socialism happen will decide the form that socialism takes. Socialism formed by elites, even well-meaning ones, will take on a hierarchical form, while socialism driven from the bottom up will result in a more democratic governance, of society by society.

From the Chartists, friendly societies, mutuals and co-operatives of the nineteenth and early twentieth centuries, through to the various new lefts that emerged from the 1950s, the 1960s, and most decisively in 1968, there has always been in the UK a strong strain of liberal and plural left politics. In the 1980s, this tradition found expression in the Labour-led Greater London Council (GLC), in which John McDonnell was such a key player. This flowering of radical, liberal socialist experimentation from yesteryear seems to have little active presence in the consciousness of the left and Labour today – which is a tragedy. Bennism itself – the early 1980s movement of the left within Labour in which Corbyn developed his political identity – championed democratic ideals and policies, especially in the economic sphere. At the same time, outside of Labour, the new social movements around feminism, peace, environmentalism and race recognised and practised an open, tolerant and negotiated form of politics. But where can we find much, or any, of this in and around Corbynism, or anywhere else in Labour today?

In the UK and around the world, we are witnessing organisations and parties struggling to experiment with new formations and ideas that can bend the complex networked modernity of the twenty-first century to accommodate older values of solidarity, equality, democracy and sustainability. The Women's Equality Party has set term limits for its leaders and welcomes members of other parties – who do not, at least not yet, reciprocate, thus sadly making such pluralism unworkable for the time being. The Green Party has a fully democratic conference and decision-making process, and has two joint leaders to provide permanent gender balance at the top. In Spain the rise of Podemos is a direct attempt to combine movement politics with a new party formation fit for the twenty-first century. It started with a flourish, but has since been bedevilled by more traditional leadership rivalry and factional problems. Syriza in Greece presents another, more community-based, model for change – born in dire economic struggle, it offers glimpses of what could be. And of course one of the biggest new ventures is Momentum, which was an incredible byproduct of the first Corbyn leadership campaign, but which struggles to demonstrate a strong internal democratic culture, and has limited influence over the leadership. Despite the best efforts of some within Momentum, the organisation has not sufficiently moved on from being Corbyn's loyal outrider, rather than an independent force for radical change on the left. Perhaps this was inevitable, given that Corbyn himself was the spark that created Momentum, rather than a new leader emerging from the twenty-first century elements of a new bottom-up movement. Finally, there is the Labour Party itself – defying the predictions of those who wrote off the very idea of the mass party, but struggling to retain its members, to know what to do with them, and along the way to carry out the urgent task of eradicating the intimidation and bullying that sometimes threatens to characterise the modern left, of which antisemitism is only the most obvious and hateful expression.

Labour's dramatic growth in membership since 2015 is the context for this book, but it should not have come as such a big surprise. Before the Corbyn surge there were surges in the memberships of other progressive parties; first the Liberal Democrats before the 2010-15 coalition disaster, then the Greens in 2015, followed by the Scottish National Party (SNP) after the 2014 independence referendum. In each case, these parties saw big increases in their membership – driven by their moment in the news, the ease with which people could now sign up online, and the aggregating impact of a politics driven first by social media and on occasion by social action too. In an era typified by the 'ice bucket challenge' viral video charity campaign and #metoo, surges and swarms of support for various versions of politics, not all of them progressive, are now commonplace.

WHERE IS CORBYNISM?

From the start Corbynism was a contradictory project, and it remains so: it contains elements of both the wind and the sun. But the predominant cultural form feels more like the chill of the wind than the warmth of the sun.

To understand why, we need to see Corbynism as a striking product of three contextual elements. The first of these was the small group of committed parliamentary socialists in and around the Campaign Group who, up against the tired nostrums of ultra-cautious Blairism, offered, almost accidentally, Jeremy Corbyn as the only name on the ballot paper for the 2015 Labour Party leadership committed to change. And we should not forget that it was in the spirit of pluralism that some MPs who did not support him nominated him, in order to get him on the ballot and foster a more inclusive debate.

The second element was the social movements that carried the spirit of the twenty-first century with them. The often-younger activists who surged into the party to back Corbyn from 2015 came from places such as Climate Camp, UK Uncut, the student movement against tuition fees, and the anti-war, anti-racism and anti-austerity movements. They had been the hackers and social media campaigners, the designers, organisers and activists of the social movements, who now saw in Corbyn something different from the usual reformist parliamentary politics.

The third element in the Corbyn victory was a product of the 2008 crash – a new emerging class, the precariat[7] – mostly young people, often with university degrees, suffering big debts, low wages, insecure jobs and little hope of ever owning a home. This emerging social formation had felt the moral pain of the Iraq war, and had no faith in any kind of revived Blairism. Many had voted Liberal Democrat in 2010, only to be let down over student fees in particular, while others had joined the Greens and the SNP, but now saw in the Corbyn project a chance to influence the national debate as never before. For these reasons and more, they piled into Labour and joined Momentum. These are people quintessentially of the twenty-first century – never knowing a world before social media – willing and able to speak their own minds, to innovate and create. They join a dozen different groups each week on Facebook and WhatsApp, their values are deep, but their loyalty and identities are much more fluid than those of my generation, for example, formed in the more politically rigid 1980s.

The sheer dogged persistence of Corbyn, and the remnants of Labour's hard left around him, meant that when he stood for the Labour leadership in 2015 they could benefit from these movements and these people to win the leadership. This then posed a fundamental question for Labour – beyond the choice of leader, but more broadly, about its future as a party and a movement – would the party be transformed and the membership empowered, along with its external relations with civil society and the social movements? The new leadership walked into an old hierarchical institution, the Labour Party, and has led it in largely the same vein as every previous party leadership. The policies have been slightly, though not dramatically, more left wing than those under Ed Miliband, but the party has not been transformed.

Let us be honest: making such choices, then or now, is not easy – there are no certainties – but in 2015, what I called 'the Corbyn wave' seemed to offer exciting possibilities. This 'wave' of movements and people gave a window into what was possible. Its energy was breaking up the permafrosted soil that for thirty years had been too harsh for our dreams to grow in. Labour as a party and a movement cannot survive electorally or politically unless it holds out the hope of radically changing society. On this point, time had caught up with New Labour. If the best on offer was slowing the pace at which the poor got poorer and the planet burned, then it was obvious that what was on offer was not going to be enough to sustain us. A party needs high ideals and deep organic roots in society if it is to transform that society. This cannot be done from the top down, but only when a party meets a groundswell from below.[8]

The result was a shock to everyone – including Jeremy. But as the product of a union of these three very different political cultures – the fellow-traveller MPs, the new anti-capitalist movements, and the precariat – the art of political leadership in this context would be to learn how to connect with and ride this wave, with Corbyn as the surfer, and the new-generation membership and their allies the wave.

In terms of party formation, what has happened since 2015 has been disappointing, although probably not surprising, given the political genesis of the Corbyn project. While the shift to the left in terms of policy is to be welcomed, especially on the economy, the party, its structure and culture have changed little. Labour's 2018 Democracy Review,[9] having proclaimed its goal to be to look at how the party's hugely expanded membership might become a mass movement that can transform society, has delivered little of the sort. There have been a few tweaks here and there to how the National Executive Committee (NEC) and the party's leadership are elected, plus a little more leeway has been offered to Constituency Labour Parties to organise themselves differently, but that has been about it.

There has been no attempt at a thoroughgoing re-examination of the form and function of a twenty-first-century socialist party. Instead of starting with a blank sheet of paper, the Review became a vehicle for special-interest lobbying – not least by the trade unions. The unions deserve a strong voice in the party, but not at the expense of individual members. Policymaking is still not decided by the membership, or even by the opaque National Policy Forum, but by the leadership. This is all a huge disappointment.

Meanwhile, the leadership decided from the get-go, almost without notice, that there would be no return to the practice of MPs electing members of the Shadow Cabinet, rather than their being selected by the leader's office, a centralisation of power previously opposed by the same left MPs who are now enforcing it. Of course, a hostile parliamentary party made an elected Shadow Cabinet problematic, to say the least, for Corbyn, but democracy is not something to be turned on or off just because you think you might lose the vote.

The party's annual conference can now look forward to a few more votes on the floor, but apart from these small adjustments, nothing much has changed in relation to the setpiece stage-managed conference event. Meanwhile, around the corner, The World Transformed festival bubbles with energy and ideas – but where are the connecting fibres between the small group who appear to decide everything around the leader's office, and this more vibrant force?

An example of this tendency to insularity at the top was the 2018 selection of a new party general secretary. Rather than undertaking an open selection of all the talents, the post was filled by a Unite trade union figure already in the leader's circle. This clearly political position could and should have gone to a vote of the membership, with candidates vying for the post on the basis of ideas and credentials, not a back-room arrangement. In these respects the Labour leader's office today is at least as powerful, and unaccountable, as it was under Blair and Brown. Whatever else it is, this is not bottom-up democracy.

Indeed, much of the good work in Labour happens despite the central party, not because of it. The following took place during the switch-over period between the old regime and the new, but an example of this kind of good work can be seen in the 2017 general election, when a number of vibrant, mass target-seat campaigns were run by activists who had been instructed by the party to campaign in other seats. Battersea was won because activists on the ground knew it was winnable and defied party orders. In Chipping Barnet, members were told the seat was unwinnable, they saw resources go to nearby marginals, but they still came within a handful of votes of winning. There are countless other examples of seats won in spite of instructions not to bother with them. In this volatile voting age, local knowledge is key, and local parties should be given the autonomy to do as they see fit. Momentum's 'My Nearest Marginal' app inspired thousands of activists, Labour Party members and others, to get involved in electoral politics. The potential of this kind of culture of local autonomy that could help Labour win the next general election has still not been fully grasped by the party.

It is welcome, therefore, that Labour does now have a properly resourced and staffed Community Organising Unit. The idea was first introduced under Ed Miliband, who brought in US community organiser Arnie Graf,[10] but it has now been revived and reinvented with more than thirty full-time organisers working in marginal seats, mostly 'held-back towns' and former industrial areas, to build a new activist base and reconnect with voters who have lost the party's trust. The potential here is to support local party leaders and candidates by building up members' own organising skills and confidence in campaigning. The initiative is a good start, but it remains too small scale and too electorally focused, and is not connected to any wider programme of party reform. This resource should not exist, as it currently does, as an adjunct to the leader's office, but should instead be accountable to the whole party, and its focus should not only be to elect Labour MPs – that should come as a very welcome byproduct – but rather to build a broader civic capacity to achieve social change. What we need to see is local Labour parties helping people solving problems in the here and now, not simply saying – elect our candidate to do it for you.

None of this is to deny the necessity of facing up to certain political realities. A media and Parliamentary Labour Party largely hostile to Corbynism cannot simply be ignored. Electoral imperatives, the urgent need to get Labour into a position to win the next general election, must be recognised. But who seriously believed that once Corbyn was elected leader it was going to be easy? Corbynism, fashioned in the face of the open hostility of most of Corbyn's own MPs, must nevertheless at some point stop – as Rosa Luxemburg famously accused the Bolsheviks of doing – 'making a virtue of a necessity', and move on; opening up and out. Leadership must be about building bridges and trusting others – expanding the circle, not seeing it contract. In part, because it trusts too little, Corbynism now feels like a defensive project, not an optimistic and expansive one.

Certainly, there should be a sympathetic understanding of the difficulties of managing a national political project – especially when the leader himself has next to no experience of running a big complex organisation. But it is now time to say that what has happened since the summer of 2015 is simply not good enough. And, in particular, what has happened since the surprisingly good election result in 2017 is far from good enough. 2017 was the moment, from a new position of strength, to reach out and start to devolve power downwards, to trust others and thereby win back trust and support. Of course, some never accepted the leader's legitimacy – but they would have been more effectively marginalised had there been a reaching out to others who did want to work constructively. But that moment has been missed. To reiterate, what Corbyn does with the party is likely to be a precursor to what he does with the country. The party is the only thing he has dominion over, and as such it should be used to try out both governance and democracy ideas, thereby showing the country which sort of leader he is, the wind or the sun.

Members of the Labour Party today may be largely delighted with the shift in tone and policy under Corbyn, an enthusiasm and confidence that was confirmed by 2017. But members' organisational and cultural experience of the party remains little different to that experienced before Corbyn became leader. There has been no transformation of Labour's organisational culture. How much longer are members expected to wait for this to happen? What further excuses about Rosa's 'necessity' are members going to be given? The party has stopped growing and, according to every membership secretary you speak to, is almost certainly now shrinking. It was great to reach 500,000 members by 2017, but why not aim for a million or more, to counter the hegemony of the right? The party appears content with decline as long as the grip on the leadership is held firm.

For those who do join, being a member of the Labour Party ought to be a rich, vibrant, cultural and convivial experience. For how many members does this match the experience of their local branch, or constituency Labour party? The vast majority of members don't ever engage apart from carrying a party card, and the party seems entirely content with this. There is an incredible wealth of talent in Labour's vast and diverse membership; a huge range of practical experience and tacit knowledge.[11] The party should be seeking ways to tap into and utilise the best resource it has – its membership. Members should be provided with the training and support to unlock this experience and knowledge that otherwise goes to waste. Power and resources should be devolved down to the local level to enable this to happen, but instead these are being held tightly at the centre. We are seeing a pattern whereby the new members who were attracted to Labour because of Corbynism are attending fewer and fewer meetings and becoming less and less active. The moment is being lost as an old and out-of-date organisational culture that doesn't feel like the new politics that we were promised persists. Rather than gentle and kind, what we have feels as hard, remote and brittle as ever. It feels like the chill wind, not the warmth of the sun.

Of course, this is not all Corbyn's fault. Tom Watson was elected deputy at the same time in 2015, and promised specifically to renew the party. He has utterly failed. Now leader and deputy seem locked in a battle to the death, both sides representing the culture of the wind – 'As long as I'm in charge, all will be well.' It is all about them, and what they will do for us and to us.

A NEW CONCEPTION OF POWER

But at the same time as these old battles play out, all around us are examples of new ways of deciding and doing things that are in tune with the twenty-first century, and from which Labour could learn, forms of self-organising and collaborative action that reflect the cultural zeitgeist.[12] Caring, sharing, funding, creating and deciding are increasingly being done in new, collective ways, often powered by new technology. Plenty of people will be familiar with BuzzFeed and others like them as news providers using this kind of participative model, but what of Buurtzorg,[13] a Dutch organisation that uses collaboration to provide social care? The most successful twenty-first century organisations harness the power of citizens and activists. Labour should be learning from these organisations; attracting the people who work in and around them as members, supporters and future leaders.

What these entities have in common is that they are new – they are born with the collaborative DNA of the twenty-first century coursing through their veins. That DNA is trusting, participatory and kind. But Labour is not new, it is an old party, with much old and cold industrial baggage weighing it down. Jeremy Corbyn himself is not a new politician. Far from it. He has been saying and doing the same things for decades – which is, of course, exactly what made him look so attractive and authentic up against the failed politics of Blairism. But now?

Labour's problem is not its alone, but is shared with just about every other social democratic party in the world: all were creations of the same mechanical cultural moment. Perhaps real cultural transformation is impossible for any organisation still framed by the twentieth century in which it was founded – after all, when an old institution is failing, it's usually better to stop and start again. But Corbynism was supposed to be different. To be truly different, however, means taking risks and giving up the comfort of old command-and-control systems and levers of leadership, becoming instead servant leaders, first of the party membership and then of the country's citizens. Such a step is a huge and risky leap, of letting go and trusting others. But, ultimately, all the risk for Labour lies in not changing and not transforming. Because, while we can and must fight many things, what we must not fight is the spirit of the age – and that spirit is for participation, collaboration and negotiation.

OFFICE IS NOT ENOUGH TO EFFECT CHANGE

A Labour or Labour-led government is, of course, a necessary step on the way to transforming society but, increasingly, it is insufficient. The challenges any progressive government faces will be complex and daunting. In 1945, Labour could only build council houses, the NHS and the welfare state through the top-down culture of the day. Now, the challenges of climate change, the fourth industrial revolution, mass and permanent migration, issues of identity and belonging in a global world, an aging population, and much else are vastly more complex than the challenges of the past. They can only be confronted through the negotiated bottom-up culture of this age.

But cultural change is always the hardest kind of change to enact. It cannot be forced, and can only happen through the actions of people who recognise the need for the shift – who already practise it. It must, by definition, emerge from below. Ultimately, this

is all about a different conception of power. Labour should therefore begin its transformation by embracing Mary Parker Follett's
distinction between 'power over' and 'power with'. Follett, a feminist management theorist from the early years of the last century,[14]
offered, in effect, a theoretical basis for Aesop's wind and sun fable.
'Power over' is power as domination: in this context, the ability,
through the state, to make people do what they would otherwise not
do. This can sometimes be necessary to ensure, for example, that
we pay our taxes and fasten our seatbelts. But in a non-deferential,
networked and complex world, 'power over' has severe limitations,
and it always fails to unleash the full potential of people, as they
remain unwilling cogs in a machine of limited creative and productive capacity.

'Power with', or 'power to', has the means to transform precisely
because it involves politicians and people in the co-creation of a
better society. At every point the future is negotiated, rather than
imposed. In such a world, knowledge is dispersed, and therefore any
project is going to be better informed and more agile. And, as the
people engaged in it, we are likely to be more committed precisely
because it is 'our project', not theirs. In a world of 'power with', no
one view dominates, meaning that politics can become much more
creative to meet the challenges of the complex world we now live in.
Pluralism, the recognition and embrace of the fact that two or more
principles or sources of authority can coexist, is vital to any notion
of change from below. Labour must be plural, both inside the party
and outside it – constantly negotiating change with others. This is
how the twenty-first century works.

As the author Terry Pratchett wrote: 'You can't go around
building a better world for people. Only people can build a better
world for people. Otherwise it's just a cage.'[15] This does not mean
that the politics of complexity is easy or straightforward – clearly, it
isn't. But if this is the governance culture of the twenty-first century,
then we had better get used to it, and faster and better than the right
does. Indeed, the only alternative to this task is populism.

What this means is giving up the old model of party control
and moving on from the belief that the Labour Party alone must
sort out everything, for everyone, all the time. This is a difficult,
even impossible, challenge for Labour as long as it has an all-or-

nothing approach to power. Following the 2010 hung parliament, Labour chose to be in opposition rather than share power in coalition with others. At the 2017 general election, the party refused to countenance any notion of a 'progressive alliance'. Such an alliance nevertheless helped to defeat the Tories in more than twenty seats, but it could have been even more effective if Labour had supported it, instead of campaigning against potential allies, among them Green MP Caroline Lucas.[16] It seems likely that the party will practise the same all-or-nothing approach at the next election – what price an outright majority then?

Here is the Corbyn contradiction: Corbynism was born out of movements such as UK Uncut, Occupy, Climate Camp and Stop the War. It borrowed people, inspiration and ideas from the Scottish independence campaigns, the Greens and even the young Liberal Democrats. And yet it cannot seem to drop the 'monopoly socialism' approach, and return to the wave that carried it to victory in 2015. Corbyn himself was always better known as an extra-parliamentary campaigner than as an MP. But the pluralism that he once demonstrated by working across campaigns and parties, on issues such as peace and international solidarity, is not being translated into attempts to reach across to different parties, or even across different groups inside Labour.

A return to both Corbyn's own personal experience and these roots of his support would have overwhelmingly positive consequences. From his position as party leader – and notwithstanding the ongoing hostility of some of his MPs – and drawing on the huge support he retains across the membership and most of the trade unions, Corbyn could reach out and express solidarity with those who are not Corbynites but who share many of his beliefs, both within Labour and in different parties.[17] Such a move would lay the groundwork for the kind of broad progressive bloc that incorporates – both inside and outside Parliament – members of other parties and none. All the lessons of history tell us that radical change requires this kind of co-operative bloc-building.

When, in contrast, Corbynism clings to the remnants of a monopoly socialist politics, it threatens to kill off co-operation and collaboration. Just think of the forces that will be unleashed against any Corbyn-led government, resisting the radical policies that are now being developed. It will take not just all of Labour, but social liberals, Scottish and Welsh nationalists, Greens, and many more to fight back. None of these groups are going to work with Labour on the basis of being commanded from above.

Out there, where it matters, in communities and civil society, in social enterprises and in the best of the public sector, individually and collectively, there are plenty practising the culture of the sun – because it is the best way to meet our human needs in the twenty-first century. Labour can and must set an example by carrying out a bottom-up revolution, starting with the party itself, encouraging all its public representatives, including every MP, elected mayor and local councillor, to see their role primarily as empowering others. This culture must underpin the manifesto for the next general election. The extent to which it is able to understand the leadership as facilitator, supporter, enabler, servant and champion of emerging radical forces for change will be key to Corbynism's success, or its failure.

All viable political projects are the product of contradictions solved via compromise. Those that are not are purist failures. Corbynism is the product of particular contradictions, of an older vanguardist-style tendency and a much newer participatory ethos. This is the clash of cultures within it. Will it be a monopoly socialism that eventually dominates, but dies in the process, or a plural and radically democratic socialism that triumphs, giving life to infinite new possibilities? As ever, we must note the dictum of the Italian socialist theorist Antonio Gramsci, that the challenge of modernity is to 'live without illusions, without being disillusioned'.

Maximum social change usually comes at the start of a political project when the energy and vitality is at its height. The first flush of Corbynism did not deliver, and it still has not. But, in all probability, this won't be the end of the story. Corbynism may be remembered as a vital and necessary break with the failure of Blairism and centrist social democracy more widely, and a bridge to something very new and very different. To fulfil that ambition, to paraphrase another of Gramsci's famous epithets, we will need to balance the pessimism of Labour's here-and-now, whose character is largely out of our hands, with an optimism for a future that we, the people, will make for ourselves. Let's see.

NOTES

1. George Fyler Townsend (ed.), *Aesop's Fables*, reproduced at www.fablesofaesop.com/the-north-wind-and-the-sun.html.
2. Zygmunt Bauman, *Liquid Modernity*, Polity: Cambridge, 2000.
3. For useful background, see John Harris, '*Marxism Today*: forgotten visionaries whose ideas could save Labour', *The Guardian*, 29 September 2015.
4. Stuart Hall and Martin Jacques (eds), *New Times: The Changing Face of Politics in the 1990s*, Lawrence and Wishart: London, 1989.
5. Charles Leadbeater, *Living on Thin Air: The New Economy*, Penguin: London, 2000.
6. See Manuel Castells, *The Rise of the Network Society*, Blackwell: Oxford, 1996.
7. See Guy Standing, *The Corruption of Capitalism: Why Rentiers Thrive and Work Does Not Pay*, Biteback: London, 2017.
8. For the original 2015 version of this argument, see Neal Lawson, 'If Jeremy Corbyn is to succeed, he's got to ride the wave', *New Statesman*, 15 September 2015.
9. Labour Party, 'Democracy Review', September 2018.
10. See Rowenna Davis, 'Arnie Graf: The man Ed Miliband asked to rebuild Labour', *The Guardian*, 21 November 2012.
11. On the radical potential of tacit knowledge, see Hilary Wainwright, *A New Politics from the Left*, Polity: Cambridge, 2018.
12. Lawson, '45° change: Transforming society from below and above', Compass, February 2019.
13. See Jos De Blok, 'Buurtzorg – Could it work in England?', King's Fund, 12 July 2016.
14. For a useful introduction to Mary Parker Follett's work, see Pauline Graham, *Mary Parker Follett: Prophet of Management*, Harvard Business School: Boston MA, 1995.
15. Terry Pratchett, *Witches Abroad*, Corgi: London, 2013, p.317.
16. For background on the 'progressive alliance', see Barry Langford, *All Together Now: The Progressive Alliance and the 2017 General Election Campaign*, Biteback: London, 2017.
17. See Lawson, 'Beyond monopoly socialism', Compass, Thinkpiece 94, March 2018.

An Extra-Parliamentary Affair

Lindsey German

Long before he was elected Labour leader, Jeremy Corbyn was a familiar face on just about any protest I have been on. From supporting Chagos Islanders reclaiming their homeland, to showing solidarity with the Mau Mau's victims of British torture in Kenya, Corbyn was there. He was arrested demonstrating against apartheid South Africa, and has marched countless times for Palestine. Over many years, he played a central role in the leadership of the Campaign for Nuclear Disarmament (CND). And he was, from the beginning, identified with the Stop the War Coalition, which campaigned against the 'war on terror' from 2001, and which organised the biggest-ever British protest,[1] against the Iraq war in 2003, where he was one of the speakers at the closing rally.

That Corbyn's involvement in movement politics could now have such an impact on a mainstream political party like Labour is itself a product of the turn towards various forms of activism, as interest and involvement in parliamentary politics has seen a decline. From the last third of the twentieth century onwards, the tendency has been for fewer people to vote, and for more people to engage in various forms of non-parliamentary political activism, including signing petitions, and joining consumer boycotts, unofficial strikes, and demonstrations.[2] The impact of various movements has been considerable in the twenty-first century, as there has been more reliance on do-it-yourself change, especially from a younger generation. The 1999 mass protests against the World Trade Organization in Seattle marked a new international awareness of the effects of globalisation and neoliberalism, and the beginning of the century saw the big anti-globalisation and anti-war movements (the mass protests in Genoa against the G8 summit were just two months

before the events of 9/11), in which Corbyn was a central participant. Since then, there have been continuing campaigns on these
and other aspects of globalisation. UK Uncut, Extinction Rebellion
and the school-student strikes against climate change, and the
People's Assembly, for example, have raised issues of austerity, the
environmental crisis, tax evasion and much more, and have had an
impact on wider politics and popular consciousness, which in turn
has fed into the Labour Party.[3]

Corbyn has, therefore, helped to create a situation where the
political impetus of the movements has led to the paradox we see
today, of the only major social democratic party in Europe, the
Labour Party, with a clearly left-wing leader. Despite the continued
denigration Corbyn faced from some of his own MPs and from
the media, Labour's 2017 general election vote was a good deal
higher than that of most of Europe's other comparable parties. The
German SPD, the French Socialist Party and the Italian left have all
seen their vote slump to much lower levels than Labour's. Corbyn's
election as Labour leader reflects many of the same concerns and
political developments that led to the rise of, variously, Syriza in
Greece, Die Linke in Germany, Podemos in Spain and Mélenchon's
La France Insoumise. Despite the considerable differences between
these organisations, they have all reflected a disillusionment with
traditional social democracy and its absorption into the neoliberal
project, offering in its place a determination to break with that agenda
from the left. And each has also, like Corbyn, been influenced and
galvanised by a range of extra-parliamentary movements.

EARLIER DAYS

Attempts to form a left alternative to Labour first became evident
after disillusion with Tony Blair's government led to the formation of
the Socialist Alliance, the Scottish Socialist Party (SSP) in Scotland,
and eventually Respect in England and Wales. Despite some important victories for the SSP in elections to the Scottish Parliament,
and for Respect, which scored several of the biggest swings away
from Labour recorded in the 2005 general election and saw George
Galloway elected in Bethnal Green and Bow, these ventures did not
succeed in sinking long-term roots. Instead it could be argued that

their electoral success led to a crisis for this form of politics, at least in part because of the tensions between parliamentary and extra-parliamentary activity.

As one of the candidates who achieved a major swing to Respect and came second to Labour in Newham with 20 per cent of the vote, I would argue that the party suffered firstly from failing to achieve a sufficiently significant split from Labour when it was set up, and secondly from a lack of roots within the working-class communities in which we stood. This plus the highly unfavourable first-past-the-post electoral system (something which the SSP did not have to encounter) made it extremely difficult for the left to find a voice and electoral success.

The failure of these organisations meant there was no meaningful electoral alternative to the left of Labour, but the sentiments which had driven their creation remained. It is this which helped lead to Corbyn's remarkable victory in the 2015 Labour leadership election, as many former members rejoined the party or signed up as 'supporters' to vote for him. In this sense, his leadership can be seen as part of a pattern where large sections of left opinion want an alternative to the established social democratic parties. The uniqueness of Corbyn's position is that he has won over this following while remaining *within* a traditional social democratic organisation. To seek comparisons with this we need to look back to the 1980s, to the phenomenon of Bennism, or to Ken Livingstone's early success as Labour leader of the Greater London Council (GLC). Neither of these, however, came close to the scale of Corbyn's achievement – Tony Benn narrowly lost to the right-winger Denis Healey in the 1981 deputy leadership campaign, while Livingstone became GLC leader through a coup within the Labour group rather than mass support, and was eventually defeated by Margaret Thatcher's successful campaign to abolish the elected metropolitan authorities.

CHALLENGES WITHIN LABOUR

When the surprising summer of 2015 happened there was much talk about Corbynism as a social movement. That was, after all, much of the point of Momentum, which was originally conceived of as involving both party members and supporters. However, while

Momentum was often spoken of in these terms, it soon became an organisation for Labour Party members only, and its main orientation is towards mobilising for electoral gain, rather than other forms of activity. There have been exceptions to this, for example when it organised against Trump's visit in the summer of 2018, or organised opposition to far-right activist 'Tommy Robinson' and his supporters, but neither event was on anything like the scale of Momentum's electoral-focused work, such as its 'Unseat' days, aimed at dislodging Tories and others from marginal seats.

Few around Labour talk anymore in terms of Corbynism as a movement. Whereas the enthusiasm of the early days encouraged the idea of much activity taking place outside the parameters of mainstream politics, now nearly all of Labour's activity is within them. Outside of a general election, Corbyn's mass rallies are few and far between – in contrast to the strategy of, for example, Donald Trump who, despite being president, sees the importance of continually mobilising his base. Corbyn now only rarely speaks at protests and demonstrations. His relative success in the 2017 election has helped to push the party's priorities back in a different direction from mass mobilisation.

A relentless onslaught on Corbyn's background in extra-parliamentary campaigns and movements has led to compromise from Corbyn and some of the left over a range of causes Corbyn had previously so publicly backed, such as opposition to Trident, coming out of NATO, and standing for Palestine. The dominant position represented by Shadow Cabinet ministers is in support of both Trident and NATO, in spite of Corbyn's own views, and any support for Palestine has become mired in controversy over antisemitism. Most Corbyn supporters probably recognise that, in his situation, some compromise may be necessary. That is not the same, however, as abandoning long-held principles, for example accepting that criticism of Israel's policies may be construed as antisemitic. When Corbyn has refused to do so, he has been subject to the most incredible attacks, with some of his supporters making far too many concessions.

The furore over antisemitism has led to the accusation of racism being directed at pro-Palestine campaigners, and disciplinary proceedings being threatened, and in some cases taken, against them. It has thrown the Palestine solidarity movement onto the defensive at a time when Israel's attacks on the Palestinians have been growing. Corbyn's opponents now talk openly about the Labour Party being institutionally antisemitic, despite the fact that a systematic breakdown of antisemitism allegations and complaints to Labour shows a very different picture.[4]

Momentum's founder Jon Lansman is among those who have expressed the view that antisemitism is a pervasive issue for the party:

> I do think we have a major problem, and it always seems to me that we underestimate the scale of it. I think it's now obvious that we have a much larger number of people with hardcore antisemitic opinions, which unfortunately is polluting the atmosphere in a lot of constituency parties and in particular online, and we have to deal with those people.

He attributed this in part to the fact that 'The party trebled in size, we took in 300,000 and more new members, and amongst those members are members who are attracted towards conspiracy theories.'[5]

Labour's figures demonstrate the reality of antisemitism inside the party, but they also indicate that the problem is being dealt with seriously. Between April 2018 and January 2019, 400 complaints were made against individual members, which represents 0.07 per cent of the membership. Margaret Hodge MP has personally reported 111 individuals for antisemitic abuse, of whom 91, or 82 per cent, were found not to be members of the Labour Party.[6] Lansman's response overlooks the actual facts about the incidence of antisemitism cases, while the mainstream media bandies accusations, but all too rarely dissects the evidence. Conspiracy theorists there are on the left, certainly, but there is no evidence that they are a significant force in Labour or indeed among the wider left. There is, in my experience, a good record of the left rebutting such theories, whatever their provenance. And surely the far right – with their anti-Soros theories that reek of antisemitism – are more of a source of these ideas than are those on the left.

As well as this political retreat, there has been the downgrading of extra-parliamentary protest by many on Labour's left. The important battles are now seen as being those internal to Labour – reselection of MPs, the composition of committees, questions of who controls the apparatus, and of what happens at Conference. While these are all sometimes important questions, they are about how Labour is run, not about how it campaigns within the wider movement for change, nor how it relates to the mass of working people who are potential Labour voters and supporters. The current emphasis on these questions has two effects: it consumes many activists' time in matters which are not about mobilising or campaigning, and so can cut them off from the wider movement; and it means that the concern that Labour members feel about austerity, wars, job losses, the environment, is not harnessed to organise wider numbers of activists who might not be Labour members, or even Labour voters.

LABOUR AND THE MOVEMENTS: A PARADOX

Labour is a large membership party with over half a million members – and that is a tremendous advance on where it was before Corbyn became leader – but there are between six and seven million trade unionists, hundreds of thousands of people with recent active involvement in campaigns, and tens of thousands of people who identify with left politics not restricted to Labour, or who choose not to join Labour. It therefore makes little sense to see Labour as the only vehicle for change, or to demand that everything is done through the Labour Party, to the exclusion of other parties and none. Indeed, such a view leads not to an inclusionary approach, but to one which sets those outside Labour as somehow apart from any movement. The left outside of Labour has always seen movements based on self-organising as central to its project, which explains the concentration of far-left activists in trade-union organisations, anti-war and peace movements, anti-austerity and anti-racist campaigns, and thousands of local campaigns and activities.

The problem of Labour looking inward rather than outward is made particularly intense by the fact that the Labour Party is a bureaucratic party, and one where much power lies with trade union leaderships and MPs. These two groups have traditionally led opposition to left-wing politics within the party, although more recently a number of trade unions have been broadly supportive of Corbyn. Nevertheless, the majority of Labour MPs and peers remain hostile to the left.

The attempt to pull Labour to the left has achieved some major successes, but is still hampered by the idea that the party must prioritise elections over everything else and that it must constantly move to the centre ground in order to do so. This is very much the logic of Labour's concept of a 'broad church', an ideal which seeks to incorporate both left and right, but which in practice is traditionally dominated by the right.

The nature of the Labour Party and the overwhelming priority it gives to electoral politics, coupled with the right-wing persuasion of many of its elected representatives, highlights, therefore, the importance of independent movements, which include within their ranks many Labour members, activists and supporters, but which also encompass many who might vote or support Labour, but who are outside the party. It is essential that those movements have their own dynamic that is not dependent on the parliamentary timetable or arithmetic, or under the control of any particular party or fraction of it. This is not special pleading on behalf of the movements, nor a mere preference for street politics over time-consuming Labour Party committee meetings. It is rather a recognition that there is a tension between Labour and the movements, which we need to understand in order to try to overcome.

Labour's whole history can be seen in a sense as one of benefiting electorally from extra-parliamentary movements, while at the same time being inimical to fostering and creating them. The original Independent Labour Party (ILP) was formed following the mass radicalisation of the new unions in the late 1880s. Labour grew again from the periods of industrial struggle before and after the First World War, the radicalisation produced by the Second World War, and the upsurges in struggle of the 1960s and 1970s. That Labour benefits as a result of these movements, rather than being organically part of them, is a feature of the party which those of us involved in the movements must recognise.

So there is a paradox in the present success of Jeremy Corbyn's Labour. Many of his supporters look with pride and enthusiasm on previous movements. Yet there remains a tension between these movements and Labour. Britain's major social movements of the twentieth and twenty-first centuries have in nearly every case neither been initiated nor sustained by Labour. Indeed, they have sometimes operated in the teeth of opposition from Labour bodies. The fight against fascism in the 1930s, especially the Battle of Cable Street, the campaign to Aid Spain, the support for national liberation movements, CND, the movements of 1968, the big industrial struggles of the 1970s, the Anti-Nazi League, the anti-poll tax movement, Stop the War, the student movement and the anti-austerity movement – all of them involved large numbers of Labour voters and members, but none of them were initiated or organised by the Labour Party.

THE OUTSIDE LEFT

Labour's involvement came overwhelmingly, and unofficially, from the Labour left. Many individual members of the Labour left played a big role in Stop the War, and there were probably tens of thousands of such people on the up to two-million strong march in February 2003, but they weren't there, for the most part, as the Labour Party. At the core of many of these movements, rather, were people from parties and organisations to the left of Labour: in the 1930s the Communist Party, and to a lesser extent the ILP, then later, in the 1960s, the International Marxist Group, International Socialists, and after that, the Socialist Workers Party (SWP) and the Militant Tendency. While in recent years there has been less organised left involvement in such groups as, for example, the Occupy and environmental movements, these groups still reflect a political orientation that is external, if not in opposition, to Labour.

My own experience of involvement in the left and in a number of movements and campaigns has convinced me that the most dynamic movements have been organised and given leadership and direction by the extra-parliamentary left. This was true of the Vietnam Solidarity Campaign, the National Abortion Campaign, anti-apartheid, CND, the Anti-Nazi League, and the campaign against the poll tax, as well as the Stop the War Coalition. The organisational backbone and often the flair and imagination of these campaigns came from that section of the left. Of course, many

Labour left figures have been involved in these campaigns, including Tony Benn and Jeremy Corbyn, and they have been supported by many more rank-and-file Labour members and activists. But it is hard to imagine these and similar campaigns being established or flourishing from within Labour alone. And it would be equally hard to argue that such campaigns were marginal to British politics. In fact, they have played a key role in addressing issues and changing opinion on a range of questions.

The Stop the War Coalition was established initially by myself and other then-members of the SWP. It was supported from the outset by Labour MPs, in particular George Galloway and Jeremy Corbyn, as well as some Labour-affiliated unions, for example Aslef and CWU. Many thousands of Labour voters and members were amongst the movement's initial supporters, as were members of some other left parties and groups. Unsurprisingly, Tony Blair's Labour Party never supported it. The Greens took some time to come on board, but did so eventually. And then Liberal Democrat leader Charles Kennedy spoke at our big 2003 demonstration on the eve of the Iraq war. But most of all the movement was galvanised at an unofficial, localised, grassroots level. This is what helped to give it its strength. One important aspect of this was the involvement of the Muslim community from the beginning of the campaign. All of this was achieved by informal contacts from below, from the beginning. This, then, is another paradox: the lack of official Labour support can allow a fast-moving and inclusive campaign to develop. Just so long as it involves and welcomes those from Labour and makes clear that its fight is not with the party as such, but with its leadership or policies, a left movement such as Stop the War can positively thrive in the absence of official Labour support.

The fact that leadership in the movements tends to come from those outside and to the left of the Labour Party is in part due to the commitment of those on the far left to extra-parliamentary activity and to their understanding that such movements play a big part in wider social change. However, there were always wider political reasons, too, why this has been the case. They have to do with the orientation of Labour and other social democratic parties towards reform by parliamentary means, rather than extra-parliamentary campaigning. Around Labour, there is always a tension between the two. This tension arises partly over questions of time and personnel – do we campaign or canvass? – and partly over differences about political goals. Can movements themselves achieve their stated aims and other transformative goals, or can these only be attained via electoral and parliamentary change? And will electoral efforts be hampered by commitment to extra-parliamentary action, including the militant kind?

If there is a choice to be made between the two, the balance sheet in all these cases has, for Labour, always come down on the side of electoralism, rather than extra-parliamentary action. It is for this reason that movements are so often led by those on the revolutionary or far left, and why they usually come into being and often live out their entire existence without any official input from Labour.

This section of the left of course has its own problems in relation to movement-building. Historically there have been divisions within and among the far left over how to build the movements, in particular over the relationship between the broader movement and each group's own political organisation. A frequent source of tension and sometimes conflict, in my experience, is the perception by some in a socialist group that the group has failed to immediately capitalise on its involvement in the movements. Far left organisations judge success in a number of ways, but one prominent one is size of organisation, and whether activity leads to recruitment to the organisation. This is doubtless an important test, but it is not the only one, and this view tends to downplay the importance of influence or hegemony, and the extent to which socialists can strengthen support for their ideas in ways other than direct arithmetical growth. I would argue that it is their focus on self-organising and the lack of bureaucracy that gives these movements the opportunity to grow; further, that a shift of the focus away from the demands and priorities of electoralism allows movements to seize on issues that have the potential to mobilise people on a scale that can begin to have an influence on wider politics. On the whole, the Labour left doesn't share this experience of doing politics, and the record of the Labour Party has been to treat these movements as insignificant, or even at times to oppose them.

Yet social movements have been key in effecting social change. The experience of the 1930s campaigns against fascism and in

solidarity with Republican Spain showed that it was mass mobilisations that began to turn the tide against the far right, and that
these were always organised by grassroots activists from below,
for example at the Olympia rally in 1934 and at Cable Street in
1936, where the Communist Party and others on the left organised in the face of opposition from official Labour. The turning
of the tide against fascism in the 1970s was due to large numbers
of on-the-ground mobilisations against fascists, and the SWP's
creation of the Anti-Nazi League. These mobilisations were all
too often denounced at the time – for example by leading Labour
left figure Michael Foot, who described the activist left as 'red
fascists'. Yet they attracted growing numbers of Labour members
and supporters. This was because there was a much wider understanding among the party's rank and file than there was among
its politicians that the threat of fascism could not be dealt with by
a Labour government or electoral means alone – indeed, Labour's
policies of wage restraint and tightening immigration laws helped
to boost the fascists' support.

Movements such as those described above did not emerge out of
thin air – they came from socialists developing insights about how
best to mobilise, coupled with high levels of activity on the ground.
Major demonstrations are the result of thousands of individuals
organising to bring out far greater numbers – booking coaches, leaf-
leting workplaces and communities, passing resolutions, debating at
public meetings. It is this practical engagement that the far left has
prioritised in terms of building events and it is this, rather than any
internal party process, that has built successful movements.

OUT OF AUSTERITY

The major campaigning focus of the past few years has been opposition to austerity and what is happening to public services. Many
organisations have taken part in anti-austerity campaigns, including
the People's Assembly, UK Uncut and the Occupy movement.
But there has been no such campaign on an organised scale from
Labour. MPs turn up and speak and share platforms, Constituency
Labour Parties bring banners, but Labour does not organise as a
campaigning party. Indeed, Labour councils have implemented

austerity measures as a result of Tory government cuts, rather than trying to mobilise their communities to oppose them. This has led to councils disregarding local people's concerns over housing, public services and schools, and a pattern of deals being done with private developers that have overwhelmingly benefited those developers at the expense of the public good. It was just such a pattern that led to the huge protests about the development of council housing in Haringey, and which culminated in the deselection of prominent councillors involved with the deal. Here, there were welcome and influential campaigns involving both Labour left activists and those on the extra-parliamentary left, which combined mobilisations with internal pressure on the Labour council that proved decisive in achieving change.[7]

A similar story can be told of two of the biggest industrial disputes of recent years – those of the junior doctors and NHS nurses. These were popular and attracted widespread support, including from Corbyn and his allies, but there was no wider Labour involvement or wider mobilisation around the NHS, which could have led to huge numbers on the streets, the resignation of then-Health Secretary Jeremy Hunt, and a much greater public awareness of what is happening in the NHS and consequently a renewed ability to campaign against it locally.

The contradictions involved in these processes have led to a further paradox, whereby many of those engaged in social movements and industrial disputes are also supporters of Corbyn, and sometimes active within the Labour Party. Yet the party as a whole has little involvement in such movements and some prominent actors in the party machinery, such as councillors, oppose them. It could be argued further that the Corbyn phenomenon, despite its roots in the movements, has not helped to strengthen those movements but has in many ways weakened them, as the focus of political campaigning switches more sharply to Labour. This process has been accompanied by a weakening of the extra-parliamentary left in recent years, in part because many of its potential support base and erstwhile members have joined Labour, inspired by the phenomenon of Corbynism. This tendency has been fairly widespread, involving a wide range of old and new activists. It reflects the attraction of a rising left within Labour, and echoes the rise of Bennism in the late

1970s, when many former members of left groups took the same step of joining Labour.

ASKING THE RIGHT QUESTIONS

The relationship between parties, organisations and movements is a major question for the whole of the left because it points to a key question of political strategy: the relationship between parliamentary socialism and extra-parliamentary social change.[8]

There is a great deal of tactical fluidity on the Marxist left over this relationship. This reflects a recognition of the need to be responsive to the demands of specific situations, and follows in the tradition of Marx himself, who found himself involved in a revolutionary organisation in the 1840s, but who consciously built a very different kind of organisation in the 1860s, in the form of the First International, which he considered fitted the needs of the situation, and which was very far from being a revolutionary organisation. He wrote to Engels in November 1864 about writing the founding principles: 'It was very difficult to frame the thing so that our view should appear in a form acceptable from the present standpoint of the workers' movement...It will take time before the reawakened movement allows the old boldness of speech.'[9] Lenin, too, shaped the organisations of which he was a part and chose who he worked with according to the needs of the situation. Lenin's political work is a lesson in strategy and tactics. Tariq Ali writes of his adaptability:

> Lenin was a product of Russian history and the European labour movement. Both posed questions of class and party, of agency and instrument. The synthesis developed by Lenin was thus determined by the intermingling of two very different currents that can be characterised, broadly speaking, as anarchism and Marxism. He played a crucial role in the triumph of the latter.[10]

While there was room for manoeuvre around modes of political organisation, Marx and Lenin learnt through direct experience that they could not be so flexible when it came to confronting the state machine and unelected power. The importance of this confrontation remains true today, and highlights the ongoing need for an organisation founded on ideological clarity on this matter.[11] The socialist campaigning journalist Paul Foot expressed the power of this state and associated circles of power well in his book *The Vote:*

> The blatant assaults on elected Government by a whole host of state representatives – notably by the common law made over centuries by judges who clung relentlessly to the values of their class, or by the media, which throughout the process was almost universally owned and directed by particularly corrupt members of the same class, by generals and police chiefs whose class loyalties have never been in doubt, and by a civil service whose mandarins, despite the screens of neutrality behind which they hide, have been uniformly loyal to their class. The unimaginable power wielded by this combination of industrial and financial chieftains, their toadying press, their police chiefs, their generals and admirals and their judges is incomparably greater than the formal powers wielded by elected Governments.[12]

For social democratic and left reformist parties, there is no similar critique of unelected power, instead all emphasis is laid on the need to take over institutions within the state, most obviously Parliament. In the words of Ralph Miliband, introducing his great 1972 work, *Parliamentary Socialism*, 'Of political parties claiming socialism to be their aim, the Labour Party has always been one of the most dogmatic – not about socialism, but about the parliamentary system.'[13] Elections remain paramount. Everything about these parties is geared organisationally towards a timetable of national, regional and local elections, which then each create their own political priorities. Support for extra-parliamentary movements is always subordinate to that timetable. For parties that are mainly extra-parliamentary, however, there is a different set of priorities, which are to develop strategy and tactics that raise left consciousness through self-organising, whether via trade union and workplace organisation, or through participation in broad movements. These movements then operate to influence electoral politics at the level of candidates, manifestos and campaigning. As a result, the extra-parliamentary left places great emphasis on political education, the development of theory and encouraging the formation of a 'cadre', or embryonic leadership – an organisational culture quite different from what exists in the Labour Party.

PREPARING FOR A BACKLASH AGAINST A CORBYN GOVERNMENT

The future success of any left government will depend heavily on the support that it receives outside Parliament. Even if it has a clear parliamentary majority, it will from the outset be beset by threats. This was true even for governments much more centre left in character than one led by Corbyn, such as the 1960s Wilson governments.[14] There is not usually the luxury of being able to govern 'in normal times', because these are never normal times. Usually, as well, left governments come to office in periods of crisis and instability – and this would certainly be the case were a Corbyn government to be elected within the next few years.

So left governments are typically elected against a highly contested and polarised background. The threats they face come from a variety of sources. The media is for the most part unremittingly hostile and, in very many cases, in the hands of ideological right wingers. Big business and the money markets react violently to the advent of left governments, with runs on the stock market, investment strikes and threats of all kinds posed against even quite moderate levels of nationalisation and state intervention. Any or all of these can force a retreat on left policies, and in a party like today's Labour Party would help to reinforce the right wing of the party, which would become the mouthpiece of 'moderation' in the face of such attacks.

There are two other possible dangers. The first of these is direct state intervention to prevent a left government from carrying out its policies. While some on the left dismiss this as a possibility, we have both the evidence of history, and some evidence about the nature of the current state machine to suggest that this is, in fact, all too likely. The gradualist and parliamentary character of British politics should not be allowed to obscure the role of those who would try to destabilise or even remove an elected government. In the early 1970s, Harold Wilson faced serious plots from forces within the military and the secret service.[15] Representatives of the military have already made clear – albeit anonymously – their refusal to accept a Corbyn government or its policies. Protection against any such attempts to weaken or remove a Corbyn government will not come from Parliament, nor can we accept the idea of a neutral judiciary or monarchy. Protection will only come from the millions of supporters of such a government and its policies, mobilised on the streets.

There is of course another danger that a Corbyn government would face – opposition from its own side. Within the existing constitutional rules, there is nothing to prevent candidates from standing and being elected as Labour and then declaring themselves something different, while continuing to sit as MPs, as first John Woodcock and Frank Field did, followed by the more spectacular departure of Chuka Umunna and his friends in February 2019. Despite the apparent failure of Change UK, if a version of this tactic is used from within what remains a mainly anti-Corbyn Parliamentary Labour Party following the next general election, it would in all likelihood either deprive Labour of a majority, or make a minority Labour administration very difficult to form. This would, of course, be its profoundly undemocratic purpose.

In the event of any single one or combination of these attacks on a Corbyn government, the minimum requirement would be that trade unionists organise industrial action in defence of a government voted for by millions of working people; students and school students walked out and took to the streets; and local organising committees drove back the attacks on government. All on a scale not seen in Britain for a very long time. This would mean a high level of convergence between parliamentary measures proposed by the left and the activities of the working-class movement outside Parliament.

NO TO ZERO-SUM SOCIALISM

The long-standing debates within the left about the possibilities and limitations of 'parliamentary socialism' – or reform versus revolution – would then be put into practice in the most concrete way. The phenomenon of a left-led Labour Party has forced a reassessment of the left as it has been composed since the 1960s. The majority of those on the far left in Britain have been extremely welcoming to Corbynism, whether we have joined Labour, been prevented from joining, or simply chosen to support from the outside. We believe Jeremy Corbyn has helped to create the very real possibility of a government that attempts significant reforms and tries to shift the balance of wealth and power towards working people. At the same time, our ideological belief remains that such a reforming government would come up against undemocratic forces in society that control wealth and power.

This is an issue that cannot be avoided, and must be recognised and prepared for. Corbynism may incorporate different models of socialist change, but there should be general agreement that such change will not take place without a confrontation with those forces. The main mode of confrontation should be the assertion of popular power in the streets, in the squares and, above all, in workplaces.

The development and practice of Labour's left since Corbyn was elected leader has involved too little thinking about this; too much concentration on changing internal structures and particular personnel within the party, and not enough work to develop our alternative sources of power to set against everything the Establishment lines up against us. This orientation only serves to undermine the long-term strength of the left, and leave it isolated from wider movements that can bring change. We are in the midst of a huge crisis in British politics – the rise of Corbynism is just one expression of this. The outcome of that crisis, if it is to benefit working people, will depend on forces mobilised well beyond Westminster. Momentum has played an important role in organising doorstep campaigning, canvassing and getting out the vote, but has failed to develop as a wider movement. Both Momentum and Labour more generally have, of course, a much greater reach than have the far-left organisations outside Labour, and the campaigns we have helped initiate. But there must be a coming together of all these elements, to address these wider questions of political power that affect a layer of working-class society immeasurably bigger and broader than the Labour Party and its activists alone.

The experience of Corbynism so far has shown the potential of socialists organising within Labour, but also the very clear limitations to this project. Labour has always held together in tension those who are happy to accommodate fully to the parliamentary system, and those who see the extra-parliamentary as central to change. Managing that tension is now central to the success or otherwise of Corbyn's Labour. What is needed now is a minimising of the former, and maximising the latter approach.

The problem is that the left is unlikely to have the luxury of working on a long-term strategy for doing so. The attacks from the right, the constant criticisms of Corbyn, and the likelihood of further splits and defections by MPs, have all heightened and sharpened the crisis and tensions within Labour. This is no time for the left to retreat. Instead, we should be going on the offensive, stressing the importance of democratic socialist politics, and taking the fight to the Tories over the parlous effects of austerity on our lives. If this means a confrontation with some in the Parliamentary Labour Party, it is better to be prepared and organised, than allow the right to gain the advantage.

This battle is not going to be won within the corridors of Westminster. Corbyn's success has been as a movement and as an insurgency from the streets. He has brought a new hope and new enthusiasm to hundreds of thousands of Labour members and much wider numbers of potential Labour voters. We need to return to that street-level insurgency if we are to defeat the attacks on him and mobilise grassroots support.

NOTES

1. Alan Travis and Ian Black, 'Blair's popularity plummets', *The Guardian*, 18 February 2003. The article uses figures from a *Guardian*/ICM poll and states that 'at least one person from 1.25 million households went on Saturday's anti-war march in London'; a separate YouGov poll for the *Telegraph* found that four per cent of the population demonstrated on 15 February 2003 – both polls point to 1.5 to two million on the march. *Telegraph*, 19 February 2003.

2. See Pippa Norris, *Democratic Phoenix*, Cambridge University Press: Cambridge, 2002, and Adrian Cousins, 'The crisis of the British regime', Counterfire, 27 November 2011. For a very good short overview of these developments in British politics, see Chris Nineham, *How the Establishment Lost Control*, Zero Books: Winchester, 2017.

3. For details, see Alex Nunns, *The Candidate: Jeremy Corbyn's Improbable Path to Power,* Chapter 7, OR Books: New York, 2016.

4. David Rosenberg, 'What do Jennie Formby's stats tells us about antisemitism in the Labour Party?', *Morning Star,* 14 February 2019.

5. Jon Lansman, speaking on the *Today* programme on BBC Radio 4, quoted on www.politicshome.com, 25 January 2019.

6. Rosenberg 2019.

7. Phil Jackson, 'Momentum isn't staging a coup in Haringey, this is about housing, not Labour factions', *Independent,* 29 November 2017.

8. For recent discussions of this classic dilemma, see for example *Socialist Politics and Electoral Strategy: A Report,* Verso: London, 2019; Kevin Ovenden, *Syriza: Inside the Labyrinth,* Pluto: London, 2015; Leo Panitch and Greg Albo (eds), *Rethinking Revolution: Socialist Register 2017,* Merlin Press: London, 2016.

9. Karl Marx and Friedrich Engels, *Selected Correspondence,* Progress: Moscow, 1982, pp139-40.

10. Tariq Ali, *The Dilemmas of Lenin,* Verso: London, 2017, pp1-2.

11. For an interesting discussion of parties and movements, see Jodi Dean, *Crowds and Party,* Verso: London, 2016. See also Karl Marx, 'The civil war in France', in David Fernbach (ed), *The First International and After,* Pelican: London, 1974 for a contemporary, highly incisive account of the destruction of the Paris Commune; and V.I. Lenin's *State and Revolution* for a classic response to this enduring question.

12. Paul Foot, *The Vote: How it was Won and How it was Undermined,* Viking: London, 2005, p.435.

13. Ralph Miliband, *Parliamentary Socialism,* Merlin Press: London, 1972, p.13.

14. Wilson himself claimed that in all but one of the years he was in government in the 1960s, the administration was plagued by a balance of payments problem that led to 'frenetic speculative attack', quoted in Miliband 1972, p.361.

15. Peter Wright, *Spycatcher,* Heinemann: London, 1988.

Class, Racism and a Vacuum

Satnam Virdee

The neoliberal consensus crafted by both conservative and social democratic political parties since the 1980s was dramatically unsettled by the financial crisis of 2008. The subsequent imposition of austerity aggravated already damaging social inequalities, producing a polarisation of social forces in the political field. It has been the far right, first and foremost, that has capitalised on these developments. From Sweden to Switzerland, from Belgium to Bulgaria, a tide of reactionary populism is sweeping across the European mainland and beyond; a tide which promises nothing less than a restoration of a mythical golden age of sovereign nation states defined by cultural and racial homogeneity.

Significantly, Britain is not inoculated from this economic and political turbulence. The most striking manifestation of it here has been Brexit. On 23 June 2016, Britain voted narrowly to secede from the EU; by 52 to 48 per cent. Alongside the fantastical visions of imperial restoration crafted by aging Etonians – Britain as the best in the world – was the altogether more insular Powellite vision of an independent sovereign nation state: Britain for the British. At Brexit's core were concerns around immigration, with the migrant represented as not just an economic threat, but a security threat as well. Unsurprisingly, given the deeply entangled history of immigration and racism in British history, following Brexit, there has been a disturbing wave of racism directed not only at migrants, but also at settled communities of black and brown Britons.[1]

Yet alongside this increasing drift to the hard right in British politics there has been the altogether more positive shift to the left represented by the election of Jeremy Corbyn to the leadership of the Labour Party. The significance of Corbyn's ascent is twofold. On the one hand, it represents a left-wing break from the neoliberal consensus and the decade-long programme of austerity which has devastated so many multi-ethnic working-class communities. At the same time, it is a welcome riposte to the right – that when it comes to anti-racism, there are resources of hope, that all is not lost. At a representational level, this nod towards a more inclusive way of doing politics has been reinforced by Corbyn's commitment to diversifying the composition of the Shadow Cabinet and shutting down the worst of the migrant detention centres. Given this, it is all the more dispiriting to witness a Labour Party leadership team encompassing Jeremy Corbyn, Diane Abbott and John McDonnell supporting restrictions on freedom of movement on the grounds that such freedom lowers the wages of British workers.[2]

We need to understand how Labour's new-found inclusive conception of social justice regardless of ethnicity coexists with its reproduction of anti-migrant discourses. The reasons for this contradiction in the Corbyn project are to be found in deeply embedded structural factors that were crucial to the party's foundation, as well as in more immediate instrumental concerns around building successful electoral coalitions.

THE STRUCTURAL CONTRADICTIONS OF THE LABOUR NATION

A historical perspective on the present reveals why this contradiction is not new, but is inherent to the logic of the Labour project. Throughout its history, the Labour Party's demands for economic and social justice have been wilfully entangled with questions of national belonging. While Labour's conception of the nation was undoubtedly broader than those forged by the imperial elites, and in that sense represented an ambition to democratise society, it nevertheless did so by offering a vision of the working class that identified certain racialised others as neither fully of that class nor of the nation. In the first half of the twentieth century, it was Jews who could not be imagined as British. Such Labour antisemitism drew on a long prehistory too often ignored in accounts of socialism. As Brendan McGeever and David Feldman show, it can be found in:

> Chartism in the 1840s and in the pages of Keir Hardie's *Labour Leader*, which in 1891 proclaimed that imperialist wars were being planned to suit the interests of 'hook-nosed Rothschilds'. Jews were good when outcast, a long way away and suffering from Tsarist oppression. But many of the same socialists and radicals who protested against pogroms were first in line to pronounce the Boer War an expression of Jewish conspiracy.[3]

And Labour's failure to take account of this legacy has had deleterious consequences politically, which are now becoming increasingly and publicly apparent: 'In failing to acknowledge this inheritance, Labour leaders disavow a painful and dishonourable aspect of the movement's past'.[4] 'Painful and dishonourable' is also an entirely apt description of Labour's record on racism in the second half of the twentieth century, as demonstrated by the party's inability to imagine workers of Caribbean and Asian descent as British. These racialised versions of national belonging acquired their legitimacy among parts of the working class precisely because they helped to frame elite conceptions of national belonging as unjust because they excluded those working-class people who understood themselves as 'racially British'.

By the time 400,000 migrants from the Indian subcontinent and the Caribbean arrived between 1948 and 1962, a century of incremental democratising reforms had helped secure the mental as well as material integration of much of the working class into the imagined British nation.[5] Working-class power was then at its zenith, encompassing a bipartisan commitment to a common citizenship and the welfare settlement, including full employment and the National Health Service. Looking back on this period through our neoliberal present, many contemporary socialists seem to understand this moment as a golden age, a yardstick for the kind of ethical society we may wish to live in today. On the dustjacket of a recent book on Corbyn's rise to power we are told: 'post-war Labour England wasn't a bad place to live'.[6] However, when the period is viewed through the eyes of Caribbean and Asian workers, there is little room for such misty-eyed nostalgia. Attachment to the twin racialising nationalist projects of imperialism and socialism was so comprehensive that there was simply no institutional space in British political culture, including working-class culture, to make sense of the presence of these so-called 'others'. Consequently, what these social groups faced was an unrelenting and sometimes violent racism from all social classes, which was combated only occasionally by abstract appeals to 'tolerance'.

Alongside party political and state racism, Caribbean and Asian workers were confronted with practices of social closure on the part of the organised working class who, in opposition to their presence, had come to reimagine themselves as white. Trade unions used the closed-shop tactic to limit migrant workers' access to skilled work, while colour bars were actively enforced from below, including at Ford car plants and British Railways.[7] If these were breached by the employers, wildcat strikes were initiated by workers to bring their employers back into line – a sort of DIY racism which helped enforce a hierarchical ordering of the working class based on colour. When racist employment practices came under threat of being breached, white workers took industrial action to defend them. In February 1955, in the West Midlands, employees of the West Bromwich Corporation Transport system began a series of Saturday strikes in protest against the employment of an Indian trainee conductor. In the same year, transport workers in Wolverhampton decided to ban all overtime in protest at the increasing employment of black labour, and the breaching of the 5 per cent quota for black workers agreed by the trade unions with their employers.[8] In this period the long-standing principle of 'last in, first out' when redundancies were threatened was abandoned if it meant white workers would lose their jobs before black workers, with one official of a general union confirming 'that in the event of redundancy occurring his members would insist on coloured workers going first'.[9]

What distinguished this post-war period up to the mid 1970s was the extent to which the British state, employers and workers had come to internalise a common British nationalism, underpinned by a shared allegiance to whiteness. The racialising nationalism shared by both the ruling class and too many socialists profoundly scarred British society and the working class within it. Its effects

could be traced through the political and cultural spheres, as well
as the economic. From the creation and consolidation of a stratified
division of labour in the workplace, to the informal regulation of
intimate social relations in the community, racism's reach was all-
encompassing. And over time, it became institutionalised, which
meant it no longer always required active enforcement, because the
structures and institutions of society came to reflect this distorted
understanding of the world. This was an all-pervasive, suffo-
cating racism that ranged 'from the massive to the substantial',[10]
and its effects were such that, irrespective of their cultural capital,
Caribbean and Asian workers found themselves located overwhelmingly at the bottom of the British class structure, carrying
out unskilled manual work.

The racialised other, then, was the unwitting foil against which
the Labour Party legitimised its efforts to include the majority of
the working class marked as white. And each time the institutional
boundaries of the post-war nation were stretched to encompass more
members of the white working class, this was simultaneously accompanied and legitimised by a racialising nationalism that excluded
the more recent 'non-white' arrivals. What gave this racialising
nationalism its power to reach deep into the working class was that
it emanated from political organisations and leaderships that had
emerged out of the organic struggles of the working class itself. This
gave these leaders and the positions they adopted a degree of authenticity, and helped consolidate the parallel efforts of the imperialist
state to integrate workers through relentless propaganda drives and
the invention of national traditions.[11]

THE DECOMPOSITION OF CLASS, THE RACIALISATION OF CLASS

This contradiction at the heart of the Labour project has been
further worsened by a pattern of heavy defeats since the 1980s across
a range of industries, combined with a technical decomposition of
class through deindustrialisation, which has increased the damage
to, and in some cases entirely destroyed, the spirit and combativity
of working-class communities. Overdetermining this has been a
process of political class decomposition, including the incremental

disappearance of once-powerful cultures of solidarity and socialist infrastructure that had been built up over the course of the post-war welfare settlement. And with this has gone the language of class, such that now we find a strong sense of class disassociation, if not dis-identification, meaning that for many working people today class has become 'a category loaded with negative connotations, a category by which they believe they are mis-recognised and from which they dis-identify'.[12]

This story of class decline and dis-identification is intimately connected to the racisms currently unleashed amid the political crisis of Brexit. In recent years, the prospect and often brutal realities of downward mobility have produced a set of class injuries that have been recast through a politics of *ressentiment*.[13] Decline is necessarily a multi-ethnic process, yet for many it has been experienced and made sense of through a racialised frame of nationalism. Often, it is the politics of English nationalism that have captured this sentiment. While the British National Party (BNP) and, more recently, the UK Independence Party (UKIP) have at times ridden this wave, it is the political mainstream that has played the decisive role in bringing to life these racialised resentments.

In the vacuum remaining after defeats inflicted during the Thatcher years, a powerful narrative emerged – from New Labour to the Conservatives – that claimed the principal losers from globalisation were a category referred to as the 'white working class'. For New Labour's think tanks, this categorisation formed part of its modernisation project, of refashioning the working class of welfare capitalism as classless subjects suitable for a neoliberal economy underpinned by a commitment to state-led multiculturalism. In this imaginary, the term 'white working class' was used as an ethno-racial label to denote a social group whose alleged culture of welfare dependency and accompanying social excesses (e.g. criminal inclination, racism and so on) had to be combated through a raft of remedial social policies aimed at making them fit for the precariat workforce[14] of twenty-first-century capitalism.[15] At the same time, while class remains a fundamental source of inequality, a post-war working-class militancy that briefly emerged in the 1970s and early 1980s has also been comprehensively defeated. Further, the idea of socialism as an emancipatory political project lost much of its appeal amid the collapse of the state socialist regimes in Eastern Europe in the late 1980s, such that today it has little purchase among large swathes of the working class. And the traditional party of the working class – Labour – responded to such changes via the Blairite model of modernisation discussed above. The result was not just the jettisoning of the original, and totemic, Clause Four commitment to common ownership of the means of production, but the forsaking, in effect, of any lingering commitment to the forging of a democratic socialist society.

If this vision sought to 'domesticate' or 'tame' a fraction of the working class, another vision sought to unleash its allegedly instinctive aversion to immigration. From 2001, the BNP began to make minor yet unprecedented electoral gains in working-class districts of local councils, and then, in 2009, it had two MEPs elected in the north of England, on the back of the slogan 'rights for whites'.[16] This was followed a few years later by UKIP achieving much greater gains, locally and in the European elections.[17] Whatever the differences between the BNP and UKIP, they shared a broadly similar anti-immigration message, amplified by the right-wing press whose aim was to erode support for state multiculturalism. While these elements weren't uniform and were often in conflict with one another, what they did collectively was help reinforce the racialised idea of 'the white working class'.

Thus, the long-term absence of multi-ethnic class narratives and erosion of working-class agency, combined with New Labour attempts to racialise class politics, and its subsequent complicity in imposing austerity, helped carve open this space for the injuries of class to be recast through the politics of racist resentment. Rather than challenging the presuppositions that underpinned such politics, key intellectual currents emergent in the past decade, such as Blue Labour, reinforced them. Founding figures of this movement such as Maurice Glasman and Jonathan Rutherford spoke of the 'paradoxes of Labour's tradition', arguing that Labour needed to 'address the crisis of its political philosophy and to recover its historic sense of purpose' by 'rebuilding a strong and enduring relationship with the people'.[18] The suggestion was that working-class voters would be won back to Labour through a rediscovery of its socially conservative roots, with an approach that emphasised concern for 'family, faith,

and flag'.[19] But such a conservative message is only likely to reso-
nate with certain categories of workers, in particular those who are
concerned about questions of race, immigration and Europe. And
this view's narrow conception of the working class fails to consider
how such a message might play to a working class in England that
today is increasingly characterised by ethnic diversity.[20] What Blue
Labour, and others like them, fail to understand is the structuring
power of racism throughout English society, including within
parts of the working class, and the extent to which visions of 'the
people' have been deeply racialised over a long period. Any progressive political project that attempts to invoke notions of 'the people'
today must actively seek to both acknowledge this contradictory and
complex history of racism, and plot ways of moving beyond it and
its structuring effects.

The consequences of these developments for socialist politics
have been catastrophic. Today, real working-class pain – which in
Britain is necessarily a multi-ethnic pain – has come to be understood by substantial numbers of mainly older people through a
racialised anti-immigrant focus. And this was no more clearly seen
than during the Brexit referendum, and now in its aftermath. What
immediately becomes obvious when analysing the Leave vote, town
by town, is how closely it maps onto those working-class communities that went down to a series of historic defeats in the 1980s at the
hands of the neoliberal offensive we then referred to as Thatcherism.
Typical are the former mining towns from Barnsley to Bolsover,
Rotherham to Doncaster, which felt the full force of Thatcherism
during the 1984-85 miners' strike. Former steel towns like Redcar
and Scunthorpe, along with others like Hull and Grimsby, where
once-thriving fishing industries were destroyed by neoliberal capitalism, all voted strongly to leave, as did a string of former mill
towns in Lancashire. And should anyone think this represented
a north-south divide, one could point to the 'garden of England',
Kent, where towns like Gravesend, Gillingham, Chatham and
Dartford – once home to powerful groups of workers employed in
cement manufacture, paper mills, coal mines, the railways, and the
Royal Navy dockyard – all voted overwhelmingly for Brexit.[21]

An understanding of the multi-ethnic working-class subject is
fundamental to transformative social change, but this cannot be to

the exclusion of attention to the question of working-class support for reactionary projects that seek to racialise class politics, and divide the working class along lines of race and citizenship. Of course, not everyone who voted for Brexit in these localities or, for that matter, in London or Manchester, is a dyed-in-the-wool racist. Rather, in the context of the historic defeats of movements for working-class emancipation and the resultant disappearance of class narratives, many working-class people marked as white remained indifferent to the ways in which the Brexit visions put forward during the referendum were racialised and shaped by anti-immigrant sentiment. And they were indifferent because they were operationalising visions of 'them' and 'us' which were based on affiliations to British, and more specifically, English, national belonging.

And herein lies the political limitation. Labour under Jeremy Corbyn has come to an understanding that if it is to forge the kind of historic bloc that can win a general election, it will need to soothe the concerns about immigration of a crucial segment of that potential bloc. It is for this reason, and in spite of their own long-standing commitment to anti-racism, that Corbyn, Abbott and other figures of Labour's 1970s and 1980s anti-racist left now find themselves articulating and justifying restrictions on freedom of movement from the EU. This fundamental tension at the heart of the Corbyn project – between anti-racist class politics and sustaining the party's potential voting bloc in order to bridge the Brexit divide – came into full view in 2017, in a series of interventions by Corbyn. Most notably, in July, he announced that Labour's post-Brexit Britain would see 'the wholesale importation of underpaid workers from central Europe' prohibited. Instead, jobs would be advertised 'in the locality first'.[22] What adopting such a strategy does, however unwittingly, is to feed the assertion, now increasingly dominant in British politics, that it is migrant workers who undermine working conditions. In so doing, Corbyn concedes crucial ground in the confrontation with anti-immigrant racism. Corbynism undoubtedly contains within it the resources for an alternative way of doing class politics, but as presently constituted, it retains intact a particular left understanding of the nation state that has been a feature of the labour movement since its formation, and which is now being reprised through the crisis of Brexit.

THE RECOMPOSITION OF CLASS, AND AN INDIFFERENCE TO DIFFERENCE

Raymond Williams once remarked that 'to be truly radical is to make hope possible, rather than despair convincing'.[23] And there is hope. This rising tide of racialised class politics has not gone completely unchecked. If one fraction of the working class has shifted towards projects framed by anti-immigrant and sometimes racist narratives as part of a long-term process of technical and political class decomposition, what has been striking is how another element has remained largely unmoved by such politics. Part of this working class emerged under neoliberalism, in a process of technical class recomposition that saw many of the children of the manual working class acquire high levels of cultural capital, yet be ruthlessly pushed into precarious forms of employment. Other important fractions include the state proletariat of teachers, civil servants, health workers and local government officers, that first came to prominence in the 1970s cycle of protest. While it survived Thatcherism relatively intact, this fraction has found itself under attack since the imposition of austerity.

These working classes are to be found disproportionately in large cities and university towns; they tend to be younger and, significantly, they are both a multinational and multi-ethnic working class, comprising three key elements. The first is recent migrants from Europe and elsewhere. The second, black and brown Britons. And third, the white British who reject the tying of this identification to racist projects. What is significant about all three is that they are resident in locations that were at the epicentre of the cycle of anti-racist protest that occurred between the mid 1960s and the late 1980s, including London, Manchester, Liverpool and Glasgow. While that wave eventually subsided, it left traces such that those who grew up in the slipstream of these actions encountered spaces that had been transformed by the real gains of the anti-racist movement, among them state support for multiculturalism. However much these achievements are being rolled back by austerity and new modalities of racism, their imprint is still traceable in the ease with which many young people handle the lived realities of multi-ethnic life in urban Britain.

What is striking about Corbynism's break with neoliberalism is that a significant component of the activist base that drives the project forward is drawn from these social layers. They form an important element of the potential coalition around a Corbyn-led Labour Party, and any renewal of the left that coalition sparks will be bound up with the fortunes of this multi-ethnic and multinational working class. However, if this renewal is to be truly effective, it will require an urgent reckoning with Labour's current positioning on questions of immigration, and antisemitism as well, because, as McGeever and Feldman point out, 'anti-racism is not divisible'.[24]

At the same time, this emergent working class is profoundly disconnected from its past. Perhaps because of this, it has not challenged Corbynism's contradictory position on freedom of movement as vigorously as might have been expected, nor found a path out of the antisemitism crisis. A major factor in this is that it emerged as a class fraction under the most unfavourable of circumstances: the historic defeat of the antisystemic cycle of protest and the stigmatisation of socialism, especially Marxism. Consequently, we have a political left ill-equipped to deal with a rising tide of racism and the likely emergence of a form of right-wing politics that parallels developments on the European mainland, where populist parties of the right campaign on an increasingly anti-immigration, Islamophobic agenda. Brexit seems to have energised such social forces. This is the vacuum that racism fills in the absence of class politics.

To respond effectively therefore requires a working class conscious of itself as a class with interests in common, regardless of race, gender or faith. Class, as the historian E.P. Thompson described it, is 'a happening':[25] for this emergent left not only to consolidate itself, but to tackle the racialising dimensions of the crisis and effect meaningful social change, class will have to happen, and in a way that actively absorbs the differences inscribed into the working class.

NOTES

1. Satnam Virdee and Brendan McGeever, 'Racism, crisis, Brexit', *Ethnic and Racial Studies*, Vol. 41, No. 10, 2018, p.1808.
2. Helen Lewis, 'Jeremy Corbyn: "Wholesale" EU immigration has destroyed conditions for British workers', *New Statesman,* 23 July 2017.

3. Brendan McGeever and David Feldman, 'Labour and antisemitism: What went wrong and what is to be done?', *Independent*, 18 April 2018.
4. *Ibid.*
5. Virdee, *Racism, Class and the Racialized Outsider*, Palgrave: Basingstoke, 2014.
6. Mark Seddon and Francis Beckett, *Jeremy Corbyn and the Strange Rebirth of Labour England*, Biteback: London, 2018.
7. Virdee 2014.
8. *Ibid.*, pp102-3.
9. Leslie Stephens, *Employment of Coloured Workers in the Birmingham Area*, Institute of Personnel Management: London, 1956, p.16.
10. William Daniel, *Racial Discrimination in England*, Penguin: London, 1968, p.209.
11. Virdee, 'Racialized capitalism', *Sociological Review*, Vol. 67, No. 1, 2019, pp.3-27.
12. Beverley Skeggs, 'Class disidentification, singular selves and person-value', Goldsmiths Research Online, 2016, p.1.
13. Vron Ware, 'Towards a sociology of resentment: A debate on class and whiteness', *Sociological Research Online*, Vol.13, No.5, 2008.
14. See Guy Standing, *The Precariat*, Bloomsbury Academic: London, 2011.
15. Chris Haylett, 'Illegitimate subject? Abject whites, neoliberal modernisation, and middle-class multiculturalism', *Environment and Planning D: Society and Space*, Vol. 19 No. 3, 2001, pp351-70.
16. James Rhodes, 'White backlash, "unfairness" and justifications of British National Party (BNP) support', *Ethnicities*, Vol. 10, No. 1, 2010, pp77-99.
17. Virdee and McGeever 2018.
18. Maurice Glasman, Jonathan Rutherford, Marc Stears and Stuart White (eds). *The Labour Tradition and the Politics of Paradox*, Lawrence and Wishart: London, 2011, pp9-11.
19. *Ibid.*
20. Virdee and McGeever 2018.
21. BBC, EU referendum results, 2016, www.bbc.co.uk/news/politics/eu_referendum/results. While this essay focuses on the working-class component of the Leave vote, it was the middle class that demonstrated a greater propensity to vote Brexit overall, see for example Virdee and McGeever 2018, pp1802-19.
22. Anoosh Chakelian, '"It feels like a betrayal": EU citizens react to Jeremy Corbyn's migration stance', *New Statesman*, 27 July 2018.
23. Raymond Williams, *Resources of Hope*, Verso: London, 1989, p.118.
24. McGeever and Feldman 2018.
25. E.P. Thompson, *The Making of the English Working Class*, Penguin: London, 1991.

Farewell to the Labour Nation

Gerry Hassan

It was on May 8th 1940 that the Labour Party challenged the Chamberlain Government in the Division Lobby. 281 Tories voted for the Government, while the Labour MPs and 33 Tories voted against. The initiative of the Labour Party led to Chamberlain's resignation. VE Day came exactly five years later, on May 8th 1945.

In these five years Britain has been working to a plan. Behind this plan the whole people of Britain have been ranged ... The people of Britain must now drive home their victory in the next five years by defeating their peace-time foes of unemployment and poverty. But there must be a plan for victory in peace, just as there has been a plan for victory in war. Private enterprise could not have won the war. Nor can private enterprise win the peace.

Labour Party, *Speaker's Handbook 1945*[1]

Take One. 'Comrade Corbyn is an enemy of the British state', declares Stephen Pollard in the *Daily Express*.[2] Simon Heffer writes that 'Jeremy Corbyn has long hated Britain',[3] while David Starkey announces that Corbyn is 'a man who invariably sides with the enemies of Britain'.[4]

Take Two. The Churchill film *Darkest Hour* opens to the scene of the famous May 1940 House of Commons Norway debate that brought down Neville Chamberlain as prime minister. It homes in on Labour leader Clement Attlee savaging the Tory record of appeasement and military incompetence, claiming patriotism and fighting fascism as core Labour subjects. 1940 was many things – when a large part of the British ruling classes wanted peace on any terms with Hitler – but it was also undoubtedly Labour's finest hour, and led the way to 1945.

These two contrasting visions of Labour and its leading figures have run through how the party has been seen since its inception: as respectable and unrespectable Labour; as the party of Britishness, and that of the country's enemies and the equivalent of a virtual 'fifth column' – from the Zinoviev letter, via Tony Benn and Michael Foot as 'reds under the bed', to the anti-Corbyn hysteria in parts of the contemporary press.

Labour has understood much of this doubleplay and the problematic reclamation of its past prominent figures as national treasures, when they were seen as far from that when they lived. But, more importantly, today's Labour has ceded the ground of patriotism and national pride to its opponents, along with the very idea of Britain itself. And, in so doing, it has sold short its own story and traditions: ones that could have offered a radical counter-story to reaction.

For example, how many Corbynites know that the fate of Britain in those tense days of 1940 actually hung on the deep deliberations of Labour Party discussions? As the German Panzers advanced westwards and Chamberlain desperately clung on to office in May 1940, the annual Labour Party conference met in Bournemouth, with the prime minister trying to broaden his government through coalition with Labour. At this critical hour for Britain, Labour's National Executive Committee (NEC) – meeting at the Highcliffe Hotel – decided against coalition with Chamberlain, resulting in his resignation, Churchill coming to office, a coalition government involving Labour, and the continuation of the war.[5]

In his seminal left critique of Labour reformism, *Parliamentary Socialism*, Ralph Miliband passes over this pivotal moment in the party's and Britain's history without comment.[6] As does Lewis Minkin in his study of intra-party democracy.[7] This was the point when, in the words of Attlee's deputy Arthur Greenwood, 'the guns had come near enough to England to be heard sounding inland across Essex and Kent'; writer Nicholas Shakespeare adds the context: 'the fate of Chamberlain, Halifax, Churchill, of England too, was determined'.[8] For England read Britain, as always in such accounts.

In all the conjecture over Churchill as war hero or villain (or both),[9] where is the Labour account of the pivotal role of the party's

NEC and democratic processes in the continuation of the war and defeat of fascism? This is an acute example of a wider problem: Labour's marginalisation from its own role in history, and hence its relationship with the idea of Britain, which has come back to haunt the party and the left as UK politics have lurched rightwards over the past four decades.

Britain has, throughout its history, been dominated by reactionary ideas. These have seldom been fully understood by radicals and progressives. There is Andrew Gamble's notion of 'the conservative nation', an evoking of an England/Britain as both rural idyll and place of permanently entrenched power and privilege.[10] Then there is the British empire state, which at home and abroad practised a brutal imperialism, politics of domination and economics of extraction, both from the colonies and domestic working classes.[11] And finally, there is what David Edgerton has described as a 'warfare state', where the leading frontiers of twentieth-century innovation, research and development, and science and technology, were overfocused on the needs of the military to the detriment of the wider economy.[12]

All three strands of reactionary tradition and ideology have come to contribute to and impact on politics not just in the past, but also in the present – in the form of Brexit and the delusional, fantasyland 'Global Britain' of the hard right of the Tory Party. A long historical tailspin has led the UK to this present predicament, and to this discourse, which it will take enormous effort to counter, challenge and defeat.

A major factor in the journey to the present Brexit impasse has been the constrained nature of democracy in Britain; in which only one half of Parliament, the House of Commons, is elected by popular vote; where British people are not citizens but subjects; and there is no such thing as fundamental rights or laws – a perilous situation made more acute by the UK's impending withdrawal from the EU, which will leave unchecked the degree to which governments can legislate to abolish the most basic rights and freedoms. This restriction of democracy is reinforced, both by the sense of continuity and permanence that the British Establishment works to convey, and the character of capitalist democracy – itself a truncated form that has functioned to curtail political debate, and prevent economic and social democracy from becoming reality.[13]

THE RISE AND FALL OF 'THE LABOUR NATION'

This is the context in which Labour has undertaken its politics, a context that has proven to be, in the past and today, a hostile environment in which the party has at times achieved impressive change without ever managing permanently to alter the wider political landscape.

Within the arc of this Labour history, the party at its peak articulated what might be called 'the Labour nation'. This was a counter-story of Britain to the dominant Tory one; a story that, although it never became hegemonic, had influence and impact and, critically, affected how Labour saw Britain and acted politically.[14] The argument that such a conception existed is implicitly made in Edgerton's *The Rise and Fall of the British Nation*, although he never names the 'Labour nation' as such: 'The United Kingdom of Great Britain and Northern Ireland of the late 1940s can usefully be seen as one of the new nations which arose from the dissolution of the one empire ... A national United Kingdom arose after 1945':[15] one where the UK became a separate body from the empire and defined its own nationality, distinct from the colonies and Commonwealth.

'The Labour nation' did not exist in the legal sense of having a formal territory, of course, but it was both a political and imagined community, with a concept of its borders, a notion of where it began and ended, and even its own flags, symbols, codes and cultural references, all of which fed into a distinctive Labour ethos and outlook, which in turn informed the party's actions.[16]

First, 'the Labour nation' was founded on the principle of parliamentarianism; of the Westminster parliament as the primary and sovereign political authority. Acceptance of this principle gave legitimacy and mandate to Labour in office, enabling it to advance far-reaching change often in the face of powerful vested interests.

Second, it was built upon the idea of the advancement of equality and fairness in relation to economic and social advancement and opportunity, and the use of a powerful central state to advocate for this.

Third, a centralised politics of command and control was deemed necessary, with the role of government and the state pivotal. Only a powerful centre had the resources and political capital to pool, share and redistribute resources to those who most needed them.

Fourth, and underpinning all this, Labour had a form of democracy that was proscriptive and restrictive. Democracy flowed through the party's historic mission, mandate and popular support, and was seen to reside above all in its elected representatives, particularly those at Westminster. Hence, mainstream Labour down the decades has shown a lack of curiosity about how power and elites work in the UK; a limitation that has gone beyond the misguided Fabian belief in gradual change and conviction that through permeation, the institutions of the Establishment might be turned to progressive ends.

Fifth, 'the Labour nation' had to be governed and administered by a class of people. These were not Labour radicals, socialists, or even trade unionists. Instead, they were an insider group of experts, technocrats and managers who staffed the agencies of the state, nationalised industries, planning bodies and new centres of authority. This was not about democratising power and decisions, but a masculinist rationale based on a vision of blowing away the cobwebs of fusty old practice, introducing science and enlightenment to public service, and championing what was, in places such as Scotland, referred to as 'planned freedom'.[17]

Sixth, at times, 'the Labour nation' strayed into endorsing the idea of British exceptionalism, and with it the Whig interpretation of history about the supposed uniqueness of British institutions and their continuity and durability. Labour thought it could seamlessly come to power and use archaic bodies and practices to remake the country in an egalitarian fashion, in a way that continental European socialists could only observe with envy.

Finally, 'the Labour nation' saw the UK as a powerful force for good in the world – a view that overstated the scale of the UK's global impact post-1945. A critical period, in this mindset, was Labour's participation in the wartime coalition of 1940-45, the precursor to the 1945 government. This view can be seen in the party's support for decolonisation and the Commonwealth, along with its sporadic support for the Campaign for Nuclear Disarmament (CND) and unilateral nuclear disarmament, where the moral ground and the importance of the UK taking exemplary action was heavily emphasised by the likes of Michael Foot, in a kind of reverse imperialism.

The above visions of the Labour nation operated on often unstated assumptions about the British economy and its strength domestically and internationally – that this was one of the key economies of the capitalist order, and that what mattered most was how it was redirected and redistributed. These assumptions were severely challenged by the recurring crises of the UK economy and its relative post-war decline, which produced the 1949 and 1967 devaluations of the pound and the 1976 International Monetary Fund (IMF) crisis, all under Labour. The first two of these resulted in productionist export-focused drives, but, despite this, the party's distributionist tendencies – that is, its emphasis on how national wealth is divided rather than focusing on, say, questioning the entire growth model – have remained in the ascendancy to the present day.

Moreover, the Labour nation mindset has underpinned how Labour has seen Britain and the British state, and hence how it has interpreted Britishness and the multiple identities of English, Scottish, Welsh and Northern Irish, which also interplay with Britishness. From 1940 onwards, through Clement Attlee, Hugh Gaitskell, Harold Wilson, and more recently Tony Blair and Gordon Brown, Labour has seen the British state in neutral class terms as an institution which can be used to advance far-reaching progressive change. Even the Labour left, from Nye Bevan to Michael Foot and Tony Benn, while it showed scepticism about, and sometimes offered a critique of, the British state as a part of an Establishment that might block or even try to destabilise an elected radical Labour government, only ever put forward the most limited reforms to remake the powers of the central state. This was even true at the peak of the Bennite new left, which, for all its ultra-democracy, still proposed to retain parliamentary sovereignty, the idea of the all-powerful electoral mandate and, hence, an absolutist state.

These pillars of 'the Labour nation' gave sustenance to a political framework that shaped the party's politics and its idea of Britain throughout its key moments: 1940-45, 1964 and 1974 – the high points of Labour ascendancy pre-Blair. However, by 1997, this framework was beginning to weaken, due to the onslaught of

Thatcherism's partisan abuse of the British constitution such that it could act like an 'elective dictatorship', and in whose wake New Labour's methods and statecraft followed.

Eleven years after the financial crash and nearly a decade after New Labour lost office, 'the Labour nation' is discredited as a road map for future political guidance. The reasons for this are many, but key among them has been the morphing of central government into an unapologetic neoliberal state, a process begun under Thatcher, but entrenched under Blair and Brown, and maintained by Cameron, May and Johnson as the new normal. This political capture means that the idea of the state either as neutral, or as a political agency that can be captured and used for progressive politics, is now redundant.

The demise of 'the Labour nation' puts the party in a very different place from that of the era of stable post-war two-party politics which characterised the period 1945 to 1979. It leaves Labour in an exposed place for finding direction and strategy, but it is also an environment shaped by other mainstream political declines, including the multiple crises of Tory Britain and the wider ideas, referenced above, of 'the conservative nation', the empire state and the warfare state. This, then, is a time of both significant danger and opportunity.

AFTER 'THE LABOUR NATION'

The Corbyn leadership has talked a good talk on political change, but on political power and relationships within Britain and the character of the British state, it has been both too reticent and too conservative, still clinging to the old discredited order.

Part of the reason for this is the allure of the possibility of a future left Labour government being elected on a minority vote to a convincing parliamentary majority, and thus being able to use the institutions of monopoly state power to ram through a socialist political programme and overcome political resistance by using these institutions' undemocratic character for progressive ends, against the forces of reaction and privilege. This is, of course, a fantasy version of political power, drawing on past British crises of reactionary power such as 1931, when Ramsay MacDonald went into coalition with the Tories, and 1976, when the IMF imposed monetarism on the Callaghan government. Influential as well have been non-British crises, such as those of Gough Whitlam in Australia and Salvador Allende in Chile – in which centre-left elected governments were toppled, the first by constitutional means, the second by the military. This is the heady stuff of ex-MP Chris Mullin's novel *A Very British Coup* and similar political fictions; it is far from the realpolitik of British politics.[18]

As 1976 and other occasions underline, a radical Labour government would meet ferocious extra-parliamentary opposition both in a conventional domestic sense, and also from the markets and international capitalism. There would be capital strikes, disinvestment, runs on the pound, and the UK's international credit ratings would be at risk. All of this has been war-gamed by John McDonnell and other senior Labour figures.[19] But they would also face resistance from within Labour – from senior anti-Corbyn figures in the trade-union movement, and from a Parliamentary Labour Party in which the Corbynite left is a tiny minority, with the faultlines and fissures within the party amplified by the forces of reaction.

But more profound challenges would face such a Labour government. First, there are the problems inherent in the principle of basing monopoly political power upon a minority of votes, and of seeking legitimacy from the tired old tropes of parliamentary sovereignty and mandate-ism. Second are Britain's multiple crises and divisions – economic, social, regional, national – which will not be resolved simply by waving the magic wand of a Labour government. And thirdly, the very idea of Britain itself, including the Labour idea of the country, is in crisis and a terminal condition.

In clinging to the conservatism of the British state, the Corbyn project draws from the well of mainstream labourism.[20] Labour's continued attachment to the shibboleths of parliamentary sovereignty and the notion of a unitary-state Britain put it in agreement with both the mainstream of the Conservative Party and ultra-Brexiteers: all share a continued deference to an indissoluble political centre, and an authority that is neither restricted nor codified.

CLINGING TO THE EMPIRE STATE: UNITARY-STATE LABOUR NATIONALISM

A key aspect of this is Labour's ongoing commitment to the misguided idea of a unitary-state Britain. This may be understood as the notion that there exists a supreme political authority that can legislate, administer and do what it likes across the UK. This idea has always played a role in the tradition of Labour absolutism and the myth of a left government overcoming the resistance of the Establishment, and in Labour's concepts of Britain, unionism and the union. It happens to be completely inaccurate, as well as being bad politics.

The UK has never been a conventional unitary state as that term is understood. The UK is not a state with a standardising political centre. Rather, it is a country, not a nation, made up of four component parts: England, Scotland, Wales and Northern Ireland. This union has arisen from a series of conquests and unions as well as divisions: the union between Scotland and England in 1707, the union between Great Britain and Ireland in 1801, and the emergence of the Irish Free State in 1922, which produced the present state and its name: the United Kingdom of Great Britain and Northern Ireland, although it only took this legal name in parliamentary legislation in 1927.

In the hybrid union that is the UK, Scotland as a legal entity with a degree of autonomy and its own laws never went away; Wales was conquered, disappeared, and then reappeared as a legal entity in post-war times; while Northern Ireland practised its own home-rule one-party state between 1922 and 1972. And this is before we even get to the post-1997 round of devolution reforms.

The UK has increasingly been understood as having been a union state throughout its history, a state where pre-union rights and arrangements remain, and where there is a plethora of unions and different relationships.[21] What needs to be emphasised here is that British Toryism and its unionism was, historically, instinctively better than Labour at grasping the evolving, organic nature of the union.[22] It celebrated the union as something distinctively British; had a distrust of the state and was wary of the centre accruing powers; and it championed the local and traditional. These attitudes were based on an understanding of both the limits of the absolutist state and the patchwork nature of the union. All this contributed to the story that British conservatism was able to tell about Britain that resonated beyond Tory shires.

This presented problems for Labour, and gave an inbuilt advantage to the Tories. Labour's unitary-state Britishness was a form of inflexible unionism (and hence nationalism) that proposed a homogenised expression of Britishness as a form of citizenship and social contract. In so doing, it faced a much more flexible Tory unionism, which championed decentralisation and a differentiated Britain. If Labour and the wider left think that this account of pre-Thatcher times is unfair, consider the way Churchill and the Conservatives campaigned against the centralisation of the Attlee government. In the 1950 UK general election, Churchill in Edinburgh a week before polling stated that he would 'never adopt the view that Scotland should be forced into the serfdom of socialism as the result of a vote of the House of Commons'. Similarly, the Conservative Party made the case for the union at the time while standing against the remorseless march of centralisation, which they described as the 'amalgamation' of Scotland in the union.[23]

If we fast forward to Britain post-1979 and Thatcherism, we see this high Tory pragmatism slowly being pushed to the margins, such that it no longer has any serious influence among the Tories. Instead, they have become, as much as Labour ever was, a party of the central state, with a complete disregard and indeed lack of respect for the local and decentralisation. These attitudes present problems for both parties, considering how diverse, fragmented and non-national the politics of Britain have become, with a 'national' British politics only existing at Westminster in the form of façade and pretence – and in the name and claim of British government.

A pivotal moment for Labour was its position in relation to the 2014 Scottish independence referendum.[24] Leaving aside the question of why the Scottish Labour Party *opposed* independence and campaigned on a joint ticket with the Tories as 'Better Together', the party had an even bigger problem, and one that still haunts it: the grounds on which it defended the union.

Labour had, once upon a time in Scotland, made the case for the union in *instrumental* terms: as a means to a better end, namely that of a more egalitarian, progressive Britain. This was the compelling story of 'the Labour nation' of 1945 to 1979. Since 1979, this story has ceased to be so plausible. It is all fine and well for Gordon Brown to wax lyrically about the joys of 'pooling and sharing' resources in the UK and how this aids Scotland, but this sidesteps the realities of the neoliberal state and the UK as one of the most unequal countries in the developed world.[25]

What Labour's messaging degenerated into because of the state of the divided kingdom in 2014 was a defence of the union in *intrinsic* terms: as an end in itself, irrespective of how it advanced centre-left, progressive goals. This is a total cul-de-sac, which proposes the union as something to be championed irrespective of what it stands for in relation to inequality, poverty and power and which is, in essence, nothing more than an unreflective British state nationalism that does not have the insight to understand that it is a nationalism.

This relates to another major dilemma and problem for Labour: how to come up with a convincing story for Britain after Thatcherism, New Labour and 'the Labour nation'. The Corbyn leadership's approach to this has been to invoke the need for trans-formational economic and social change, which is imagined to emerge from a centre of state power under the direction of a mass membership party. This approach offers little in the way of detail on a number of critical questions, such as how they might go about democratising this central state in a way no previous Labour govern-ment has attempted, and how to defeat the forces of reaction that sustain the neoliberal state.

The current leadership has conformed to many traditional Labour patterns at a time when these have become more problematic. Thus one member of Corbyn's inner team, when I asked them in 2018 what thinking the leadership were doing on England, replied: 'We are not doing any thinking on England.' Similarly, until the 2017 UK election, the leadership seemed to have written off Scotland electorally for Labour, and had no discernible strategy north of the border. This changed post-2017, in that Scotland became less SNP and Labour regained a foothold in its own once-impregnable heart-land. But it is still the case that Corbyn has not found a coherent Scottish strategy, and he still zigzags on his public stance on Scottish independence: stating at one point that he is 'absolutely fine' about another referendum on the question,[26] and on other occasions seeming to reject the idea out of hand.

There has been initial movement on constitutional change, with Baroness Pauline Bryan of Partick, a key Corbyn ally, tasked with coming up with proposals for a new democratic pan-British settle-ment that abolishes the Lords and entrenches the Scottish Parliament. Bryan has suggested the Lords be replaced by a Chamber of the

Regions and Nations, while the UK would evolve in a federal direction with 'common minimum standards across the UK on human rights, employment rights, consumer protection and environmental protection'.[27] But as with federal mood music from the likes of Gordon Brown and others down the years, Corbyn's Labour Party has stopped short of a written constitution or any detailed federal plan, remaining committed instead to the absolutist state.

The snail-like pace of this evolution is in stark contrast to the crises engulfing British politics. The Labour Party is still, in its core beliefs, committed to the political authority and centre that served it from 1945 to 1979. In the forty years since the end of the era of competitive two-party politics regularly alternating in power, the party has at points oscillated towards recasting the entire political landscape and state, but it has on each occasion backed off. Such a transformation would entail the party abandoning its commitment to parliamentary sovereignty and the unwritten nature of the British constitution; instead embracing shared sovereignty, a written constitution and codified rights, with checks and balances on central power.

Constitutional change on its own is not enough to rebalance and redistribute power in the asymmetrical union that is the UK. Scotland and Wales are already salutary examples of that.[28] Both are in many ways successes as devolved public polities, but neither has engaged in fundamental economic and social change. Any constitutional reform of the UK also has to deal with the deformed nature of the central state and not only take it back from the neoliberal insider class, but transform it into a developmental state that promotes a different kind of economy, investment and business.

This is easier said than done. Such a transformation was the aspiration of successive Labour and Conservative governments pre-Thatcher, from Macmillan's National Economic Development Council to Wilson's National Plan and the first Bennite Alternative Economic Strategy of the 1970s: all failed in the face of capitalist opposition and internal resistance from the Treasury and its commitment to economic orthodoxy and short-termism. Thatcherism and New Labour gave up entirely on trying to remake the state to refashion British capitalism, and instead embraced the short-termist, rentier model of finance capitalism that produced electoral

dividends for both, but did not address any of the underlying weaknesses of the British economy.

BEYOND THE MIRAGE OF MISSIONARY BRITAIN

The crisis we are living through now goes to the heart of what
Britain is, who gains from it, who the insiders and the outsiders are,
and the very idea and survival of Britain in the near future. The rise
of the neoliberal state has been part of the capture of British politics and Britain itself by the forces of the radical right. They have
retooled politics, state and statecraft to be about the interests of a
narrow global class and their self-interests, and repurposed public
policy, political discourse and the public sphere to this end.

This grim set of realities has fed into day-to-day politics, producing
the decline of both mainstream Toryism and Labourism as ideologies, and the weakening of internal control in their respective
parties. The Tories are evolving into an intolerant English-focused
populist-nationalist party that is shedding any connection with the
old, paternalist, pragmatic unionism of its past. In contrast, the
Corbyn phenomenon is transitional; breaking with the discredited
old order, but not yet fully formed. It is a mixture of old opposition-
alists, ideologues of the hard left, and new forces of disruption and
energy, with very different and competing sensibilities.

The Corbynite interpretation of a future Britain is a work in
progress, vague on the details, although some of its form can be
identified. This is a project defined by rejection of the dominant
stories of empire and class domination at home and abroad.

Constitutionally, Labour has at least grasped some of the basics.
There is a recognition that, beyond the complications of Brexit, a
Northern Irish unity referendum will happen at some point. The
Corbyn leadership seems on balance more relaxed than anxious
about the prospect of a second Scottish independence referendum.
This leaves the huge question of what to do about England and any
pan-British governance: 'the missing England' being the historical
subject large sections of the English left have had a deep embarrass-
ment about ever talking about.[29] This is no longer sustainable, as the
avoidance of England as a political agency is one of the main ideological stalwarts maintaining the neoliberal state and settlement.

Neoliberalism has never been very popular in the UK, for obvious reasons, but it has managed to capture the political elites and win sufficient minority support in insider and popular opinion to carry the day politically. One of the drivers enabling it to sweep all before it has been the absolutist state, the extent of power centralisation and Whitehall micromanagement and, related to this, the absence of England as a democratic voice.

A POLITICS OF LIBERATION FOR THE LEFT MEANS TALKING ABOUT ENGLAND

Unlocking England is the key to remaking the UK. Labour's avoidance of the subject has come at a bitter cost in recent times: Thatcherism was both an English and British nationalism that annoyed large parts of Scotland, Wales and Northern Ireland (in the latter, in both republican and unionist communities). New Labour had nothing to say to English sensibilities beyond the mantra of offering it a supporting role in 'Cool Britannia', and its superficial cosmopolitan consumptionism. The eventual failure of both of these political moments played a significant role in the predominantly English (along with Welsh) revolt that is Brexit, a revolt that has given voice to an English reactionary, xenophobic nationalism at odds with much of the modern world.

Much has been written about English national identities since Brexit, including the occasional almost essentialist take on England, for example, Fintan O'Toole's polemic about Brexit, in which the one England that seems to be present has been captured by the Tories and right-wingers. Missing is any reference to Labour or radical England, or explanation of how these traditions have been marginalised and even sometimes written out the picture entirely.[30]

There have always been many different Englands and expressions of England, with Englishness for much of the UK's existence being subsumed within and seen as more or less synonymous with Britishness. This association has weakened in recent years, a process accelerated by Brexit. Writing about data from the 2018 Future of England Survey, Ailsa Henderson observes that 'The more English one feels, the more likely one is to express dissatisfaction with each of England's two unions: one external, the other internal' and that this and contrasting attitudes in the other three nations mean that 'The UK is not now, nor has it been for a long time, a union of shared identities.'[31]

In the near future, Scottish and Northern Irish referendums on their constitutional status seem inevitable. England is the only nation in the UK which has not been allowed to have a say in its own self-government, and is the only country in the developed world without its own form of democratic government. All the sub-national enti-ties of Europe – from Catalonia to Bavaria, Brittany to Tuscany – have their own democratic representation and voice. England is an anomaly and this, combined with the left's self-denying ordinance on the subject, has brought a heavy cost, allowing the right to speak for a certain narrow England and Englishness.

England is, of course, not just one nation in a group of equals, but by a massive margin the biggest component part of the UK, with 84.2 per cent of the population. Such asymmetry has a political cost, for no federation so imbalanced is practical. This then requires thinking equally about England, Englands and the many identities that exist within the nation.

But equally key here are the pan-British relationships, and the challenge of effecting change that is more than mere federal mood music, and tackles the problem of the undemocratic polit-ical centre. Underneath the glacial pace of Westminster, the UK is already on the move, with Scotland and Wales in a different political space already, and Northern Ireland too stuttering hesi-tantly into a different orbit.

Much more likely than the emergence of federalism and some benign grand redesign of the UK is that events, political dynamics, and the imbalances of the union prefigure a future that is already beginning to take shape now. The intransigence of the Democratic Unionist Party (DUP) over Brexit and Northern Ireland is not the politics of strength, but that of anxiety and deep foreboding about the future. Northern Ireland will, undoubtedly, become more decoupled from the UK and closer to the Republic, with the even-tual prospect of Irish reunification. Meanwhile, in its very different political landscape, Scotland remains on the brink of that second independence referendum.

A UK without Northern Ireland and Scotland would cease to

be the same country. The Union Jack would cease to be its flag, its name would have to change. There is, after all, little point in being called the United Kingdom of England and Wales.

This takes us into the uncharted waters of the slow loosening of the union that is currently the UK. This is already happening at a de facto level, with Scottish and Welsh self-government, and the unsustainable position in which Northern Ireland has found itself, dictated to by two right-wing parties, the Tories and their erstwhile allies the DUP, supporters of a hard Brexit in a part of the UK that voted to remain in the EU. Just as significantly, London has detached itself from the rest of the UK and declared a semi-independence that mirrors the relationships that world cities often have to the rest of a country, only magnified in the UK by the degree of political centralisation and the economic dominance of (London-based) finance capitalism that bears little relationship to real business.

If a unitary Labour statism does not work, mainstream Toryism is dead, and the fantasyland free market of ultra-Brexiteers is an unrealisable dystopia, where do the nations and regions of Britain go? One answer is to look beyond supposed tidy solutions such as federalism to a looser fit such as a confederation. This would allow Scotland, Wales and Northern Ireland to find their own democratic forms of self-government: the Scots a formal independence, the Welsh a powerful autonomy that may, for now, stop short of independence, and a pan-Irish set of arrangements that would see Northern Ireland slowly move out of the UK orbit.

A confederation of what is now the UK would be a hybrid – a very British solution, and a modern, bespoke one of shared and pooled sovereignties. It would be a big ask of the old traditions of Labour and Tory, and require the demise of parliamentary sovereignty and the age-old ritual practice of absolutism. It is the direction we are heading in, but it needs English voices and champions, not only the Scots, Welsh and Northern Irish. And it needs left radicals and Labour to consider how it might be possible to weave out of the wreckage that is the contemporary British state, and how we can develop a different power centre, possibly for England, and have a democratic, pluralist and collaborative set of relationships between the different nations.

THE END OF THE SPIRIT OF '45 AND THE OMNIPOTENT CENTRE BRINGING US SALVATION

Some will regard such a prospect as a defeat of British dreams, and of the spirit of '45. But many of these dreams were conservative, insular delusions: of achieving socialism through the distortions of first past the post, of 'elective dictatorship', and 'socialism in one country'. Such ideas never made any real sense, and were always a left mirror of the grotesque swagger and self-importance of the imperial state and its core class.[32]

Release from all that is, in fact, a form of liberation, which the left and Labour should not resist, but positively embrace. There will be significant turbulence and difficulty over the next few years in UK and international politics, with no prospect of a return to 'normality'. The defeat of the British imperial state and its neoliberal core could be a progressive victory, and one it is worth campaigning for and helping to happen sooner rather than later. But it also requires a political agenda and radicalism from the forces of the left to shape this future, as opposed to holding on to the old dreams, or waiting for the *ancien regime* to completely self-destruct.

The politics of nationalism(s) and self-determination increasingly prevail in Scotland, Wales and Northern Ireland, but also in England too. Politics in Scotland in recent decades has been shaped by a civic nationalism at ease with multiple identities, social citizenship and a moderate social democracy, but it is still a nationalism. Meanwhile, Brexit has been driven by a reactionary ethnic English nationalism of exclusivity, in thrall to the chimera of undiluted sovereignty.

Yet, as the UK becomes a looser entity of self-governing nations, nationalism on its own, benign or not, will not be an adequate guide. Writing about Scotland's twenty years of devolution, O'Toole suggests that 'Nationalism is a rocket fuel that can get you out of the orbit of an old order but burns quickly and leaves you dependent on much more complex and subtle systems of guidance.'[33]

The demise of the British state will finally end the idea of Britain, held onto by the neoliberal class and parts of the traditional left, as a magical place with a special destiny. Both groups display what Michael Moran has termed a 'messianism',[34] believing that Britain has a pioneering purpose – for one, of buccaneering capitalism; and for the other, of saving the people from the same, and building a socialist commonwealth in its place.

The old British state is dying along with its life-support systems and ideologies. These include those visions of both left and right that saw salvation in all things British and national, for the UK's crises are also ones that have affected its mainstream and competing politics, of conservatism, labourism and liberalism.

Related to this, some on the left still have a nostalgic yearning for a mythical 1945, partly accounted for by the subsequent years of disillusion and retreat. The myth of '45 is a left version of 'the Dunkirk spirit' mobilised by the right, often invoked without an understanding of either 1945's conservatism or its context – such as the immediate sense of disappointment many on the left felt at the culmination of the Attlee administration.[35] This sentiment was even widely articulated beyond radical circles, with journalist and broadcaster Anthony Howard reflecting in 1963 that 'the overwhelming Labour victory of 1945 brought about the greatest restoration of traditional values since 1660'.[36]

As Britain creaks and cracks and its foundations shake to breaking point, new voices and movements are emerging through the spaces and gaps, and will continue to do so into the future. Some of them, as we can already see, will neither be edifying nor progressive, but this is no reason to cling to the wreckage, or to old complacencies.

The British state is entering a period of crisis, challenge and disruption, with the ending of one state and set of nations that we have come to know. Many, including numerous left voices, will feel bereft and grieve this passing, but the demise of the British state, the idea of Britain, and belief in it as some missionary project, is long overdue and an escape from illusion. No longer can people think socialism could be built behind the walls of this empire state. That story is over, and along with it the illusions of the Fabian state of '45, of Bennite ultra-democracy coming to Whitehall, of Blairite degenerated forms of progressive governance and, as well, the Corbynite idea of an omnipotent centre pushing through radical change.

Resisting the temptation to cling to the old state means not lamenting the loss of the spirit of 1945, or 1940, or 1964, and or even, for some, 1997, or any other supposed radical moment of rupture. Rather, the moment requires an understanding of the politics of now, of crisis and rupture, and of the fact that a politics of the left cannot and should not try to put back together the increasingly divergent, loosening union of the UK.

A politics of the left, whether under Jeremy Corbyn in 10 Downing Street, or among a younger generation of Corbynista leaders, should not dissipate any of its political energies in invoking some elusive all-inclusive national spirit of British renewal. This has gone forever, and a more radical politics of our times would begin to embrace a new spirit of cohabitation and collaboration for the nations and regions of these isles. After Britain, and after the empire state, should not be a context the left is scared of, but a time to embrace a very different politics that puts at its very core counter-stories of democracy, equality and solidarity.

NOTES

1. Labour Party, *Speaker's Handbook 1945*, Labour Party: London, 1945, p.3.
2. Stephen Pollard, 'Comrade Corbyn is an enemy of the British state', *Daily Express*, 9 October 2018.
3. Simon Heffer, 'Jeremy Corbyn has long hated Britain', *Telegraph*, 28 May 2017.
4. David Starkey, *Politics Live*, BBC Two, 12 April 2019.
5. After these momentous events, the critical role of Labour increased, with nine War Cabinet discussions held over three days in which Churchill, with the support of Attlee and his deputy Arthur Greenwood, held out against the appeasers' last stand to explore a peace deal with Hitler. For the detail of this see John Lukas, *Five Days in London: May 1940*, Yale University Press: New Haven, CT, 1999.
6. Ralph Miliband, *Parliamentary Socialism: A Study in the Politics of Labour*, Merlin Press: London, 1972.
7. Lewis Minkin, *The Labour Party Conference: A Study in Intra-party Democracy*, Manchester University Press: Manchester, 1980.
8. Nicholas Shakespeare, *Six Minutes in May: How Churchill Unexpectedly Became Prime Minister*, Harvill Secker: London, 2017, p.387.
9. Gerry Hassan, 'Why Churchill still matters: The power of the past and the postponement of the future', *Soundings*, No. 70, Winter 2018.
10. Andrew Gamble, *The Conservative Nation*, Routledge & Kegan Paul: London, 1974.
11. Hassan and Anthony Barnett, 'Breaking out of Britain's neo-liberal state', Compass, Thinkpiece 43, January 2009.

12. David Edgerton, *Warfare State: Britain 1920-1970*, Cambridge University Press: Cambridge, 2005.

13. Miliband, *Capitalist Democracy in Britain*, Oxford University Press: Oxford, 1982.

14. Hassan and Eric Shaw, *The People's Flag and the Union Jack: An Alternative History of Britain and the Labour Party*, Biteback: London, 2019.

15. Edgerton, *The Rise and Fall of the British Nation: A Twentieth Century History*, Allen Lane: London, 2018, p.26.

16. Henry Drucker, *Doctrine and Ethos in the Labour Party*, Allen and Unwin: London, 1979.

17. See on this James A. Bowie, *The Future of Scotland: A Survey of the Present Position with Some Proposals for Future Policy*, W. & R. Chambers: Edinburgh, 1939.

18. Chris Mullin, *A Very British Coup*, Hodder and Stoughton: London, 1982.

19. Greg Heffer, 'Labour "war-gaming" for run on pound if elected', Sky News, 26 September 2017.

20. Tom Nairn, 'The nature of the Labour Party (Part one)', *New Left Review*, No. 27, September-October 1964; 'The nature of the Labour Party (Part two)', *New Left Review*, No. 28, November-December 1964.

21. James Mitchell, *Devolution in the UK*, Manchester University Press: Manchester, 2009.

22. Arthur Aughey, *The Conservative Party and the Nation: Union, England and Europe*, Manchester University Press: Manchester, 2018.

23. Mitchell, *Conservatives and the Union: A Study of Conservative Party Attitudes to Scotland*, Edinburgh University Press: Edinburgh, 1990, pp30, 50.

24. On Scottish Labour before the independence referendum, see Hassan and Eric Shaw, *The Strange Death of Labour Scotland*, Edinburgh University Press: Edinburgh, 2012.

25. Danny Dorling and Sally Tomlinson, *Rule Britannia: Brexit and the End of Empire*, Biteback: London, 2019.

26. Nicola Slawson, 'Jeremy Corbyn "absolutely fine" with second Scottish vote', *The Guardian*, 11 March 2017.

27. Pauline Bryan, 'Creating a constitutional moment', in Vince Mills (ed.), 'Time for a radical Scottish Parliament', Red Paper Collective, 2019 Red Paper, March 2019, p.14.

28. Michael Moran, *The End of British Politics?*, Palgrave Macmillan: London, 2017.

29. Aughey 2018, p.106.

30. Fintan O'Toole, *Heroic Failure: Brexit and the Politics of Pain*, Head of Zeus: London, 2018.

31. Ailsa Henderson, 'Brexit, the Union and the future of England', *Political Insight*, Vol. 9, No. 4, 2018, pp33, 34.

32. Nairn, *The Left Against Europe?*, Penguin: London, 1973.

33. O'Toole, 'The art of leaving and arriving: Brexit, Scotland and Britain', in Hassan and Simon Barrow (eds), *Scotland the Brave? Twenty Years of Change and the Future of the Nation*, Luath Press: Edinburgh, 2019.

34. Moran 2017, p.6.

35. Richard Crossman, 'Towards a philosophy of socialism', in Richard Crossman (ed.), *New Fabian Essays*, Turnstile Press: London, 1952.

36. Anthony Howard, 'We are the masters now', in Michael Sissons and Philip French (eds), *Age of Austerity, 1945-1951*, Hodder and Stoughton: London, 1963, p.19.

History in the Remaking

Out of the Ruins

James Meadway

There is a wonderful metaphor from Alasdair MacIntyre's *After Virtue*, in which the philosopher asks us to imagine a world hit by some terrible calamity that caused scientific and technical knowledge to be almost destroyed. What was left was smashed into thousands upon thousands of disconnected pieces, and the inhabitants of this world had to piece together their understanding of science and technology from what was lost, trying to reassemble the remnants of the earlier age from the ruins that remained as best they could.[1]

Scrabbling, ignorant, and in the darkness, they would sometimes get things right. More often, however, they would get things seriously wrong. Most of all, they had lost any sense of science as a system, depriving them not only of existing knowledge, but of the means to generate new ideas and make new discoveries.

It's an image that haunts me, repeatedly, when surveying the state of the left today. We don't live in quite such desperate times – clearly, we've inherited an enormous amount from our own past and, in particular, the major institutions of the left retain some of their capacities to shape and influence society and ideas. But it is as if we have lost something, and in its place has emerged what the Marxist historian Eric Hobsbawm highlighted in his much-maligned 1978 Marx Memorial Lecture *The Forward March of Labour Halted?*: 'It seems to me that we now see a growing division of workers into sections and groups, each pursuing its own economic interest irrespective of the rest.'[2]

At the time Hobsbawm upset many left trade union leaders by calling this trend 'sectionalism'. Today we might observe this same trend as a broader socio-political loss, or radical diminution, of what we can think of as a continuous *movement*, whose many parts may be separate, but which have some clear articulation and engagement with each other.

WHAT WE HAVE LOST

This shared movement, as a powerful and meaningful force in society, helped in turn to frame and articulate the ways in which it was possible to think about the world and how to change it. It mattered a great deal that at the time of Hobsbawm's lecture half the entire workforce was in a trade union, and 70 per cent were covered by a collective bargaining agreement.[3] And it matters a great deal if, conversely, today only 17 per cent of under thirty year olds[4] are in a TUC-affiliated union, and only 12 to 14 per cent of private-sector workplaces have even a single trade union[5] member present. It means, other things being equal, that there will be enormous numbers of people who will live, day after day, without ever knowingly meeting a trade union member or coming across any trade union activity. It means that the ways in which trade unionism and the labour movement more generally might be woven into the fabric of working-class life have frayed – in some places to the point of non-existence.

It isn't necessary to follow Hobsbawm's rather rigid economic determinism in this, by tying it to the decline of manual work. Clearly, there is no reason to suppose, as he did, that a working-class movement as such can only exist when the working class is dominated by its 'traditional' occupations of (male) manual work. It's perfectly obvious that, far from producing a widespread transition into the middle class, the spectacular shift to service-sector employment in the past few decades has remade the working class in a different image: more female, and more diverse, but also less secure and less well paid than the archetype that still exercises such an extraordinary grip on our collective imagination. Nor is it necessary to think, as Ian Jack recently suggested in a nicely observed, elegiac piece on the loss of traditional working-class culture, that we will remain trapped with a politics of negativity and sullen refusal as a result of this loss:

> Some places seem to have no point to them. We remember their public libraries, cinemas and shops, their pubs, dance halls,

Methodist chapels and Workers' Educational Association evening classes. Not least, we remember how busy the streets became at clocking-off time when people went home from work. Is it too much to speak of betrayal when this kind of town (industrial, with a Woolworths and a Gothic town hall) and this class of person (industrious, locally patriotic, manually skilled) have more or less died of neglect?[6]

But it is simply not possible, either, to deny the reality of what has happened.

Once there was the era of 'This Great Movement of Ours', recalled by writer and trade union official Francis Beckett thus:

> The days of windy, overblown trade union rhetoric. Middle-aged union officials at the annual Trades Union Congress would talk about This Great Movement of Ours (the irreverent called it Tigmoo), its rights, its duties and its responsibilities. Young firebrands demanded that the unions took their rightful place in the vanguard of the revolution.[7]

Today 'This Great Movement of Ours' no longer exists in the same way it once did. The *form* of it is still here; we still have large trade unions – membership remains around six million – but the *content* has been evacuated. To take a crude but meaningful indicator, it has been reported that strike days lost in 2017 were at the lowest level since records began in 1893.[8] There is zero evidence that Britain's workforce has become more militant since 2017; if anything, the reverse. And, as a consequence, the trade unions' decline forms part of what Phil Burton-Cartledge has called Labour's 'crisis of decomposition', in which, among other things, a fall in union membership has resulted in less participation by unionised workers in the party at both local and national levels.[9]

POLES OF ATTRACTION

What we have today is a series of partial and disparate *movements*, spread across society, with a circulation amongst them as to which appears dominant at any point in time, dependent usually on external events. For the period at least since the miners' strike of 1984-85, or, less obviously, the early 1990s, when strike levels collapsed[10] and never recovered, the record of the left in Britain has been readable as a series of singular movements, each one of which could coexist with each other one, and one of which would, for a time, become the dominant form of political activity for those on the left. The brief flaring of the pit closures campaign in 1992; the Criminal Justice Act protests; the road protest movement; anti-globalisation; the anti-war protests; the student movement; protests against austerity – the 1990s, 2000s, and 2010s for the left may be transcribed as a series of flashes in the darkness, of greater or lesser intensity and duration, leaving behind only traces.

Intellectually, this pattern – which is familiar across the Global North – has largely formed two responses, between which everyone on the left has distributed themselves.

The first response has been to retreat to a mid 1970s comfort zone and pretend that, but for a lack of 'confidence' or some other subjective factor, the working class in Britain was about to throw off its shackles and come rallying to the scarlet banner once more, in a reassuringly familiar pattern. Some shop stewards' committee[11] or other would rise from its political graveyard and come marching down London's Holloway Road, whilst dockers would once more picket Fleet Street to demand solidarity from the press, overcoming the mere happenstances that no newspapers are now produced there, and that they themselves no longer exist.[12] It would be conjectured that, although call-centre workers or Deliveroo riders are, admittedly, doing different things to coal miners or steelworkers, they would – eventually, sometime soon – adopt the same familiar tactics and forms of organisation. In 1974, the Japanese soldier Hiroo Onoda was found in the Philippines, still fighting the Second World War, unaware it had been over for close to twenty years. In much the same way, there is a not-insignificant section of the left still fighting the 1970s battles they lost four decades ago.

The second response has been to celebrate the diversity of movements as such, and to pretend that the fragmented parts added up to more than their sum, or even that fragmentation itself was a step towards a higher goal. What self-respecting would-be intellectual in the early 2000s had not read Antonio Negri and Michael

Hardt's tome against *Empire*, and their ringing endorsement of the *Multitude*[13] as the radical alternative? Who on the left had not been thrilled at the thought that even though we were manifestly and obviously losing, we were, in fact, secretly and subtly winning everything?

Even if most on the left have fallen somewhere between these two poles, what has been lacking for all is the sense of a meaningful connection to a continuous, permanent movement – because that continuous, permanent movement does not exist. Something has had to be conjured up in its place: be it a celebration of what exists, or a nostalgia for what has passed, reheated. In both cases, the future is something to be ignored. Similarly, the vast distance that has – until very recently – existed between the left and any serious prospect of political power has warped its intellectual life. It has meant that academia has provided a warm home for a generation or more of those on the left, with all the distortions that brings. For the social sciences most concerned with the questions of power in society, this has had the most dramatic effects. Chief among the affected disciplines is economics: squeezed to the margins of the academy, those economists opposing the dominant paradigm and its broadly centrist political conclusions have been reduced too often to the status of squabbling sects, indulging in esoteric debates thousands of miles from questions of power, and therefore policy.

THE LONG RETREAT

But the impact of this dispersion and retreat on the wider movement has been more significant. Jeremy Corbyn's election as Labour leader in September 2015 offered the chance to make a break with what Jeremy Gilbert has called the 'long 1990s', a period when flashes and bursts of activity occurred, only to be followed by quiescence: 'a culture in which technological change is accompanied by cultural stasis as a pretty direct expression and effect of the hegemony of the techno-financial historic bloc'.[14]

Corbyn's election, and re-election, as Labour leader has posed, and given an institutional shape to, the question not only of building a permanent movement, but of challenging for political power in the near future. Elected through a rejection of the centrist politics that supported austerity, economic questions were always going to end up centre stage under Corbyn's leadership. Gilbert points to the significance of this enduring moment: 'If the key feature of the long 1990s was the pervading sense that even on the left, the normativity of neoliberalism could not be refused, then that moment is clearly now over.'[15]

The capacity of the movement to respond and meet the challenge, however, has been limited by the decades of retreat from core economic questions. The numbers in the party with a formal training in economics are limited, and in any case an academic background in economics will have taught only the neoclassical mainstream – good enough for challenging austerity; less obviously useful if the necessity is to transform the economy; whether that means reversing rising inequality, or dealing with climate change. The number of academics or others trained in economics who engage with any part of the movement remains small. It is many years since a significant core of labour-movement-oriented economists could be sustained.

As a result, this nascent movement has had to look to its own resources. John McDonnell as Shadow Chancellor has promoted a wider discussion,[16] but clearly running any such initiative top-down can only do so much. Efforts outside Westminster have pulled together whatever is to hand from the materials available, notably from the now fragmentary and partial knowledge of the economy, and economics, that is the legacy of the older labour movement. Some parts are half-remembered, and then pieced together in peculiar (and often largely useless) new ways, for example 'Modern Monetary Theory' – a reconstruction of post-war Keynesianism minus the mass workers' movements and international political economy that helped deliver it.

Where any semblance of connection to the labour movement – let alone the tiny political institutions of the left – has crumbled, many have pulled together what they can, with the social playing a crucial role in forging these connections. But the knowledge assembled is necessarily fragmentary and isolated, and its relationship to the central strategic question of political power may be indirect, at best. We are, like the victims of MacIntyre's cataclysm, left picking through the ruins, unable to assemble a coherent whole from the parts.

But the great danger here is not that we won't be able to provide answers to current questions. The danger is that, if we do not have a functioning economics of our own, aligned to a movement, we will fail to answer the questions we don't yet know exist. As MacIntyre warned, we will lack the trained imagination needed to think not only about today's problems, but about tomorrow's – and about where tomorrow's solutions might lie.

There is an urgent and pressing need to develop that imagination. We can know the rough shape of at least some of the problems bearing down on us (climate change, digitisation, automation) and some of the answers (renewables, working time reductions, common-ownership). But we have far more work to do in developing those answers and in winning a wider understanding in the movement of the tools needed to answer them.

A mass, popular programme of education in economics – perhaps better to call it 'political economy' – is required. We need Gramsci's 'organic intellectuals', tied to and part of the movement, on a mass basis. We need the imagination, sense of possibility and commitment to making it happen that a mass movement can give to all its participants. We need reading groups and day schools in every town and city; web resources such as Open Democracy's ourEconomy[17] to host and help shape the arguments; and events like The World Transformed,[18] up and down the country. We need Constituency Labour Parties hosting events as a means by which the membership can shape this new political economy at a local level. We need an ambitious national education programme, based on participative learning, to knit all of this into what the Labour Party is about.

It is time, now, to stop picking through the ruins and start to build a mass movement for a new economy: one that places the values of solidarity, sustainability and democracy at its centre, but that has the strategic sense to know how to apply them in the reality of our torrid present.

NOTES

1. Alasdair MacIntyre, *After Virtue: A Study in Moral Theory*, Bloomsbury Academic: London, 2013.
2. Eric Hobsbawm, *The Forward March of Labour Halted?* Verso: London, 1981, p.14.

3. See Stefano Marino and Miguel Martinez Lucio, 'Trade unions – in decline or renewal?', Manchester Policy Blogs: Europe, 13 May 2014.

4. Shehab Khan, 'Fewer young people joining trade unions because they don't see they are relevant', *Independent*, 4 June 2018.

5. Brigid van Wanrooy et al., 'The 2011 Workplace Employment Relations Study', Department for Business, Innovation and Skills, 2011.

6. Ian Jack, 'The great betrayal: How Britain's industrial towns died of neglect', *The Guardian*, 9 March 2019.

7. Francis Beckett, 'United we stand', *The Guardian*, 13 June 2000.

8. Richard Partington, 'UK worker strike total falls to lowest level since 1893', *The Guardian*, 30 May 2018.

9. Phil Burton-Cartledge, 'Labour's crisis of decomposition', www.averypublicsociologist.blogspot.com, 10 March 2019.

10. Office for National Statistics, 'Labour Disputes Enquiry', www.ons.gov.uk.

11. For historical interest, see Joyce Rosser and Colin Barker, 'A working-class defeat: The ENV Story', www.marxists.org, originally published in *International Socialism*, 1st series, No. 31, Winter 1967/68, pp21-32.

12. For a typical example of this, see Dave Stockton, 'Pentonville Five: When dockers fought the law and won', www.workerspower.co.uk.

13. Michael Hardt and Antonio Negri, *Empire*, Harvard University Press: Cambridge, MA, 2001; Hardt and Negri, *Multitude: War and Democracy in the Age of Empire,* Penguin: London, 2005.

14. Jeremy Gilbert, 'The long 1990s is over', www.jeremygilbertwriting.wordpress.com.

15. *Ibid.*

16. See for example John McDonnell (ed), *Economics for the Many,* Verso: London, 2018.

17. OurEconomy at www.opendemocracy.net.

18. See @TWT_NOW.

The Revolution Will be Networked

Paul Hilder

In the Prague Spring of 1968, Alexander Dubček and his comrades launched an 'Action Programme' designed to liberate Czechoslovakia from the iron grip of the USSR. The document painted a striking and inspiring vision, one which appealed to revolutionaries all around the world: 'Socialism cannot mean only liberation of the working people from the domination of exploiting class relations, but must make more provisions for a fuller life of the personality than any bourgeois democracy'.[1] Embracing pluralistic ideas of multi-party democracy and freedom of speech, the Prague Spring insurgents started implementing bold reforms to decentralise power and move it into the hands of ordinary citizens.

Moscow could not allow this heresy to take root. By August of that same year, Soviet tanks were rolling in to crush the Czechoslovaks' all-too-brief experiment in 'socialism with a human face'. Appalled by the crackdown, Britain's Ralph Miliband, whose father had served in the Red Army, wrote to the Belgian Marxist Marcel Liebman about it. He argued:

> The democratisation of 'revolutionary' parties is essential... The internal life of a revolutionary party must prefigure the society which it wants to establish – by its mode of existence, and its way of being and acting. While this is not the case, I don't see any reason to want to see the current parties take power: they are quite simply not morally ready to assume the construction of a socialist society.[2]

While leaders like Dubček and Corbyn can open the door to transformational change, what they can never do is deliver that transformation on their own. Even the greatest of leaders will inevitably fall under the spell of that 'iron law of oligarchy'[3] to which the left is far from immune – at least as long as power is hoarded by the few in their political bunkers, and until that power is finally shared with the many.

'Socialism from above' has gathered wide support on the left, and has played a vital role in restoring faith in the possibility of a better politics. The idea of enlisting a rejuvenated state on the side of the people to confront the monsters of monopoly capitalism and degenerate markets is a potent one. But who will pull the strings of this newly muscular state? If they ever make it into government, what will our new prophets' blind spots be? How will they fall from grace, how soon? If all our chips remain on them and not on ourselves and our fellow citizens, the fallout of failure from above will not only be toxic; it will be nuclear for the prospects of twenty-first century socialism.

'Socialism from below' was the most important principle of the Prague Spring. It was similarly a central principle of Salvador Allende's Chilean movement and government, so cruelly destroyed by the US-backed coup in 1973, which made such a profound impression on the young Jeremy Corbyn.[4] And 'socialism from below', or, in Ralph Miliband's words, the 'prefigurative democratisation' of the Labour movement, is the most pressing imperative of the twenty-first century new left in Britain. What will most determine our prospects of transforming our country for good? The stifling or empowering of bottom-up movement energies, the rotting or the flourishing of an empowering political culture, and the question of whether and how we can truly share power with the many, will be decisive.

We live in volatile and unforgiving times, where politicians and movements can rise and fall in a heartbeat, where desperation is rising, where despair and abandonment are all too close at hand. With all this in mind, we need to ask Ralph Miliband's question. Is today's British Labour Party morally ready to lead the construction of a socialist society that could genuinely liberate citizens to lead larger lives and manifest our dreams together? If not, why not? What must we change before it is too late? Before the window of opportunity closes again, for yet more decades we cannot afford to lose.

Our twenty-first century reality of networked social relations and the left's abiding values of humanity and social justice both point in the same direction: toward new ways of organising our Labour movement, new ways of winning power and governing, and new ways of transforming and renewing all we hold in common. As the Italian theorist Antonio Gramsci once put it: 'the old is dying, and the new is as yet barely born'.[5]

A 'socialism from below' is growing in our movement. We could call it 'networked Labour'. This movement is ours to weave and grow; and no party apparatchik, of whatever shade of red, has any right to stop us.

HOW WE GREW THE NETWORKED LEFT

In February 2019, my friend Zack Exley came to the UK to meet with Jeremy Corbyn, John McDonnell, Clive Lewis, Rebecca Long-Bailey and other leading Labour figures. A new movement called Labour for a Green New Deal was launched during his visit, led by leading young Momentum organisers and climate activists. Zack shared some lessons from the meteoric ascent of the Green New Deal in the US, and their plan to end net fossil-fuel emissions within ten years.

The US Green New Deal had first been floated just three months previously. Immediately after the midterm elections, the youth-led Sunrise Movement organised a sit-in occupation of veteran Democratic House leader Nancy Pelosi's office to advocate for the idea. It was immediately championed by superstar progressive Congresswoman Alexandria Ocasio-Cortez (AOC) and like-minded new representatives. AOC had originally been recruited to stand by another movement, Brand New Congress, founded in 2016 by Zack with fellow alumni of the Bernie Sanders campaign in the Democrats' presidential primaries.[6]

Despite fiery controversy and right-wing attacks, the Green New Deal – a plan that includes massive state-directed investment and puts social and racial justice at its core – almost immediately secured endorsements from most of the 2020 Democratic presidential contenders, and initial support from a majority of the American public, including many Republican voters (before the Fox News hatchet jobs kicked in).[7] Interestingly, its content was modelled in part on a British initiative from 2008 led by the New Economics Foundation and involving socialist economist Ann Pettifor and Green MP Caroline Lucas, which broke important new ground back then, but was initially much less successful in influencing Labour politics.[8]

I first met Zack Exley in 2005. I had been writing about and advocating for a more open, movement-powered form of politics, and had just launched Vote4Peace – a campaign supporting MPs who voted against the Iraq war with donations and volunteers.[9] Zack had campaigned against the same war and other Bush-era atrocities as organising director of MoveOn.org, a progressive US movement, before advising Howard Dean's insurgent presidential run.[10] Zack had been enlisted by New Labour to help them prepare for that year's general election. But privately he was unimpressed, not only by the Blairites' aggressive support for Bush and all that entailed, but also by their lack of serious big ideas. We compared notes on our respective top-down political establishments, and agreed that only movements and new leadership could transform the 'Overton window'; the range of political ideas that are treated seriously.

In the following years, I helped build Avaaz and 38 Degrees, the global and UK equivalents of MoveOn.org, as well as more open campaigning platforms like Change.org and Crowdpac. I began advising many progressive campaigns and causes, and in 2011, I applied to be General Secretary of the Labour Party on a platform of movement politics. I did not expect to be shortlisted then, just as I knew the job had already been earmarked for Jennie Formby when I ran a much more public campaign for the role in 2018. But I viewed both occasions as an opportunity; a moment to share fresh ideas for building a stronger, more networked Labour movement. The new left had the energy, the reach, the culture and the ideas to build a new common sense in this country, and to win a decisive victory for Labour and progressives in the next general election – if the old left was prepared to open up and share power.[11]

In the US, Zack was experimenting with what he calls 'distributed organising' techniques, which, instead of relying on thin and extractive command-and-control campaign structures, centred on empowering networks of volunteers – as, for example, in the American unions' Fight For 15 movement (a campaign for a $15

minimum wage, which spread from city to city and state to state).
Then, in mid 2015, he joined the Bernie Sanders campaign as an
unpaid volunteer. In the following months, Zack, Becky Bond,
Claire Sandberg, Alexandra Rojas and many others built an extraordinary 'distributed organising' effort, in which tens of thousands
of volunteers stepped up to take leadership, building support for
Sanders across dozens of states long before the more traditional hierarchical field operation.[12]

Meanwhile, the Sanders digital team based at Revolution
Messaging (which included Michael Whitney, a young star of
Howard Dean's 2004 presidential campaign, who ran our US
email programme at Change.org) built a remarkable growth and
fundraising operation. By spring of 2016, they were raising tens of
millions of dollars a month in small donations, even outstripping
Hillary Clinton's legendary big-donor machine.

Back in 2005, one of Zack's main projects for the Labour Party
had been building a 'Labour Supporters' Network', dreamt up by
Peter Mandelson and his allies and inspired partly by the successes
of MoveOn. This email list swiftly grew to dwarf Labour's membership, which had shrunk to below 200,000. The Blairites' ambition
was that this circle of loosely affiliated supporters would provide
them with a more sympathetic and tractable base, helping them to
reconnect with the general public and, of course, to further bypass
an increasingly recalcitrant party membership.

Under Zack's guidance, the Labour Supporters' Network was
used fleetingly and constructively to recruit and organise campaign
volunteers. But it went downhill from there; typically for New
Labour, the rhetoric of movement-building and participatory
democracy was only skin deep. The network was neglected. Instead
of organising people and campaigning for change, the list was used
for little more than publicising poorly considered and self-regarding
screeds from Cabinet members. It was clear that Labour's culture
and organisation were too broken to understand the depth and seriousness of the party's own failings, let alone why and how we needed
to change.

The next faltering step towards a networked Labour Party was
the creation of a new category of 'registered supporters', as recommended by the 2014 Collins Review initiated by Ed Miliband in

the wake of a controversy involving allegations of vote-fixing by the Unite trade union in the selection of Falkirk Constituency Labour Party's parliamentary candidate.[13] For the first time, crucially, as 'supporters', people were given the right to vote in Labour leadership elections, but without needing to take the extra step of actually joining the party. At the same time, the Collins reforms theoretically shifted power from trade union general secretaries to the union membership at large; but far too little was then done by the unions and the party to actually sign up those members en masse as opted-in affiliate supporters with a say in Labour's politics.

When against all the odds in 2010 Ed Miliband, rather than his brother David, was elected Labour leader, he seemed authentically open to transformative policies, curious, capable of listening, and passionate about movement politics. But Ed made the mistake of surrounding himself with a conservative and Establishment Shadow Cabinet, reinforced by like-minded advisers and operators. The few experiments to build a more networked Labour movement were strangled before they even got started. Ed's strategy to carry Labour over the line without doing anything to risk the 2015 election ended up with him scared of his own radical instincts, and failing to connect, either with his own most passionate supporters, or with the wider electorate.

In a hardly crowded field, Compass, the soft-left pressure group which together with the trade unions had helped elect Ed (and backed Jon Cruddas's deputy leadership campaign too), did its best to provide him with a support network. But as a campaigning think tank, Compass was never half as good at organising politically as it was at hosting intellectual policy discussions. Latterly, some in Labour have never forgiven Compass for its decision to embrace a more plural 'campfire' politics; but it is undoubtedly the case that their 2017 general election 'progressive alliance' tactical-voting initiative played an important role in helping Labour candidates to victory in many marginal constituencies.[14]

FROM AGAINST THE CURRENT...

Throughout the Miliband years, political energy was flowing everywhere except into the Labour Party. Occupy, UK Uncut, student and anti-austerity protests and the People's Assembly built overlapping networks of radical activists, young and old; they later became the initial backbone of the Corbyn movement.

A phenomenon less often linked to the revival of the political left, but which I believe was similarly crucial in creating a fertile context, was the rapid growth of 38 Degrees.[15] This campaigning online community, similar in many ways to MoveOn in the US, gave millions of ordinary progressives a simple way to get involved in campaigns against the Tory-led coalition's austerity policies and for social and environmental justice, during a period when Ed Balls and other forces of conservatism within the party were constraining Labour's own scope for full-throated opposition. (38 Degrees also hosted the member-created petition calling for a left-wing candidate in the 2015 Labour leadership contest, which played a part in Corbyn's decision to stand.)[16]

In Scotland, the Yes movement lost the battle but won the war of the 2014 independence referendum. The Scottish National Party's membership quadrupled. Scottish Labour, which had been in long-term decline, melted down completely at the 2015 general election, losing an astonishing forty of the forty-one seats it had previously held. In England, the UK Independence Party (UKIP) made strides in coastal towns and Labour heartland towns, including the ex-coalfields; they built a loose anti-political movement around festering resentment toward immigration, Europe, and the failings of status quo politics and economics.[17]

On the left, a 'green surge' saw more than 40,000 new members pile into the Green Party, powering them to an unprecedentedly good share of the vote in the 2015 general election. This ended up splitting the left further under the Westminster first-past-the-post system, one of the key factors which cost Labour victories in must-win marginal seats.

This new politics which had sprung up from all sides threatened the cosy Westminster parlour game. It was becoming increasingly obvious that this new politics would shake the British Establishment to its foundations. The new politics had many faces, but a common origin: the growing consensus that the status quo is broken and old politics is actively disempowering. The question was no longer whether change was coming, but where it would take us.

...TO GOING WITH THE FLOW

Without all this pre-existing networked activist energy looking for a conduit of political transformation, Jeremy Corbyn's election as Labour leader would have been inconceivable. While in the end, most of those new to Labour who voted for Corbyn went on to join as full party members, the opportunity to affiliate more loosely for the price of a cup of coffee was critical in enabling this red surge.

Left and progressive networks around the country played a critical role in sustaining the red surge – first re-electing Corbyn in 2016, then achieving the transformation of Labour's fortunes in the 2017 snap general election. Momentum's role was vital. It led the offensive in many of the seats Labour ended up retaining or gaining against all expectations, mobilising an army of volunteer canvassers from Labour's new mass membership, including many who felt excluded by the sometimes clannish old-timers in the constituencies. Momentum also dominated social media with edgy, engaging videos, reaching almost a third of voters on Facebook with next to no budget.[18] A swarm of other networked campaigns played an equally crucial role below the radar in 2017. In essence, Labour's 2017 election campaign was a chaotic and delightful case study in democracy, and all the better for it.[19]

Irrespective of the scepticism and disregard coming from the tribalist tendency in Labour, powerful tactical voting campaigns – some anti-Tory, some anti-Brexit – created pathways which helped millions of voters unsure about Labour to decide to lend their votes to the party in constituencies where Labour was clearly best placed win. This meant millions more progressive votes counted in determining the outcome, rather than being wasted under first past the post.

Labour was the overwhelming beneficiary of such tactical voting, to an extent its leaders have never acknowledged. The anti-Brexit tactical campaign run by Best for Britain and Compass's anti-Tory Progressive Alliance campaign deserve credit and recognition for this, with Compass playing a key role in persuading the Greens to stand down in dozens of constituencies for Labour, a generous gift unlikely to be repeated in future without some kind of quid pro quo. Perhaps emblematically, the most influential site, which reached millions of people, Tactical2017, was a networked grassroots initiative set up independently of any party or group by Becky Snowden without any funding or institutional backing.[20]

The extraordinary general election result of 2017 that defied all the early predictions was attributable first to this networked movement, from Momentum to Tactical2017; second, to Labour's remarkable manifesto; and third, to the terrible missteps of Theresa May's campaign, which opened the door for many voters to rethink their vote. The fourth vital factor was the millions of pounds raised in small donations, added to the backbone of organisational support provided by the trade unions, Unite in particular. Jeremy Corbyn's own performance was of course both remarkable and impressive, and without him the movement and the manifesto would have been inconceivable; but he was lifted up on to the shoulders of others, by collective networked action – by 'Corbynism from below'.

This account deliberately widens the frame from the canonical left narrative of how Corbynism grew, and puts the emphasis more on the bottom-up actions of citizens and movements which have made networked Labour's successes possible. But now, a warning.

Labour leaderships traditionally disappear quite rapidly into the SW1 bunker, behaving as if the attention of the Westminster media, the circus of Parliament and the bureaucracy of the party are the unquestionable source of, and testament to, their power, and losing any sense of their own failings and weaknesses. Disturbingly, a controlling, centralising, Labourite elite dynamic that claims to have all the answers is more present in the current leadership dynamics of Corbynism than is comfortable. This will be their (and our) downfall, unless the bad habits can be changed before it is too late.

HOW NETWORKED LABOUR CAN GROW STRONG ENOUGH TO WIN

Rather than simply seizing the broken machinery of top-down control from the old right, the Corbynite left should be leading Labour towards a networked party. It is time to build a base of millions of active and empowered supporters, to fundamentally reshape our country's culture as well as our politics. Only then will Labour grow strong enough to win; only then will Labour truly deserve to. The surge in Labour's membership to almost 600,000 gave the party the activist numbers to run the Tories close in 2017. But we still fell too far short then, and the membership growth afterwards first stalled, and has now even reversed. This must change.

It is time for Labour to commit its resources and leadership to a million-member recruitment drive. New members should be asked to pay just three pounds for their first year. Labour should develop a much more attractive and imaginative presence online, making it easy to join with a click, and it should seek more continuous feedback from citizens and supporters alike. We should organise face to face on a much bigger scale in our communities, and the party should launch huge campaigns with sympathetic trade unions to sign up tens or hundreds of thousands more of their members who support Labour's cause. Most ambitiously of all, it should pioneer a more systematic engagement with the wider ecosystem of social movements and campaigns.

In the medium term, Labour should explore new ways for people with deeply held and diverse worldviews and experiences to affiliate to the party and find their own place in our movement, without feeling as if their identity or beliefs are being compromised. Labour should encourage the creation of a swarm of new movements as new 'socialist societies'. Most of those that do exist are ancient, static and in many cases declining. Few have emerged to represent new and dynamic constituencies and networks of opinion; such new groups should be actively encouraged to affiliate to Labour.

One such movement, call it the 'European left', could provide a pathway in for some of the millions of passionate anti-Brexit progressives who largely agree with the party's domestic policy agenda, but who seek a more pro-European focus in the party's outlook, fostering activist-led link ups with parties and movements on the continent.

'Blue Labour' already attempts to represent traditionally minded and anti-European Labour, but has not effectively organised beyond a small core. Why should a larger-scale affiliated movement not be organised for these voters, who are also important in our movement and our dialogue? Such groups would provide an entry point for those voters and activists who wish to engage with and influence Labour, but who may hesitate to take the step of signing up as members. And there is no reason why many of the millions of supporters of green campaigning organisations in Britain should not consider joining a Labour-affiliated movement, 'Green left', to carry their ideas into government.

The existing affiliated groups within Labour which organise around identities are too focused on developing small elite internal networks and influencing internal party elections and policy debates, rather than turning outwards to fellow citizens and communities outside the party that share their identity or interest. They should evolve into affiliated mass movements. Instead of meetings of dozens or hundreds at very best, tens of thousands of people from black, Asian and minority-ethnic origins, women, LGBT networks, faith groups and more could all be welcomed in more actively to organise around and dialogue with the Labour Party as allies.

Such an approach can call on a wide range of precedents, such as the social movements of Latin America, which provided the roots and energies that carried forces like Brazil's Workers' Party to power, or the networked movements of Spain which initially powered Podemos and more recently have given birth to municipalist coalitions such as Barcelona en Comú and Ahora Madrid.

In the US a rainbow of movements has been built with diverse identities and origins, which often swarm together in a mutually reinforcing and supportive way. It is true that the rainbow coalitions of the 1980s often degenerated into zero-sum conflict. But we are now seeing a new repertoire of intersectional collaboration emerge among the networked movements of the twenty-first century. Socialists from below cannot shy away from rich deliberation or constructively agonistic conflict; these experiences can make us stronger, and root us better in the real lived diversity of our constituencies.

Such a strategy of radical openness and welcome would make Labour more like the country it seeks to represent. It is not inconceivable that over time, millions of people might join this new network of affiliated socialist movements, in a journey of political discovery which would lead many more to work with Labour on national campaigns and local organising – on their own terms.

Some in the trade union movement might see these newly organised allies as a threat to their power and control over the Labour leadership, policies and selections. But this transactional critique would miss the far greater prize which is within our collective reach: an irreversible transformation of British society, shifting power into the hands of the many and away from the few.

Crucially it is long past the time when we can afford not to think radically about renewing Labour's most important pillar, the affiliated trade unions. Their membership remains in long-term structural decline, despite recent signs of courage and tactical successes against Sports Direct, Uber and Amazon. Labour should help by making one of the central planks of its next manifesto a vision for universal union membership, delivered through an audacious policy of union auto-enrolment, meaning that every worker, and perhaps over time even every working-age person, would automatically be opted in to union membership unless they decided to opt out. This would remove the need to fight even to become organised, deny employers the ability to veto workers' organisation, and make unions the social norm again.

This shift would at a stroke massively increase the bargaining power, organisational resources and strength of the trade unions – not only changing our workplaces, but starting to reshape the reckless financial markets and how businesses and public services are run. Such a shift is essential, as inequality, automation and the fourth industrial revolution gather pace, and as monopoly corporate power grows ever more threatening to human interests. Like the new socialist movements I have described, a trade union revival on such a scale, standing up effectively for workers' interests, would also be a fantastic boost for Labour's cause, providing an ever-expanding pool of voters, supporters and members.

Pursuing such an agenda of radical democratic participation and mass movement-building will challenge the Labour left constructively, taking us out of our comfort zone. Ever-narrowing purity tests are a dead end; exclusive and self-defeating for any party which seeks to win a decisive majority and implement a transformational governing agenda. Instead, we will need to find authentic ways to engage in two-way dialogue with a much wider diversity of constituencies, to welcome and encourage a plurality of views, and to organise open deliberation to help surface and refine the best policies and strategies.

Any such mass movement must be genuinely empowered through

a deepening of Labour's party democracy, which, despite a lengthy review under Corbyn, remains fundamentally unchanged. Labour must urgently renew its democratic and decision-making processes, and start growing a culture fit for the twenty-first century.

The party should develop a mix of representative, participatory and deliberative democratic opportunities, bringing the mass membership, trade unions, MPs and party leadership together in constructive dialogue. Innovations such as citizens' assemblies randomly chosen by lot and online democracy platforms modelled on the likes of Barcelona en Comú and Ahora Madrid should be adopted to replace the National Policy Forum (NPF), which clearly does not work well, if at all.[21]

Instead of simply creating new unrepresentative cadres and elites to do the policymaking for us, as the NPF does, or bypassing party democracy entirely, as Blair did, we need to find ways for ordinary members to get involved directly and share their views in twenty minutes or a couple of hours here and there, without having to become full-time policymakers.

Labour should start experimenting with closed primaries ('closed', not 'open', that is, limited to our registered supporters and voters – this distinction is important if it is to reboot the conversation), in which thousands of Labour members and registered supporters – perhaps even Labour voters, if it could be managed – can participate directly in choosing our parliamentary candidates. Yes, there would need to be some guidelines and checks; but provided these are adopted, Labour has nothing to fear and everything to gain from more open and democratic processes of candidate selection.

The party should start viewing elected politics as a form of public service, rather than as jobs for life for a professional political class, and ensure that elected leaders are more responsive to the grassroots. As part of this, before long we should ensure not only open selections for vacant seats, but also open reselections for all sitting Labour MPs, to check and renew their mandates.

These are all first and foremost questions of movement strategy, organisational culture, political philosophy, resource allocation and power dynamics. The best network technologies to support an organising vision fit for our networked society will change every year. They evolve as new approaches are trialled and proven, platform algorithms and affordability shift, and new infrastructure and networks are built.

One example of technology which might be worth developing or extending to empower our movement is Common Knowledge, a formally non-partisan tech cooperative created by a group of Corbyn-supporting innovators.[22] They are seeking to solve the problem of how people can better find each other, organise together and engage in political action and education in localities. Another exciting idea is Corbyn leadership campaign technologist James Darling's 2017 prototype for a distributed membership organising model, in which power and initiative can be taken by members from the bottom up and they can be empowered to communicate and organise with each other without compromising data protection.[23]

Labour's new Community Organising Unit under Dan Firth is rightly integrating a traditional model of organising, centred on community organisers and faith, labour or community groups, based on the ideas of Saul Alinsky,[24] with the accelerated digital 'big organising' innovations of the Sanders campaign, as outlined in Zack Exley and Becky Bond's brilliant 2016 book, *Rules for Revolutionaries*.[25] Together these approaches open up opportunities to transform Labour's traditional doorstep canvassing routine, turning it from a stale transactional exercise in gathering low-quality data into a rich democratic dialogue which is genuinely two way, and through which our representatives and activists can gain richer and deeper insight into the communities we seek to serve. Both Momentum's 'persuasive conversations', and the 'deep canvassing' approach recently pioneered in the US, are models to draw on.

But there remains, overall, a lack of organisational boldness in Corbyn's Labour. Too much focus has been placed on seizing the levers of a broken machine. Too much time is spent tinkering with small decisions, instead of transforming our movement's capabilities and unleashing our mass membership's talents and potential. Labour needs to change what's broken and build for the future, most of all from the bottom up. This will require fresh ideas, fresh talent, and a deliberate process of organisational change.

HOW NETWORKED LABOUR CAN CHANGE OUR COUNTRY FOR GOOD

Just over two years after the crushing of the Prague Spring, Salvador Allende finally became president of Chile at his fourth attempt, having been blocked in 1964 by a $5.6 million campaign financed by the CIA. Allende had a vision for socialism with a human face. He started trying to build a system designed to simultaneously liberate and empower individuals, and to bring them into a more equal, more joyful, more rooted set of communal and democratic relationships.

Allende raised wages, transformed public services, organised a mass campaign of popular education and took back control of national industries. He also enlisted the help of British cybernetician Stafford Beer to build Project Cybersyn, a communications network for the emergent management of economic and social systems. This 'liberty machine' was designed not as a tool of Big Brother surveillance, but as a way to give workers a hand in managing their own factories, and to empower citizens to provide continuous, transparent and anonymous feedback about whether things were working for them.

None of this was sufficient to prevent Pinochet's bloody coup, aided and backed by the CIA. But the creative humanity and systemic rigour of the Chilean experiment, poetically explored in Beer's 'Designing freedom' lectures and analysed in Eden Medina's brilliant book *Cybernetic Revolutionaries*, provides a signpost toward a transformed future. As Beer wrote of Cybersyn and the coup against Allende:

> Thus is freedom lost; not by accident, but as the output of a system designed to curb liberty. My message is that we must redesign that system, to produce freedom as an output. If we are inefficient about that, on the grounds that scientific efficiency threatens liberty, then the institutional machinery that acts in our name will fail to prevent the spread of tyranny, war, torture, and oppression. We speak of the growth of prosperity; but the growth of those four things throughout the world today is yet more real. Let us use love and compassion. Let us use joy. Let us use knowledge.[26]

A networked labour movement will help the Labour Party to forge better alliances with the growing plurality of progressive and left forces. It requires moving decisively to harness technology in the service of individuals, communities and the common good, to fundamentally and irreversibly shift power into the hands of the many. This means pioneering twenty-first century forms of public and common ownership, from rail and transport to distributed clean energy systems and housing, ideas being pioneered by former John McDonnell adviser James Meadway,[27] the New Economics Foundation's Miatta Fahnbulleh,[28] and Mathew Lawrence's new Common Wealth ideas cooperative.[29]

It means democratising the economy and innovation, and building a high-energy democracy and a common social inheritance, as outlined by a recent project from the Nesta think tank by Roberto Unger, Geoff Mulgan and others.[30] It also means taking decisive action against the new tech monopolies who are colonising and poisoning our mental and social landscapes, as the Freedom From Facebook campaign I co-founded in the US has been arguing (although our European partners may end up taking the lead on this first).[31]

There is, clearly, still a great deal of work to do. But we can already say with clarity and conviction that the future we want to build looks very different from Harold Wilson's 'white-hot technological revolution', very different too from Stalinism, quite unlike the centralising left tendencies of the 1970s, and not the same even as Clement Attlee's 'Spirit of '45'. Wilson and Attlee's politics and governance might have been mostly what was needed for their time, but not for ours.

Ours instead will be a party, and a politics, we can only build for our own times, together. It will take millions of us, with very different life experiences, perspectives and capabilities, to get it right. If we want to win decisively and govern transformationally, we must start by realising Ralph Miliband's dictum that the internal life of a radical party must prefigure the society we seek to establish in government. The hard truth is that Jeremy Corbyn's Labour Party hasn't yet fulfilled that ambition. But he opened the door and gave us the opportunity that only we can grasp. In the twenty-first century, socialism from below is not only possible; it is essential. It is time for our networked movement to embrace the hope and responsibility of building this more human future.

NOTES

1. Central Committee of the Communist Party of Czechoslovakia, 'Action Plan of the Communist Party of Czechoslovakia (Prague, April 1968)', quoted in Paul Ello (ed.), *Dubček's Blueprint for Freedom: His Original Documents Leading to the Invasion of Czechoslovakia*, William Kimber: London, 1969.
2. Ralph Miliband's 1968 letter to Marcel Liebman is cited in Michael Newman, *Ralph Miliband and the Politics of the New Left*, Merlin Press: London, 2002.
3. *Zur Soziologie des Parteiwesens in der modernen Demokratie: Untersuchungen über die oligarchischen Tendenzen des Gruppenlebens*, Robert Michels, 1911.
4. 'Jeremy Corbyn speaking on Chile forty years on', LRC Sussex (YouTube, November 2013); Oscar Guardiola-Rivera, *Story of a Death Foretold: The Coup Against Salvador Allende, 11 September 1973*, Bloomsbury: London, 2013.
5. Quintin Hoare (ed.), *Selections from the Prison Notebooks of Antonio Gramsci*, Lawrence and Wishart: London, 2005 [1971].
6. See Becky Bond and Zack Exley, *Rules for Revolutionaries: How Big Organizing can Change Everything*, Chelsea Green: White River Junction, VT, 2016; also, Letitia Stein, Susan Cornwell and Joseph Tanfani, 'Inside the progressive movement roiling the Democratic Party', Reuters, 23 August 2018.
7. Yale Program on Climate Change Communication and George Mason University Center for Climate Change Communication, 'Changes in the awareness of and support for the Green New Deal: December 2018 to April 2019'.
8. 'A Green New Deal: Joined-up policies to solve the triple crunch of the credit crisis, climate change and high oil prices', New Economics Foundation, 20 July 2008.
9. Daphna Baram and David Hencke, '£100,000 defence fund for anti-war MPs', *The Guardian*, 21 February 2005.
10. @zackexley.
11. Paul Hilder, 'I'm not going to be General Secretary, but the real fight to change Labour is only just beginning', *New Statesman*, 16 March 2018.
12. Bond and Exley 2016.
13. Alex Nunns, *The Candidate: Jeremy Corbyn's Improbable Path to Power*, OR Books: New York, 2018.

14. Barry Langford, *All Together Now: The Progressive Alliance and the 2017 General Election Campaign*, Biteback: London, 2017.
15. Rafael Behr, '38 Degrees: The real opposition?', *New Statesman*, 26 March 2012.
16. Rosa Prince, 'Why the online petition that led to Jeremy Corbyn's rise to power has surprising roots', *Telegraph*, 30 January 2016.
17. Paul Hilder, 'A new politics? How the old political consensus is melting away', *New Statesman*, 28 November 2014.
18. Personal conversations with Momentum organisers.
19. Hilder, 'The old politics is dying, people power can win the next election', *Prospect*, 11 June 2017.
20. Catriona Harvey-Jenner, 'This spreadsheet shows exactly how flawed our voting system is', *Cosmopolitan*, 21 April 2017.
21. For examples of this kind of policy thinking, see Claudia Chwalisz, *The People's Verdict: Adding Informed Citizen Voices to Public Decision Making*, Rowman and Littlefield: London, 2017; Julie Simon, Theo Bass, Victoria Boelman and Geoff Mulgan, 'Digital democracy: The tools transforming political engagement', Nesta, 20 February 2017.
22. www.commonknowledge.coop.
23. James Darling, 'Membership: A prototype', Medium, 26 February 2017.
24. See Saul Alinsky, *Rules for Radicals: A Practical Primer for Realistic Radicals*, Vintage: London, 1989.
25. Bond and Exley 2016.
26. Stafford Beer, *Designing Freedom*, John Wiley: London, 1974; see also Eden Medina, *Cybernetic Revolutionaries: Technology and Politics in Allende's Chile*, MIT Press: Cambridge, MA, 2014.
27. James Meadway, 'After the cataclysm: Why we must build a new economics from the ground up', Open Democracy, 15 March 2019.
28. Dawn Foster, 'Miatta Fahnbulleh: People's tolerance for an unfair economic model has hit a buffer', *The Guardian*, 31 October 2017.
29. Mathew Lawrence and Laurie Laybourn-Langton, 'Building a digital commonwealth', Open Democracy, 13 March 2019.
30. Roberto Mangabeira Unger, Geoff Mulgan, Madeleine Gabriel and Isaac Stanley, 'Imagination unleashed: Democratising the knowledge economy', Nesta, 18 March 2019.
31. See www.freedomfromfb.com; Madhumita Murgia and Mehreen Khan, 'Facebook, Amazon and Google in Europe's crosshairs', *Financial Times*, 7 February 2019; Wendy Liu, 'Abolish Silicon Valley', *Tribune*, 10 January 2019.

In Search of the Value-Added Voter

Paula Surridge

B ritish politics has never been more volatile. While the 2017 general election produced the largest two-party (Conservative and Labour) share of the vote for four decades,[1] it also saw the highest levels of vote switching.[2] Voters are no longer anchored to parties by enduring party identities,[3] instead, they switch between different parties and between voting and non-voting in ever greater numbers. This unstable electoral mix has been made even more potent by the destruction that the Brexit process has caused to the political parties, both internally and externally. Two 'new' parties have – so far – emerged from this wreckage. These are the Brexit Party, led by Nigel Farage, former leader of the UK Independence Party (UKIP), and Change UK, a group of MPs split from both Labour and the Conservatives. While the Brexit Party seems to be almost a like-for-like replacement of UKIP in the party space, Change UK set out to offer something different in the 'centre' of politics, though it suffered early setbacks and a split.

Some have drawn on the formation of the Social Democratic Party (SDP) in the early 1980s as a historical precedent for Change UK, suggesting that the SDP's success at the ballot box was limited and the party's formation resulted in most of the rebel MPs losing their seats.[4] But the SDP split did not occur at a time when the country was divided along multiple faultlines, and when the core issue of the day cannot easily be contained within the current party structure. While most have assumed that any fracturing of the Westminster parties is likely to have a greater impact on the left than the right of British politics, it is worth remembering that the SDP split the Conservative vote in 1983, as well as Labour's, ultimately resulting in a smaller Conservative majority than would otherwise have been the case.[5] Although initial encounters with the electorate could certainly not be branded a great success for Change UK, there does nonetheless seem to have been some similar fracturing of the Conservative vote, with the main beneficiary being the Liberal Democrats.

How any of this will play out in the next general election is highly uncertain, and attempting to suggest likely pathways is perhaps a fool's errand. But we can use the past as our guide to work out what scenarios are more, or less, likely in the future. While the parties may be changing, the electorate remains to a large extent the same as it was in 2017. The demography of a constituency does change, but it does so slowly; the age distribution, proportion of people with university degrees, or levels of White British identity, for example, and the profile of how people voted in the past, do not change rapidly, and these indicators can provide us with a way of making sense of how the electorate might respond to changing political realities based on their past behaviour.

One impact of the high two-party share of the vote in 2017 is that it at least makes clear what needs to be done to win. For Labour to win the election with the single largest number of MPs, never mind enough of them for a working majority to form a government on its own, it needs to find more voters. In 2017 few voted for parties other than Conservative or Labour, outside of the very specific case of Scotland, which we return to later. Therefore, the additional votes must either come from voters switching directly from Conservative to Labour, or Labour must convince previous non-voters to turn out and vote for them. At the same time, Labour must not lose the voters it already has – and while losing votes to the Conservatives is especially damaging, there is also the danger of losing votes to third parties. These might include a resurgent Liberal Democrat party, the Brexit Party, or indeed Change UK or a similar formation yet to be born, with such parties gaining support through dissatisfaction with the Brexit process among both Remain and Leave voters. Some voters might simply decide after being politically exhausted by the Brexit saga not to bother voting at all next time. Any of these scenarios will harm any chance Labour has of winning.

GAINING NON-VOTERS?

'Not another one!' Brenda from Bristol[6] appeared to capture the mood of the nation when she was told by a BBC News reporter that Theresa May had called the 'snap' 2017 election. Expectations were that turnout would be muted by election fatigue among an electorate that had seen a referendum less than a year earlier and a general election just two years before that. But, instead, official figures showed a small increase in turnout from 2015, continuing an upward trend since a low point in 2001.[7]

Immediately after the election, as commentators cast around for explanations for the surprise performance of Corbyn's Labour Party, the idea of a 'youthquake' was born,[8] described by the political scientists who coined the term as a 'shock result founded on an unexpected surge in youth turnout'.[9] This idea has since been debated widely in the academic literature and in the pages of newspapers and magazines. That young people were especially likely to vote Labour in 2017 is beyond question: as psephologist John Curtice argues, 'the 2017 election appears to herald the advent of a new political division between age groups and generations',[10] but the issue that has divided analysts is the idea, assumed by some, that Labour's vote share was driven by a surge in turnout among the young. In the view of some analysts, 'the idea of a "youthquake" does not tell us much about turnout at the 2017 election'.[11]

Youthquake or not, one of the paths to victory for Labour might be to further increase turnout. Non-voters are more likely to be 'Labour-leaning' than the rest of the electorate, as they are often concentrated in groups where Labour gets strong support among those who do vote, such as younger voters and those on lower incomes. However, the lessons from 2017 suggest that even when enthusiasm is high, it is difficult to have a substantial impact on turnout levels among disengaged groups. To rely on further engaging voters who have been traditionally disengaged would be a precarious strategy, to say the least.

However, there is another, untold, story about turnout and the 2017 general election, and it is one about who abstained, rather than who turned out. Evidence from a report by market research agency BMG Research suggests that there was differential turnout according to the 'values' that voters hold.[12] Suggesting that perhaps there was no 'youthquake', but instead a 'liberal tremor', the report shows that the largest increases in turnout were found among those who held the most 'liberal' social values, for example those who take a liberal stance on issues of gender identity, human rights and multiculturalism, while small decreases in turnout were seen among the least liberal groups, for example those who are in favour of rein-troducing the death penalty, against adoption by gay people, and anti-immigration.[13]

This is a key part of the story of the 2017 election, and it signals the importance for understanding political change in Britain of understanding both the role of voters' values in their electoral decision-making, and in which sectors of society different types of voters are concentrated.

TAKING VOTES FROM THE OTHER PARTIES (WHILE NOT LOSING YOUR OWN)

Despite the surface-level re-emergence of the two-party system in 2017, at the level of the individual voter, there has been a great deal of 'churn'. One of the reasons for this increased volatility is the decline of a sense of connection to political parties; what political scientists term 'partisanship'. For much of the twentieth century most of the British electorate would express an attachment, usually to one of the two major parties, and around two in five would say this attachment was 'very strong'.[14] This has been changing. The proportion of the electorate that identifies with one of the two main parties has declined from around four in five in the 1960s to three in five in the 2010s. This reflects the increased importance of other parties, in particular the nationalist parties in Scotland and Wales, the Liberal Democrats and (briefly) UKIP. Even more marked has been the decline in the proportion who identify with their political party 'very strongly'; from two in five in the 1960s to fewer than one in five in the 2010s.[15] As a result of this weakened connection between parties and voters, 'British voters are increasingly volatile and willing to switch their allegiances between elections'.[16]

As this sense of connection to parties has declined, other factors become more important for understanding voters' choices. While some observers have focused on short-term factors such as the election campaign, the perceived competence of party leaders,[17] and a posited emergence of a more 'deliberative' electorate,[18] the decline of partisanship also makes more space for 'values' to influence voting decisions.

Our values can be thought of as our deep-seated ideas about the kind of society we want to live in.[19] They concern how we would like the world to be, and are more enduring than specific evaluations of parties, policies and political leaders. While it has been commonplace to think of the party system in the UK as dominated by a single value dimension of 'left-right', rooted in conceptions of economic fairness and justice, this one-dimensional approach is too simplistic to capture the value positions of the British electorate in the twenty-first century.

Using two scales developed in the late 1980s,[20] it is possible to look at how the value positions of the electorate have evolved, and where they are now positioned. Using the scales also enables us to identify the groups Labour did well with in 2017, and compare these with the landslide electoral victory of 1997.

One of the core features of Corbyn's Labour Party has been its explicitly left-wing focus.[21] The campaigning slogan 'For the many, not the few' conjures images of an economic elite, against whom the remainder of the electorate is set. It might therefore be expected that under Corbyn's leadership Labour would do well among those voters on the economic left in favour of redistributive policies, renationalisation and an egalitarian vision of economic justice. On the measures devised by Evans et al.,[22] it is estimated that a little over half of the British electorate can be considered 'left wing', and this has been relatively constant over the past three decades.[23] Why, then, have there not been any Labour general election victories since 2005? The answer lies in the 'other' values people hold.[24] Despite the well-known adage 'It's the economy, stupid!', elections in Britain, elsewhere in Europe and in the US have seen an increasing focus on issues that do not neatly fit into packages arranged according to economic values. The EU referendum vote has been shown to be strongly correlated to these 'other' values.[25] Combining the economic values with the 'other' values allows us to create a 'value space' with nine positions. Each position on the economic scale (left, centre and right) is divided by the person's values on the other scale (liberal, centre and authoritarian).[26]

Comparing the voting behaviour of these nine positions in 'value space' in 1997 – the high point of Labour support – with 2017 shows where there are 'left-wing' voters that did not vote for Labour. The share of the vote within value positions in 1997 (Figure 1 overleaf) shows that on the 'left' of the economic value scale roughly the same proportion voted Labour, a little over 60 per cent, regardless of their liberal-authoritarian values. Among left-wing voters it did not matter what position they were in on the other scale, they were equally likely to vote Labour. Labour also had the lead among liberal voters in the centre economically, and were competitive – about five percentage points behind the Conservatives – among those in the centre on both dimensions. Comparing this with 2017 (Figure 2) shows how the connection between value divides and voting behaviour has changed. By 2017, Labour had increased its share among those in the 'liberal-left' group, but were winning less than half of the votes of those on the left economically who were not liberal on social issues. To stress this point, in 2017 a third of voters who were on the left, broadly in line with Corbyn's economic vision, but who were not also in the liberal group on the other dimensions, voted for the Conservatives. The changes in the centre of the left-right scale are even more stark: here the Conservatives in 2017 picked up more than half of the votes, and more than six in ten of votes in the 'not liberal' groups.

This would not be a problem for Labour if most of the population were in the liberal-left group in which their support is so strong, but they are not. Just fifteen per cent of the electorate are in this value group, while more than one in five voters are in the 'left-authoritarian' group.

Labour has begun to recognise this issue: party broadcasts have been rolled out on the theme of 'Our town', featuring images of key 'small town' target seats, such as Mansfield and Hastings; a clear acknowledgment of the need to win over voters in places where there are more of these 'non-liberal left' voters. However, there is a danger in these appeals to 'Brexit Britain' if such appeals turn out to be costly in Labour's other core groups.

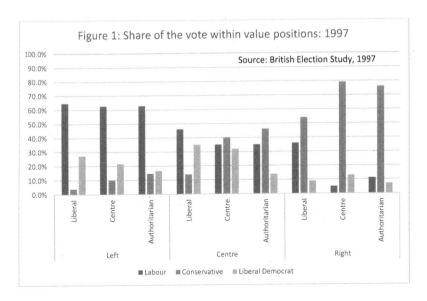

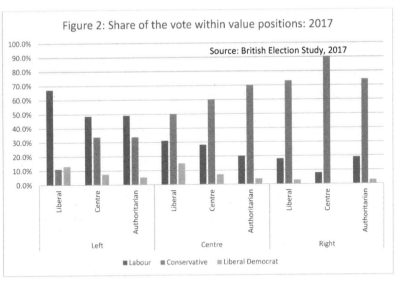

The local and EU Parliament election results of May 2019 suggest that the Liberal Democrats will be in a much stronger position going into the next general election, and with a new party leader to boot. There will also be challenges from the Greens and possibly Change UK. None of these is likely to appeal to the 'left-authoritarian' groups that Labour is trying to court in places such as Mansfield, but they are competing in a crowded 'liberal' party marketplace elsewhere. For example, in target seats such as Pudsey and Chipping Barnet, where the Liberal Democrats won over one in five votes in 2010, and in places where the Labour majority may be vulnerable, such as Stroud (discussed in detail below).

The 2017 British Election Study asked people to say how likely they were to vote for each of the main parties on a scale from nought to ten. A score of six or more was taken as a 'positive' likelihood to vote for a party. Among voters with left-liberal value positions, almost one in three said they assessed the likelihood of them voting for any one of three (or more) different parties at six out of ten or higher. This poses a real danger for Labour. Many of the voters who Labour needs to win over consider that there is only one party they are likely to vote for, with four out of ten of those in the left-authoritarian group holding this view, and for many of these, this party is not the Labour Party. Those whom Labour needs to hold on to, who are unlikely to be sympathetic to messaging that appeals to 'Brexit Britain', have a much wider range of options, most usually holding a choice set that includes Labour, the Greens and the Liberal Democrats.

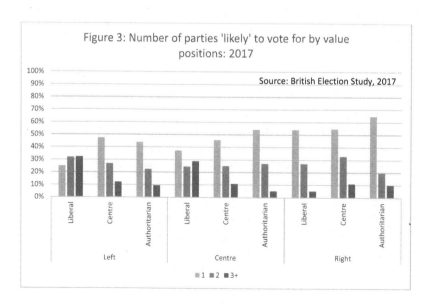

Figure 3: Number of parties 'likely' to vote for by value positions: 2017

Source: British Election Study, 2017

This, then, is the core of the problem for Labour. It reflects the difficulty the party faces over Brexit, but it is also part of a wider fracture among voters on the left.[27] The party cannot win on the votes of the liberal-left alone; yet in trying to win over other groups, it risks those liberal-left voters returning to minor parties that are less driven by a need to hold together a broad coalition of interests.

HOW TO READ A CONSTITUENCY

These patterns are informative and tell us much about how individual voters are positioned. But it also matters where they are located geographically: campaigns focus as much on areas as they do on individuals. The 'road map' to Number Ten for Corbyn runs through constituencies that must be won (and those that must not be lost); converting lots of Conservatives or non-voters in places Labour is already winning will not help at all. This is the basis of the target-seat strategy, which identifies those seats where additional Labour voters would make a material difference to the outcome.

Unfortunately, we do not have measures of the values of the electorate at the level of constituency. It is not possible to know precisely how many 'not liberal-left' voters there are in Mansfield, for instance. This makes it difficult to apply what we have learned about values and vote choice to predict what might happen in the next general election. However, we do know both how the constituency has voted in the past, and how these value positions are connected to voting in elections over time. In 2015, UKIP gained around one in five votes of the 'left-authoritarians', therefore in places where the UKIP vote was strong in 2015, we would expect there to be on average more of this type of voter – and for the Brexit Party to be able to win similar levels of support. Similarly, at their high point in 2010, the Liberal Democrats were the most popular party among the 'liberal-left', so places where they did well in 2010 are a good guide to where these voters are concentrated.

Different values groups and their relationship to 'other' parties make it very difficult to use a single measure of 'uniform' swing across constituencies. For example, in 2017 those constituencies which previously had very high vote shares for UKIP were especially volatile as this vote collapsed. Polling companies have begun to tackle this problem using 'multi-level regression and post-stratification' (MRP) modelling techniques. During the 2017 campaign YouGov's MRP model predicted, to widespread derision, that Labour would win Canterbury, which of course it did. It is very likely that these models will be used extensively in the next general election campaign. They have already been used by the polling company Survation to assess the size of Leave and Remain votes in individual constituencies.[28] These models rely on two types of data – one that we all have access to, and one that is collected, at significant cost, by polling companies seeking a competitive advantage in the crowded polling marketplace. MRP models combine things we know about constituencies with things we know about the behaviour of individuals. At a basic level, they work out, for example, what percentage of those aged eighteen say they will vote Labour, and then combine that with official data on the number of eighteen year olds in each constituency.[29] To do this requires data with a substantial sample size, so as to get good estimates of the voting behaviours of relatively small groups in the electorate: in other words, a standard opinion poll of one thousand to three thousand people would not have a large enough number of eighteen year olds to give a reliable estimate of how eighteen year olds might vote.

In the absence of this bespoke data, the interested observer of Labour's target seat and defences list[30] can instead look at the characteristics of a constituency and how electoral behaviour has been related to that shown in earlier elections. In this way, the past can be used as a guide to the future, with knowledge of the socio-economic drivers of people's core values being used to look for particularly pertinent indicators.

To illustrate how this might work, it is useful to study two types of constituencies: ones where Labour won in 2017 and now needs to defend a small majority; and ones that Labour needs to win at the next general election. There are many seats like these across the country, here the focus is on two which have not been a mainstay of political analysis post-Brexit vote: Stroud and Worcester. Stroud was won by Labour in 2017, having been held by the Conservatives in 2015 and 2010. It is estimated to be a pro-Remain area, with around 46 per cent voting in 2016 to leave the EU.[31] In contrast, Worcester has been a Conservative-held seat at each of the last three elections, and it voted to leave the EU in 2016, with an estimated 54 per cent Leave vote share. Should Labour succeed in winning Worcester at the next general election, the party would be approximately two thirds of the way through its list of target seats.

Worcester is a prime example of the need to take votes directly from the Conservatives in order to win. With a two-party share of the vote of over 91 per cent in 2017, there are few third-party votes left to squeeze. The battle here is to convince those who voted Conservative in 2017 that their interests are better served by voting Labour next time. The constituency saw a UKIP vote of 12.8 per cent in 2015, and it would seem that the votes of both the main parties here could be vulnerable to the Brexit Party. However, the Liberal Democrats also did well in Worcester in 2010, their high-water mark of support, gaining almost one in five votes in the constituency at that election.

Although a majority Leave-voting constituency, with an esti-mated Leave share of the vote of 53.7 per cent in 2016, Worcester is clearly also home to significant numbers of Remain voters. It is likely that a significant number of these voters supported the Lib Dems in 2010. Both Labour and the Conservatives will need to be cautious here about where the 46.3 per cent of the constituency's EU referendum voters go. As the initial two-year period of Brexit negotiations provided for in Article 50 of the Lisbon Treaty drew to a close in March 2019, an online petition to revoke Article 50 gained more than six million signatures. These signatures can be analysed by constituency, and they add an additional layer to our constituency analyses. Acting as a measure of 'mobilised Remain' support, this data gives an indication of places in the country where pro-Remain parties in competition with Labour might be expected to gain votes. In Worcester, the estimated share of constituents signing the peti-tion was below the national average, at 8 per cent, suggesting that the Remain voters here may prioritise other issues above Brexit when casting their votes. Should the Liberal Democrats not gain support here, it is possible that a flow of votes from the Conservatives to a Brexit-favouring party could be enough for a Labour win.

Stroud provides an example of a very different type of constitu-ency. This is one of the seats that Labour must hold on to at the next general election to secure a path to Number Ten. Losing Stroud would be a sign of a very bad election night for the Labour Party. As with Worcester, there are few third-party votes left here to squeeze, but the danger here might instead be from a flow of votes away from Labour. Stroud saw a much lower vote for UKIP in 2015 than did Worcester, but there was also a notable presence of the Green Party here, with almost one in twenty voters supporting the Greens in the 2015 general election, and the party coming third (with 14 per cent of the vote) in district council elections in 2016.

This is also a Remain constituency, with 54 per cent of those voting in the 2016 referendum voting Remain. These Remain voters also appear to be more mobilised than those in Worcester: an estimated 12.7 per cent of the Stroud electorate signed the petition to revoke Article 50. Given the relative strength of the Green Party in the constituency and the mobilisation of the Remain vote, there is a real danger here that Labour's ambiguous position on Brexit could cost enough votes to lose Labour the seat (the Labour majority here was less than 700 votes).

These two seats highlight the challenges for Labour. Can the party convert Leave voters in Worcester? Or perhaps the Brexit Party will gain enough votes from the Conservatives to deliver this seat for Labour without the party needing to increase its own vote share at all. This will be a necessary win if at the same time Labour's own votes become vulnerable to renewed challenges from 'liberal'-leaning parties. While in Stroud, this seems most likely to come from a swing to the Green Party, elsewhere the Liberal Democrats are waiting to pick up disillusioned Labour votes too.

WHAT ABOUT SCOTLAND?

Having made almost a clean sweep of Scottish seats in 2015, it was always likely that the Scottish National Party (SNP) would suffer at least some losses in 2017. Scotland also had more cause than other parts of the UK to feel election fatigue, having voted in not one but two referendums, a redefining 2015 Westminster election, and Holyrood elections, all in the previous three years. The impact on turnout in Scotland was clear: it was the only region of the UK to see a fall in turnout between the 2015 and 2017 general elections.

Election night in Scotland proved a little less dramatic than it had in 2015, though there was perhaps some surprise at the strength of the Scottish Conservative performance, a gain of twelve seats – double the number gained by Labour in Scotland. It was quite a turnaround to see a Westminster Conservative Party kept in power by the Scottish seats it had gained. The result of the four-way party competition in Scotland is that there are more marginal seats here; eighteen of Labour's sixty-six 'target' seats and four 'defences' are north of the border.

The danger here is clear. A focus on 'English' towns is likely to further alienate Labour's Scottish voters, in a party system that is realigning around the results of not one, but two highly divisive referendums. It is by no means certain that patterns of voting in Scotland will follow those in other parts of the UK. If they don't, and this works to Labour's disadvantage, then without those eighteen extra Scottish seats that the party is targeting, a majority for the Labour Party seems very unlikely.

HOW TO LOOK FORWARD TO THE NEXT TIME

There are of course many uncertainties in this diagnosis. Although it is likely that at least some parts of the Brexit process will be ongoing at the time of the next election, whether it is held in 2022 or before, the changed political landscape in a 'post-Brexit' election will be unpredictable, and potentially hugely volatile. If a resolution has been reached, it is not clear who voters will hold responsible, either positively or negatively, for the outcome of the negotiation process, while if it has not, voters will certainly look for who is to blame for the ongoing impasse. It is also unclear what the parties themselves will look like; further new parties and additional fractures of the two main parties do not seem unlikely. It would be foolhardy to suggest that anything that is true of the political preferences of the British public now will remain so when the reality of this period sets in.

The unexpected, and in many quarters unwanted, elections to the European Parliament held in May 2019 clearly demonstrate the electoral challenges set out in this chapter. Usually considered by psephologists to be a 'second-order' poll, elections to the EU Parliament are commonly low-turnout. While we should bear in mind that non-voters outnumbered voters in the May 2019 elections by almost two to one, those elections nonetheless provide a touchstone for analyses of how British politics may be reshaping as the Brexit process continues to cast its shadow over parliamentary business. As was widely expected, the Brexit Party topped the poll, with almost one in three of the votes cast; in most regions this represented a small increase on the share of the vote gained by UKIP at their peak in the previous elections to the European Parliament in 2014. While Change UK failed to emerge as a significant challenger to Labour, the Liberal Democrats and Green Party certainly did not fail, with the Liberal Democrats taking second place for overall vote share and the Green Party only narrowly behind Labour. Perhaps most telling of all for the future fortunes of Labour, the Liberal Democrats topped the poll in London, while Labour were pushed into fifth place in Scotland.

Much remains uncertain in post-referendum Britain, but one thing is clear: Labour must undertake a difficult balancing act to maintain, let alone improve upon, its 2017 general election vote. This is a difficulty only likely to be increased by renewed competition for votes from a resurgent Liberal Democrats, SNP and quite possibly Plaid Cymru too – the Brexit Party complicates this still further. It is also unlikely that the Conservatives will ever run as hapless a campaign as they did with Theresa May at the helm in 2017, but their vote, too, is fragile. As with the Labour vote, the Conservatives face challenges from the Brexit Party for their dissatisfied Leave voters, but there is also a significant challenge from the Liberal Democrats for those Conservatives who voted Remain in 2016. The next general election may well be a competition to see which party can retain its 2017 support most effectively in order to have the most legitimate claim to lead a potentially highly fragmented hung parliament.

NOTES

1. John Curtice, 'General election 2017: A new two-party politics?', *Political Insight*, Vol. 8, No. 2, 2017.
2. Jonathan Mellon, Geoffrey Evans, Edward Fieldhouse, Jane Green and Christopher Prosser, 'Brexit or Corbyn? Campaign and inter-election vote-switching in the 2017 UK general election', *Parliamentary Affairs*, Vol. 71, No. 4, 2018.

3. Russell Dalton and Martin Wattenberg (eds), *Parties without Partisans: Political Change in Advanced Industrial Democracies*, Oxford University Press: Oxford, 2002.
4. Ivor Crewe and Anthony King, *SDP: The Birth, Life and Death of the Social Democratic Party*, Oxford University Press: Oxford, 1995.
5. *Ibid.*, p.290.
6. BBC News, 18 April 2017.
7. Noel Dempsey, 'Turnout at elections', House of Commons Library Briefing Paper, 26 July 2017.
8. This was in part driven by reports of a figure of 72 per cent turnout among 18 to 24 year olds, a figure subsequently shown to be entirely fictitious, and one which no one seems to quite know the source of.
9. James Sloam, Rahib Ehsan and Martin Henn, '"Youthquake": How and why young people reshaped the political landscape in 2017', *Political Insight*, Vol. 9, No. 1, 2018.
10. Curtice 2017.
11. Prosser, Fieldhouse, Green, Mellon and Evans, 'Tremors but no youthquake: Measuring changes in the age and turnout gradients at the 2015 and 2017 British general elections', SSRN, 28 January 2018.
12. Michael Turner, Robert Struthers, Christopher Terry and Clive McDonnell, 'Fractured politics: A new framework for analysing political division in Britain', BMG Research, 2018.
13. The research uses a wide range of measures; those listed here are illustrative only. For a complete list, see *ibid.*
14. British Election Study 1964-2017, www.britishelectionstudy.com.
15. *Ibid.*
16. Prosser, 'The strange death of multi-party Britain: the UK general election of 2017', *West European Politics*, Vol. 41, No. 5, 2018.
17. Harold Clarke, David Sanders, Marianne Stewart and Paul Whiteley, 'Valence politics and electoral choice in Britain, 2010', *Journal of Elections, Public Opinion and Parties*, Vol. 21, No. 2, 2011.
18. Dalton, *Democratic Challenges, Democratic Choices: The Erosion of Political Support in Advanced Industrial Democracies*, Oxford University Press: Oxford, 2004.
19. Milton Rokeach, *The Nature of Human Values*, Free Press: New York, 1973.
20. Geoffrey Evans, Anthony Heath and Mansur Lalljee, 'Measuring left-right and libertarian-authoritarian values in the British electorate', *British Journal of Sociology*, Vol. 47, No. 1, 1996.
21. Mark Perryman (ed), *The Corbyn Effect*, Lawrence and Wishart: London, 2017.
22. These include attitudes to the redistribution of wealth, big business and trade union power, Evans et al. 1996.

23. Paula Surridge, 'The fragmentation of the electoral left since 2010', *Renewal: A journal of social democracy*, Vol. 26, No. 4, December 2018.

24. These include attitudes to the death penalty, censorship and tolerance towards unconventional lifestyles. Evans et al. 1996.

25. Eric Kaufmann, 'The indicators that show who voted for Trump and Brexit', *Prospect*, 29 November 2016; Surridge, 'Brexit, British politics, and the left-right divide', *Political Insight*, December 2018.

26. For full details of the scales, see Surridge, 'The social roots of values and their influence on voting', Medium, 2018.

27. Surridge, 'The fragmentation of the electoral left since 2010'.

28. Chris Lees, 'What does the British public now think about Brexit?', Survation, 5 November 2018.

29. Further technical details on MRP modelling can be found in this brief explainer by Survation, 'What is MRP?', 5 November 2018: www.survation.com.

30. See Perryman 2017 for a complete list of these seats, pp252-6.

31. Chris Hanretty, 'Areal Interpolation and the UK's referendum on EU membership', *Journal of Elections, Public Opinion and Parties*, Vol. 27, No. 4.

Beyond the Labour Fragments

Hilary Wainwright

Excuse me if I'm personal. I want to start from an apparently trivial thought about Jeremy Corbyn: that, with a few months' difference, he is the same age as I am.

We are of the same generation. We have lived through the same political moments: the foundation of the Campaign for Nuclear Disarmament (CND) in 1957; the global events of 1968 that shattered the Cold War order; the 1970s feminist movement; 'Bennism' and the fight for democracy in the Labour Party; the struggles of workers around alternatives to unemployment and factory closures; the civil rights movement and military conflict in Northern Ireland; Ken Livingstone's Greater London Council (GLC), with its support for initiatives outside the Labour Party – especially, but not exclusively, those of ethnic minorities and the feminist and gay and lesbian movements; the 1984-85 miners' strike, the solidarity movement and women's role in the fight against pit closures. Then, in more recent memory, the resistance to austerity and privatisation, as well as Blair, New Labour and its discontents, and specifically the movement against the war in Iraq.

INSIDE AND OUTSIDE THE LABOUR PARTY

However, although we share broadly the same radical transformative socialist perspective, we experienced these historical moments from different political vantage points. Jeremy Corbyn was, from 1965, a member of the Labour Party. In contrast, like many of my age group (I was twenty in 1969), I made a positive decision not to join. It seemed to me that the party could not be transformed into a means of achieving the radically democratic, participatory socialism that, through the international experiences of 1968 – the Soviet repression of the 'Czech Spring' as well as the US war on Vietnam – had become my political vision. I put my energies into social movements, the student, anti-war, feminist and grassroots trade union movements that had helped to shape my vision. Corbyn was active in movements such as CND and the trade unions and later became part of a diminishing band of socialist MPs, championing these struggles inside Parliament and working relentlessly to change Labour into a genuinely socialist party. By contrast, though working with Corbyn, Tony Benn, Ken Livingstone and many local Labour activists whose radically democratic socialist ideas I shared, I became increasingly convinced, influenced by Ralph Miliband,[1] that these movements could only achieve the political support needed for their transformative goals through a proportional electoral system and an alternative to the Labour Party as we've known it.

But I also believed that, in the meantime, the divisions between the left inside and outside the Labour Party were not fundamental and, where there was principled political agreement, non-sectarian collaboration made sense between those left activists working inside the party and those whose main commitment was to social movements independent of it.

THE POTENTIAL AND PROBLEM OF LABOURISM

The possibility of this blurring of the boundaries between the inside and outside of the Labour Party stems from the party's distinctive origins and characteristics in the broader labour, especially trade union, movement autonomous of parliamentary politics.

These origins, however, also laid the foundations for problems that are now emerging in attempts to consolidate and expand the movement that grew so rapidly (outside the party as well as inside it) in support of Corbyn and the 'new, participatory politics' that he symbolised. For at the same time as favouring a certain openness, fluidity and non-sectarianism, the origins of the Labour Party have also produced a problematically tribal and exclusive approach to electoral or party politics.

The crucial factor here is the party's presumption of a monopoly on working-class – or 'labour movement' – political representation. The result is a tension between the culture of collaboration between socialists inside and outside the party in social and economic campaigning and the closing down and constraining of collaboration in electoral politics. This tendency is reinforced by the non-proportional, winner-takes-all nature of the Westminster electoral system and the highly centralised nature of executive power.

ELECTORAL POLITICS AND MOVEMENT POLITICS: THE TENSIONS

A dilemma now faces Corbyn's leadership and the extraordinarily energetic movement that originally rallied to grasp the opportunity of a political leadership that empowered their self-organisation rather than patronised it. The dilemma is that of a movement based on principles of popular democracy and militant direct action engaging in the electoral politics of a parliamentary system designed to disempower, and exclude, radical politics rooted in the lives of disaffected citizens outside Parliament – whether in workplaces, communities, or indeed whole regions and nations beyond London and the south east.

It is for this reason that the contrast, described above in personal terms, between the vantage point of social movements and that of Labour Party politics is relevant to understanding the future of 'Corbynism from below' – a phenomenon through which the parliamentary left and extra-parliamentary rebellions momentarily converged.

THREE STRATEGIC IDEAS

Three strategic ideas arising from these movements as they sought to transform society, and especially as they engaged with the state, stand out: prefigurative politics; the notion of being 'in and against' the state; and the concept of a party of movements.

How might these ideas contribute to overcoming this dilemma that arises for Corbynism from below due to the nature of Westminster-style electoral politics? Could they contribute, for example, to radicalising the nature of the relationship between the

Labour Party and the working-class movements from whence it came, or to deepening the democracy of the Labour Party itself?

PREFIGURATIVE POLITICS

The first of these strategic ideas is that of 'prefigurative politics'– the process of making changes now to illustrate the society-wide changes we are working to achieve in the future; or of claiming now, in particular struggles, rights we aim to achieve systematically in the future.

This approach was particularly characteristic of the women's liberation movement in the 1970s, which had a formative influence on my politics and my life.[2] It is alive now in the growing movement for employment rights among precarious workers and in the mass movements of young people taking increasingly militant and creative action on climate change, experimenting with their 'pop-up' people's assemblies and other forms of direct democracy around how we might address the climate emergency and put maximum pressure on the slow 'business as usual' habits of Parliament.

IN AND AGAINST THE STATE

The second strategic idea is that of being 'in and against' the state – working with the considerable resources and powers of redistribution, provision and regulation of the state, but at the same time, and ideally drawing on the prefigurative relationships of social movements, seeking to transform its character and the relationships through which it is constituted. This idea was developed in practice and in theory in the 1980s as activists from social movements ended up uneasily working for the state and/or, equally warily, campaigning for its resources while at the same time being determined not to abandon their autonomous social movement commitments and values.[3]

Being 'in and against' summed up the contradictions they were attempting to straddle. Similar contradictions and determination to work within and outside of the existing state are evident now in, for example, the Labour Party's rediscovered commitment to public ownership. This is combined with an acute awareness of the limitations of the hierarchical 1945 forms of public ownership, and the necessity to respond to the aspirations of recent generations of workers and users, who have a strong consciousness of their own capacities and a desire for self-government.

John McDonnell, the future Chancellor of the Exchequer in any Corbyn government, talks frequently about preparing to work 'in and against the state', emphasising that public ownership must be different under the next Labour government, and involve the empowerment of workers and users, instead of merely replacing one set of managers with another.[4]

McDonnell intends this concept to be an appeal to social and labour movement activists actively to prepare for a radical Labour government – and the opposition it will face – by acting to shift the balance of power now towards working people and their organisations, rather than abrogating responsibility for change to the would-be Labour prime minister and Cabinet.

McDonnell's hope is that by organising for victories and alternatives in the present, not only will we illustrate future possibilities, but we will also build the alliances and base of support that will provide a counter-power to the corporate pressure likely to block radical change. He and Corbyn know that the election of a radical Labour government will not of itself be a sufficient condition for genuine economic and political transformation.

A PARTY OF MOVEMENTS

The third strategic idea has been more of a vague aspiration than a clear concept: the desire for a new kind of party, or at least a new kind of political representation, responsive to the ideas and innovative organisational forms of radical movements. The concept of a 'movement party', inadequate though it is, comes closest to conveying this line of thinking. In other words, a party, or form of representation, rooted in social movements and struggles, for which it provides a resource and parliamentary voice, as opposed to a Labour Party that, pre-Corbyn, was becoming increasingly integrated into a political class separate from the people.

Although the Labour Party has historically been above all a parliamentary – or, as Ralph Miliband would emphasise, a *parliamentarist*[5] – party, with a pragmatic, ameliorative, social democratic politics, there have always been elements of a more radical, transformative party struggling to survive in and beyond it. Generally, the imperatives of unity in the face of the enemy, carried over from the requirements of industrial struggle, have subordinated this more challenging tradition, and key victories, such as the coming to power in 1945 and subsequent achievements of the Attlee government and, to an extent, the victory of Harold Wilson in 1964, have legitimated this overriding imperative of unity around electoral priorities.[6]

But as the conditions of the Keynesian economic compromise between private capital and the social state began to break down, the cohabitation of the ameliorative and transformative traditions became increasingly tense. From 1974 until the defeat of the miners' strike and abolition of the GLC in 1985/86, the Labour Party appeared to be what I have described as a 'tale of two parties',[7] a phenomenon which burst out of the confines of party membership to involve the labour movement more generally.

In the early to mid 1970s, there was extensive activity around the radical industrial policies inspired by Tony Benn and fellow Labour MP Stuart Holland. This included many initiatives of a prefigurative kind coming especially from the networks of well-organised trade unions across the engineering industry, who developed alternative plans for socially useful employment for their industries and companies. These were sometimes to provide a positive focus for resisting redundancies and factory closures, and sometimes in response to contact with Benn as he prepared his plans for bringing shipbuilding and aerospace into public ownership. Interestingly, these trade unionists converged, shared experiences and discussed tactics and strategy through a loose, low-key, but much-used organisation, the Institute of Workers' Control, that had no party affiliations or constraints. Rather, it had a working relationship with Benn, who, although deeply loyal to the Labour Party, never asked people for their party cards before working with them.

Here was a movement that was simultaneously prefigurative, and working in and against the state (through Benn and his close ally Holland[8]). Many of its activists were at the same time working for its policies through the Labour Party, at both a constituency level and through working groups of the left-dominated National Executive Committee. As a network/movement, though, they were autonomous from and unconstrained by the Labour Party, rooted in the trade union movement but developing links with feminists, anti-racists, critical scientists and cultural activists of different kinds. It was an interesting hybrid example, with lessons for today's networks and initiatives that through Corbyn's leadership are close to the Labour Party, but not of it.[9]

Another example of this second, subordinate but transformative party cohabiting with the Labour Party emerged during the miners' strike, when especially the women campaigning to defend the mining communities against a devastating closure programme turned to their local Labour parties for active solidarity.[10] These local parties were only too eager to be actively involved and turned themselves into an effective support network, mobilising the support of local councils, helping to enable a militant and practical process of 'twinning' between the mining communities and urban centres of left and trade union organisation, and gathering material and political support.

The Labour Party nationally, under the leadership of Neil Kinnock, was actually hostile to the leadership of the National Union of Mineworkers (NUM), seeking to dissuade other unions from giving it the solidarity it needed. It was a vivid chapter in the tale of two parties. The one responding directly to injustice, engaging in immediate and practical forms of support, prefiguring at a local level the principles of solidarity envisaged for a future society, and making use of (local) state resources wherever possible to support the struggle. The other, hostile to such a radical defence of working-class interests and seeking instead to act exclusively at the electoral level, competing with the Conservatives to manage the status quo on a more humane basis.[11] Again, at a local level, and across the country, the Labour Party showed the capacity for change, for becoming in practice 'a movement party' and doing so in the local sphere with considerable autonomy from the national leadership and party apparatus. But without this national support, this localised 'movement party' could have only limited effect.

This tension between the potential for transformative dynamics locally and the constraints of the electoral pressures dominating the

Labour Party nationally will reappear, as we consider the current dilemmas facing Corbynism today.

AN EBBING OF ENERGIES

The widespread sense of expectant energy and enthusiasm generated by 'movement' and electoral politics was seemingly in sync up to and including the immediate aftermath of the 2017 election campaign, when Corbyn was able to present himself as a prime minister in waiting, with all this meant for supporters' sense of opportunity and self-confidence.[12]

There is still hope, energy and persistent creative activity among those who were drawn into the movement for change that Corbyn's leadership stimulated. The many (mainly unpublicised) meetings that Corbyn and McDonnell speak at across the country still attract an excited mass attendance of activists who leave fired up to argue and organise. There are many creative initiatives across the nations and regions of the UK, both through local Labour parties and branches of Momentum, as well as a wide range of struggles and initiatives – some local, some national – stimulated in part by commitments by the Labour leadership or the inspiration and hope generated by Corbyn's leadership. At the same time, however, there are patches of frustration and demoralisation felt by many activists who had previously organised much of what could be called 'Corbynism from below', especially among parts of Momentum.

In a sense, a certain ebbing of energy is to be expected after the intensity of the incessant campaigning of 2015 to 2017. The 2017 election campaign was a particularly dramatic break from electoral politics as usual. The familiar approach of appealing to the centre ground, focusing on floating voters in marginal seats, on election day only reminding your certain supporters to vote, would have effectively ruled Corbyn out of the competition.

THE RADICALISM OF THE 2017 CAMPAIGN

The radicalism of the 2017 campaign, on the ground as well as in policy, was both a product of necessity and of the momentum generated by the second leadership campaign, which vindicated

Corbyn's legitimacy as leader. Necessity because the mainstream media were still effectively working with the template for Labour politics set by New Labour. They had long assumed that Corbyn and his ilk were not a credible force and had no chance of even giving the prime minister a close fight. It was only the broadcasting rules for election campaigns – plus the generally loyal Labour tabloid, the *Daily Mirror* – that resulted in any mainstream coverage for Corbyn at all.

Labour, and especially Momentum activists, realised they had nothing to lose – and as it turned out, everything to gain – by campaigning in the way they knew best: direct contact under the media radar, on the streets, in outdoor rallies, using door-to-door and other face-to-face persuasion, reinforced by social media and radical cultural initiatives. They put together a powerful force, which threw normal electoral caution to the wind and took Westminster psephology by storm. They campaigned from the left, reaching out to the disenfranchised and taken-for-granted; and promoting the party leader not so much as a 'safe pair of hands' but as someone who speaks his mind, believes in the capacities of working people, and would share power rather than monopolise or concentrate it.

PARLIAMENTARY BUSINESS AS USUAL

Following the 2017 election – which left Theresa May without an overall majority, bribing and grovelling her way to remain prime minister, while Labour gained its largest vote since Tony Blair became prime minister in 1997 – Corbyn seemed unassailable. But as it became clear that another election was unlikely, Parliament returned to its archaic and inward-looking business.

Corbyn also persisted in his routine, making sure he left Parliament for at least a couple of days a week to meet voters with particular concerns in different parts of the country, especially outside London. The Brexit time bomb also began to tick that year, with the invocation of Article 50, and indications of the problems it would cause for Corbynism began to emerge as several of his supporters in the Shadow Cabinet resigned.

CONTINUED HOSTILITY FROM WITHIN THE PLP

Most importantly, hostile members of the Parliamentary Labour Party (PLP), who simply could not accept that Jeremy Corbyn, the backbench rebel of no account, would be the next Labour prime minister, began to grasp any opportunity to knock him off course. The party's traditions of unity, by which the left had generally abided, were disregarded by the right and traditionalist centre as these MPs knowingly risked their party's immediate electoral prospects to end what to them was an aberration, a nightmare produced by 'outside forces', as if the members of their party who had so wanted the new leadership counted for nothing.

The hostile MPs used every opportunity to spread disaffection, from complaints about Corbyn's lack of deference to royalty to Labour's supposedly 'weak' EU referendum campaigning for Remain. Most significantly, a toxic exploitation of stupid social media remarks by careless activists and ill-considered acts of solidarity undertaken, and then apologised for, by Corbyn was used to launch an accusation of antisemitism. This provided fuel for a relentless attempt to discredit Corbyn by attacking him where he should have been strongest – his long record of anti-racism, which included support for parliamentary measures to outlaw antisemitism, a background as a spokesperson for numerous international solidarity campaigns, and a belief that all faith communities are part of the kind of multicultural society he has championed all his life.

Scarcely noticed, large numbers of Jewish supporters of the left rejected the way that opposition to antisemitism was being deployed for the purpose of destroying Corbyn.[13] And underlying these attacks was a hostility to Corbyn's support for the rights of Palestinians and his forthright and long-standing criticism of the Israeli state. These attacks on Corbyn were amplified and often exaggerated by a predominantly hostile media.

THE TYRANNY OF THE IMMEDIATE

The result of these relentless attacks has been that the energies of Corbyn and his team have been constantly drawn into firefighting rather than working strategically on policy and party transformation. They have been in constant danger of falling victim to a 'tyranny of the immediate', at the expense of the positive transformative leadership that a radical politics needs.

The onslaught on Corbyn and the movement comes as no surprise. Indeed, the closer he comes to becoming prime minister, the worse it will get. But because his leadership is the product of a movement, his opponents find themselves up against sources of power they do not understand. The key question is whether these sources of power are sufficient not only to enable Corbyn to reach Downing Street but, once Labour is in office, to secure the process of social and economic transformation to which the party is committed.

The defeat of the attempted coup against Corbyn by a section of the PLP in 2016 and his seeing off a leadership challenge with ease shortly afterwards indicates that the movement behind Corbyn has considerable power to mobilise numbers – numbers at rallies, numbers to protest, numbers to vote and to persuade others to vote. The same capacity to mobilise creatively in large numbers was evident to impressive effect in the 2017 election.

But this is only one form of power. It is clearly effective in dealing with one-off challenges like the second leadership election. And the relationships and support built in these mobilisations is of lasting benefit. But is this form of counter-power sufficient to deal with the more systemic activation of the bias built into Britain's political institutions, including the Labour Party, against challenges from below, from organised citizens determined to break the power of the ruling elite?

Here, we have to go deeper than the concepts of 'movements' in general, or 'Corbynism from below', and distinguish the different kinds of power that movements can mobilise. In other words, insofar as Corbynism from below concerns the development of a movement with the capacity to reinforce and sustain the radical dynamic of Corbyn's leadership (which cannot thrive on policy alone), it is about building forms of power beyond the specific and limited power of political representation, and we need to understand what this might entail.

THE DISTINCTIVE POWER OF SOCIAL MOVEMENTS

A broad distinction helps between power as domination – what others have called 'power over' (the kind of power involved in government) and power as transformative capacity – what others have termed 'power to'. This is the kind of power evident in the prefigurative initiatives of social movements, which, rather than merely refusing – or, worse, reproducing – oppressive relations, create alternative relationships which not only achieve changes and improvements in people's lives in the present, but also help materially to shift the balance of power to achieve radical change in the future.

These two sources of power are not necessarily counterposed; they can be combined to enhance the power to achieve a common goal, with power as domination, power over resources and legislation, acting as a resource for power as transformative capacity. But they are distinct sources of power, with distinct dynamics and conditions under which they can thrive. Power as transformative capacity requires specific conditions under which people's capacities can be enhanced, the level of popular participation maximised and the extent of transformation deepened. This involves the sharing of knowledge; self-education; solidarity and collective care; participatory democracy, in which no voices are marginalised and in which everyone is disciplined and self-restraining; a focus on creating alternatives rather than only opposing the status quo, or defending minimal gains bargained for within the existing system; reaching out beyond the initial group, spreading and reproducing.

For power as transformative capacity to be successfully created, there has to be a significant autonomy from the pressures of hostile political institutions, and the way that, unreformed, these institutions work against the creation of power as transformative capacity through imposing a reactive agenda, a constraining timetable and an instrumental, short-term political culture.

A PLETHORA OF AUTONOMOUS INITIATIVES

On the ground, there is a wide range of initiatives that are often both autonomous from the Labour Party and prefigurative. Though organisationally distinct from the Labour Party, many of them have been stimulated by the prospect of a Corbyn government and the indications already given of the support that would be forthcoming from such a government.

An example here is the spreading organisation and militancy of precarious workers refusing the super-exploitation of major corporations such as McDonald's and Wetherspoon's, from whose picket lines McDonnell publicised the commitment of a future Labour government to end zero-hour contracts and legislate for full employment rights for part-time workers and the self-employed.

Local movements for democratic public ownership have also been stimulated by McDonnell's commitment to worker and user participation in the programme of publicly owned industries to be introduced by the next Labour government. Norfolk for the Nationalisation of Our Railways is a good example. Formed three years ago by an ex-London Underground worker, Dave Welsh, who also worked on transport issues at the GLC's Popular Planning Unit, and several local Labour activists with an interest in transport, with the support of the local RMT branch, it has drawn up a charter for a 'People's Railway' system, with a regional and national focus. It has helped to organise support for guards resisting redundancies and a nearby rural community resisting the closure of a station by the regional private train-operating company Abellio Greater Anglia, and generally seeks to be thorn in the side of the franchise, while at the same time working on the public alternative. Most ambitiously, it is considering the idea of a 'people's plan for Norwich station' that would propose improvements that could be won now, alongside more long-term plans that would require a change of government.

This is the process of building power as transformative capacity; a slow process, with minimal resources, but representing a collective commitment to an idea and a shared enthusiasm to turn such a vision into a practical outcome. This develops out of a more traditional defensive politics by encouraging a reorientation towards a positive vision and, in effect, a more political trade unionism.

Another initiative that is spreading – and could be said to put a feasible kind of utopianism into practice – is the idea of 'community wealth-building'. The idea originated when Preston Council built an alliance of local public sector organisations – 'anchor institutions' like NHS trusts, the police and a local university – who were willing, following the council's lead, to use their procurement budgets to support local companies, especially co-operatives, to generate good local jobs and to insist on decent wages. The results have been impressive, both in terms of job creation and higher wages, which have in turn increased consumer demand, creating a virtuous circle of local economic wellbeing.[14] Two years ago, the Labour leadership created a Community Wealth Building Commission comprising trade unionists, councillors, co-operative movement activists, research organisations and individuals working on related ideas to support and spread the idea.[15]

THE PARTY TRANSFORMED?

These localised initiatives that bring about changes here and now, and help to shift the balance of power and belief in what is possible, seem in practice to be changing the Labour Party mainly from below. By visible example and cross-fertilisation, facilitated in particular by the political-education initiative The World Transformed, born of Momentum but autonomous from it, they influence many party activists, who in turn take the experience or way of organising into their local parties. There is an emergent trend, partial and limited but certainly present, towards constituency Labour Parties being influenced in practice by movement political cultures – engaging in direct action and supporting local struggles, rather than invariably directing their political decision-making upwards to the party leadership. Party culture and priorities are also being influenced by the prefigurative approach explicitly encouraged by the party leadership via the community organisers' initiative. The idea is that the dynamic of cultural and political change will come from the influence of working examples of transformation in practice.

But vibrant, transformative local parties and a leader with radical policies and vision will only get so far if the parliamentary party remains conservative and hostile to radical change. This is all the more the case if the leadership team imprisons itself in an exclusively electoralist perspective imposed by Westminster's undemocratic, non-proportional electoral system, and is reluctant to take the risks that a transformative strategy requires.

The institutionalised political environment in which the party works at Westminster exerts a pressure that pulls MPs, whatever their politics, away from the transformative dynamics of the base.

This distorts the Labour Party's ability to represent the public, express our aspirations and champion our needs.

BREXIT: A SYMPTOM, NOT A CAUSE

Brexit has stripped these problems bare – and it will continue to do so regardless of the final outcome. As the political system has broken down, as it has been doing since the EU referendum result was declared in June 2016, neither Labour nor anyone else has been able to come up with even the foundations of a constitutional alternative to the crisis we have all found ourselves in.

A referendum in a centralised parliamentary system is not an instrument of democracy. This is especially so in a political system in which voters are so rarely asked for their opinion on an issue where it could actually matter. A referendum treats people as a homogeneous mass capable of only a simple yes or no. In reality, as we now know, people voted 'leave' and 'remain' for many different reasons. Broadly, Leave voters fell into at least two very different categories. First, there were those, especially from working-class communities in the north of England, who voted against a political class, Labour and Tory, that had destroyed their sources of livelihood and then the means of welfare and survival, while looking after their own in London and the south east. A year later, many of these same people voted for Jeremy Corbyn's Labour Party, not least because the party's new leadership was committed to reversing the consequences of the past forty years of austerity, and its leaders appeared to be on the same side as working people and did not take them for granted.

At the same time, across the country – in the north as well as the south, but concentrated in the south east – were those Tory and UKIP voters who voted Brexit because they wanted rid of social regulations and immigrants and desired a return to the 1950s and an era when the Britain was still 'great'. Similarly, those who voted Remain were not a homogeneous phalanx of Europhiles. Many were highly critical of the neoliberal economics that, partly under the influence of British prime ministers, were built into EU treaties from the Maastricht Treaty of 1992 onwards.

The electoral system did not allow these complexities to be

expressed any more than the referendum allowed for real debate and accurate information about the complexity of options. Leavers and Remainers of different sorts are to be found in both parties. The result on the left is that the different levels of argument over Europe cannot in practice be distinguished.

PORTUGUESE LESSONS

The contrast with Portugal is telling. There, a democratic constitution written in the aftermath of the overthrow of the dictatorship provided for a proportional electoral system in which the main social democratic party, the Socialist Party, does not have a monopoly of left political representation. Two smaller parties, the Portuguese Communist Party, rooted in the older working-class communities, rural and urban, and Bloco Esquerda (the Left Bloc), based among public-sector workers, young intellectuals, and feminist, environmental and LGBT movements, have significant parliamentary representation. Sufficiently significant, at any rate, to be able to make an alliance with the Socialist Party to prevent a right-wing, pro-austerity coalition from remaining in office.

The important point here in relation to the Labour Party is that this alliance was based on reversing the austerity policies of the previous government, and doing so as a member of the EU. Here was an agreement to work both 'in and against' the EU – the EU tried unsuccessfully to block this alliance and frequently opposed (again unsuccessfully) particular anti-austerity measures, but there was never any discussion of leaving the EU. The process also stimulated self-organisation and militancy amongst the many.

The two small left parties in the alliance had long been opposed to the EU because of the neoliberalism written into the Maastricht and Lisbon Treaties. The proportional electoral system enabled them to maintain their opposition and remain autonomous from the Socialist Party, while at the same time offering support that was conditional on the government implementing the agreed anti-austerity policies. Such political pluralism would have benefited Labour, allowing unity on particular issues while fundamental disagreements could be voiced without risking the electoral success of the left as a whole.

MORE THAN JUST FRAGMENTS

The movement that converged actively to support Corbyn for leader
and then for prime minister has shown its capacity to multi-task. At
first, when Corbyn was the outsider, and later, too, when it was faced
with attempts to marginalise it, the movement was able to mobilise the sheer momentum of determined and energetic members,
new and old, to make him internally invincible and then, in 2017,
publicly a prime minister in waiting.

Since then, the movement has found its own ways of continuing
to organise the counter-power that a transformative leadership
needs. This Corbyn-supporting movement is not a kind of fan-club
crowd that projects all its hope onto a populist leader. It is, in the
majority, one of self-organised socialists and campaigners for social
justice, who before Corbyn's name was on the leadership ballot,
were themselves organising for change through their unions, their
chosen campaigns, community groups, co-operatives, local Labour
parties and so on. We supported Corbyn because we knew that he
supported us and that with him as leader, our varied individual and
collective efforts could become a project for socialist transformation
that would go way beyond the sum of its parts, or 'fragments', as we
once called them, never imagining that the Labour Party would be
the vehicle to take us beyond them.[16]

Away from Westminster, all kinds of movements and initiatives
have gained confidence and momentum through the prospect of
a Corbyn-led Labour government and the support they get from
McDonnell and Corbyn. These scattered movements and struggles
do not gather around one organisational form. In many localities and some national campaigns, Momentum and, increasingly,
local Labour parties and the more radical unions provide sources of
support and wider connections, but none of these provide a unified
political framework. The ability of this diffuse 'movement' and of
the leadership itself to reach out to a wider public could well see
Corbyn's Labour into government. The rampant, rivalrous lust for
office tearing apart the Conservative Party could also help – though
never underestimate the capacity of this party of the ruling class to
unite when it faces the likely loss of office.

However, if Labour, having won office in the name of democracy, continues to work through what is now understood to be a profoundly undemocratic Westminster system, all the leadership's radicalism will be strangled by the conservative power of a system still substantially unreformed since its days of empire.[17]

The democratic reform of the political institutions that now serve to protect the economic and political elite and exclude citizens from even knowing how they are ruled, let alone enabling them to practise self-government, is an absolutely necessary condition for the economic and social transformations that movements are campaigning for and prefiguring in their practice.

Without such change Labour's transformative project will fail. 'Corbynism from below' will come to nothing, and we'll end up grateful for small reforms. But if we get it right, Labour could combine the transformative capacity of movement activists with democratic control over public resources to such an extent that we achieve a genuinely transformative politics, fulfilling the dreams of those who worked to make Corbyn Labour leader and then supported him to become Labour prime minister.

NOTES

1. See Ralph Miliband, *Parliamentary Socialism: A Study in the Politics of Labour*, Merlin Press: London, 1964.
2. See Sheila Rowbotham, *The Past is Before Us: Feminism in Action since the 1960s*, Pandora: London, 1989.
3. See the London Edinburgh Weekend Return Group (Cynthia Cockburn, John Holloway, Jeanette Mitchell and others), *In and Against the State*, Pluto: London, 1979.
4. Hilary Wainwright and John McDonnell, 'The new economics of Labour', Open Democracy, 25 February 2018.
5. Miliband 1964.
6. See Leo Panitch, David Coates and Colin Leys, *The End of Parliamentary Socialism: From New Left to New Labour*, Verso: London, 1997.
7. Wainwright, *Labour: A Tale of Two Parties*, Chatto and Windus: London, 1987.
8. Stuart Holland, *The Socialist Challenge*, Quartet: London, 1975.
9. See also: Hilary Wainwright and Dave Elliott, *The Lucas Plan: A New Trade Unionism in the Making?*, Allison and Busby: London, 1982; and Wainwright and Huw Benyon, *The Workers' Report on Vickers*, Pluto Press: London, 1979.

10. Benyon (ed), *Digging Deeper: Issues in the Miners' Strike*, Verso: London, 1985.
11. Wainwright 1987.
12. For the best description and analysis of Corbyn's winning of the leadership, the nature of the movement that he inspired and his first years as leader, see the second edition of Alex Nunns, *The Candidate: Jeremy Corbyn's Improbable Path to Power*, OR Books: New York, 2018.
13. For example, www.jewishvoiceforlabour.org.uk.
14. See Aditya Chakrabortty, 'Preston hit rock bottom: Then it took back control', *The Guardian*, 31 January 2018.
15. For an excellent analysis of the history and likely future importance of 'community wealth-building', see Christine Berry and Joe Guinan, *People Get Ready! Preparing for a Corbyn Government*, OR Books: New York, 2019.
16. See the third edition of Sheila Rowbotham, Lynne Segal and Wainwright, *Beyond the Fragments: Feminism and the Making of Socialism*, Merlin Press: London, 2013.
17. For a brilliant account of the disastrous consequences of the UK's anti-democratic institutions see Anthony Barnett, *The Lure of Greatness: England's Brexit and America's Trump*, Unbound: London, 2017.

Below the Line

An A-Z of Corbynism

Attlee, Clement, Labour leader 1935-55. Labour prime minister 1945-51, skewers Chamberlain and the Tories for their appeasement of Hitler, joins wartime coalition government serving as Churchill's deputy. In one of the biggest political reversals of all time, defeats Churchill in landslide 1945 general election win for Labour. Under the slogan 'And now – win the peace', Attlee's Labour government establishes the post-war consensus, creates the NHS and free secondary and university education for all, nationalises rail, coal and public utilities, and initiates a council-house-building programme.

Block vote Means by which trade union general secretaries cast millions of votes at Labour's annual conference 'on behalf of' their members. Used by left-led, right-wing, and in-between unions alike. Doesn't fit well with the idea of a mass, individual-membership party, but the historical roots of Labour's distinctiveness as a political party lie in the affiliation of trade unions.

CLP One of many acronyms used in Labour activist speak. Otherwise known as Constituency Labour Party. One per parliamentary constituency in England, Scotland and Wales (for historical reasons, Labour doesn't organise in the North of Ireland), these are the constitutional organising units of the Labour Party, and their roles include electing delegates, sending resolutions to the party's annual conference, and selecting prospective parliamentary candidates (PPCs).

Decarbonisation Process of shifting from fossil fuels to renewables, including solar, wind and wave power. At the core of Labour's

Green New Deal to deliver a sustainable economic strategy to tackle climate change.

Exit poll 10pm, Big Ben's bong, bong, bong, the nation waits to hear likely outcome of the general election, which won't actually be finalised until all the votes are counted by the early hours of the next morning, with Sunderland South for some reason always being the first to declare.

Fully automated luxury communism *abbr.* FALC. Coined by Novara Media founder Aaron Bastani, a futuristic manifesto combining new technology with liberation from the work ethic via automation for a land of milk and honey where robots are unionised.

Get Out the Vote *abbr.* GOTV. Part and parcel of Labour's people-powered election machine. Involves knocking on doors to remind, in politest possible terms, those who've previously promised to vote Labour to pop down the polling station and put their X in the right (well, actually, left) box. If desperate, providing cars to physically drive them there helps too. *See also: #LabourDoorstep*

Hegemony Widely associated with early twentieth-century social theorist Antonio Gramsci, popularised again in the 1980s often to counter the wilder simplicities of Bennism, now enjoying a revival amongst some Corbynite ideologues. Basic idea is that for the left to win it must be the leading force of ideas in every section of society, including politics, economics, culture and morality. *See also: Gramscian (confusingly, may be used as term of approval or disapproval)*

Identity politics Term first became current in the 1980s following the waves of women's, gay and black liberation movements in the preceding decade. Widely embraced on the left and popularised at the time as a 'rainbow alliance'. Now the term tends to be used more critically, to denote the practice of emphasising identity at the expense of a broader politics, threatening to undermine the dynamic of liberation. *See also: intersectionality*

Jazz hands Pointy-finger, shouty politics with mainly male platform speakers telling us what we already know doesn't do it any more, if it ever did. Sitting in circles, listening to one another, replacing clapping with wavy 'jazz' hands, palms forward, fingers splayed, much preferred by many, if not the few.

Keynesianism Bedrock of Labour and mainstream economic thinking in the decades following the 1945 Labour landslide. Full employment as first priority, guaranteed by supply and demand of public expenditure and taxation. Ideas abandoned by the neoliberal consensus from 1979.

Labourism Damned by critics as timid, statist, bureaucratic. Tony Blair promised to modernise it via the moniker 'new', and use of bold typefaces. Corbynism similarly unimpressed with its own party's 'ism', however, what will come to replace it remains to be decided, though it probably won't involve the word 'new', or a change of typeface. Helpful to be able to quote chunks of Ralph Miliband's (David and Ed's dad) *Parliamentary Socialism* to prove credentials of any critique.

Momentum Formed after success of getting Jeremy Corbyn elected Labour leader. Described by some critics as Corbynism's Praetorian Guard and by others as 'Trots', neither togas nor transitional programmes seem very much in evidence. Hugely successful in winning internal party elections, turns out thousands to canvass too. Organises annual, and now local versions too, of The World Transformed festival, a kind of mix of a club night and a counterculture seminar. *See also: Jon Lansman*

NEC Another handy acronym. The National Executive Committee in theory manages both the day-to-day affairs of the Labour Party and its strategy. Made up of members' representatives, voted in by an all-members ballot, most if not all are currently Momentum supporters. Plus trade union representatives, MPs, socialist-society and youth reps, elected, or not, by various other means. Appoints the party's general secretary, who runs Labour outside of Parliament. Other useful party acronyms include CAC (Conference

Arrangements Committee), LOTO (Leader of the Opposition's Office), NCC (National Constitutional Committee).

Open primaries Aka 'open selections', novel(ish) idea first pushed at 2018 Labour annual conference. Idea is that members vote to select their parliamentary candidates, and if a sitting MP, reselect too. That is, all members, registered supporters and, in some versions, Labour voters too. Used in US by the Democrats and seems to work perfectly well there. Useful related acronyms include AMM (All-members Meeting), GC (General Committee – delegate-based, not an all-members meeting), OMOV (one member, one vote).

PLP Acronym for 'Parliamentary Labour Party', aka Labour MPs plus unelected Labour lords and ladies. Hotbed of anti-Corbyn discontent, launched ill-fated 2016 coup that led to – also ill-fated – Owen Smith leadership challenge. Following 2017 general election, displayed gradual shift towards a more sympathetic position on the direction Corbyn is taking party, but key word here is 'gradual', i.e., painfully slow, bordering on non-existent.

Queer Potentially confusing use of what was once an insult as, now, a badge of pride (literally). Over the decades from Stonewall to Marks and Spencers gay sandwiches, 'queer' has held up the tradition of radical protest. *See also: LGBTQ (lesbian-gay-bisexual-transgender-queer)*

Resolutions Aka 'motions'. Passed by all levels of party from branch (BLP, branch of the Labour Party), CLPs, regions, policy bodies (NPF, National Policy Forum), to annual Labour Party conference. Often 'composited', which means various opinions on a subject, broadly in agreement, merged into one. Sometimes 'referred back', that is, given to some committee to mull over. Of varying significance in actually deciding what Labour might or might not do as a party and/or in government. *See also: resolutionary socialism*

Sectionalism A critical term to denote left politics and trade unionism in which the interests of some are prioritised over a broader constituency, under the guise of militancy. Historian Eric Hobsbawm was one of the first to observe this. Modern examples could be said to include the defence of jobs in environmentally damaging industries, prompting the retort from Green New Dealers that 'there's no jobs on a dead planet'.

Tactical voting Not popular in most Labour circles. Means voting for party you don't believe in (usually Lib Dems) against party you detest even more (always Tories) because party you'd rather vote for (Labour) hasn't hope in hell. Largely replaced by target-seat strategy; going to nearest marginal and campaigning where Labour has actual chance of winning and is the only contender to topple sitting Tory MP, aka 'Unseat'. *See also: progressive alliance, proportional representation*

Universal Basic Income One among a raft of new ideas on economics being considered by Shadow Chancellor John McDonnell to pep up popular 2017 general election manifesto to win the next time. A payment for all, not based on dependency, means test or work. *See also: four-day week, co-operative models of public ownership, free solar power for all houses*

Virtue signalling Making a conspicuous show of being right on, without achieving any changes to the status quo. *See also: political posturing*

Woke In contrast to virtue signalling, being 'woke' denotes actually doing something about how race, gender and class divide society. Like earlier terms 'right on' and 'politically correct', not always used approvingly. *See also: prefigurative politics, the personal is political*

Xenophobia Hatred of all things European and not too keen on anything foreign from other parts of the world either, yearning for age of (British) empire, what did the rest of the world ever do for us? Yes, really. Do mention the war, a lot, but leave out any mention of USA, Canada, Australian and New Zealand forces, Red Army, Polish aircrew, French resistance, et al. *See also: Basil Fawlty, Boris*

Johnson, Nigel Farage, assorted hangers-on, unfortunately too many to mention

Youthquake As pollsters everywhere know, young people never bother to vote, too busy staying in bed or some such. Strange, that, as at the 2017 general election, millions did get out of bed, and bother to vote Labour – although how many, and whether they will the next time, remain the subject of some dispute. *See also: Milifandom (2015) 'Oh, Jeremy Corbyn!' (2017), and 'Where's Jeremy Corbyn?' (2018-19)*

Zero hours Victorian-era contractual obligation to be at beck and call of employer but with no fixed hours, revived for twenty-first century. *See also: gig economy, precariat*

Learning from Below:
Further Reading and
Other Resources

To start off with, two books which give a very good grounding in the recent meaning of a 'politics from above'. Richard Power Sayeed's *1997: The Future that Never Happened* effortlessly recreates and deconstructs the moment of the Blair landslide. In another seamless mix of politics and culture, *Authentocrats* by Joe Kennedy is an extended polemic against a model of political leadership that proclaims the need to 'live in the real world'.

We need to delve a little further back in time to understand the politics of Thatcherism, the last time in British politics that the old consensus was broken and a new one put in its place – not to ape these politics, of course, but to learn how. The classic account was provided by the 1980s magazine *Marxism Today*, its articles variously collected in books including *The Politics of Thatcherism*, edited by Stuart Hall and Martin Jacques, and *The Great Moving Right Show and Other Political Writings* by Stuart Hall. *The Free Economy and the Strong State: The Politics of Thatcherism* by Andrew Gamble explores the beginnings of what was to become neoliberalism in this country, while Beatrix Campbell sets out how both the new right and the old left used, and abused, 'identity politics' to varying ends, in *Iron Ladies: Why do Women vote Tory?*

For a historical perspective on the Bennism of the current Labour leadership, and its connections and disconnections, read the 1982 *New Left Review* interviews with Tony Benn, *Parliament, People and Power: Agenda for a Free Society*. By way of an introduction to

Ralph Miliband, see his collection of selected writings, *Class War Conservatism and Other Essays*.

Since Corbyn was elected Labour leader in September 2015, there has emerged a growing, and sympathetic, literature on all things 'Corbynism'. The preceding volume to this book, *The Corbyn Effect*, also edited by Mark Perryman, was published in the immediate aftermath of the 2017 general election. Around the same time, new and updated editions of two of the seminal reads of this early period also came out: Richard Seymour's *Corbyn: The Strange Rebirth of Radical Politics* and from Alex Nunns, *The Candidate: Jeremy Corbyn's Improbable Path to Power*. Both remain essential reads. Steve Howell's *Game Changer: Eight Weeks that Transformed British Politics* provides the definitive insider's account of the 2017 general election campaign, while *Rise: How Jeremy Corbyn inspired the Young to Create a New Socialism* by Liam Young helps explain one of the most significant apparent features of that campaign; the 'youthquake'.

For a very good short history of the Labour left from which Corbyn emerged, see Andy Beckett's *Guardian* essay 'The wilderness years: How Labour's left survived to conquer'. For the comprehensive history, feast yourself on David Kogan's *Protest and power: The Battle for the Labour Party*, or for an admirably partisan version, *The Fall and Rise of the British Left* by Andrew Murray.

Since the aftermath of the 2017 election, a range of writers have pushed the theoretical limits of Corbynism. Hilary Wainwright's *A New Politics from the Left* connects the 'new' with the 'old' via a compelling account of the continuities, good and bad, and discontinuities, good and bad, between current and older forms of British leftism. *In Our Own Hands: Corbynism Beyond Corbyn* from Tom Blackburn and Tom Gann is a kind of manifesto for 'long-revolution Corbynism', and testament to the deep and productive thinking in this quarter. J.A. Smith's *Other People's Politics: Populism to Corbynism* seeks to provide a theoretical framework for understanding Corbynism's emergence and appeal. *Corbynism: A Critical Approach* by Matt Bolton and Frederick Harry Pitts is a thoughtful critique of all things Corbynite. It will make the open-minded reader think, including when disagreeing with it.

For a regular diet of ideas, try the left-reformist – I don't use

the term pejoratively – quarterly *Renewal*. And for further stimu-
lating fare, see the more social-movement-oriented *Soundings*. For
not only a transatlantic perspective, but also impressive coverage
of the European left, a daily visit to the online edition of the US
magazine *Jacobin* should do the trick, at www.jacobinmag.com.
Likewise for the Labour left, daily visits to www.tribunemag.co.uk
and ww.w.labourhub.org.uk offer a well-informed Corbynist view
of our world. A critical, extra-parliamentary left focus is provided
by www.counterfire.org. For a broad and global view of the social
movements, try www.redpepper.org.uk.

The annual The World Transformed festival, on the fringe of
Labour's annual party conference, is a practical and hugely impressive testament to a resurgence of creative thinking in and around
Corbyn's Labour Party. Most encouragingly, this is now being repli-
cated by local events of similar intent and ambition. To keep up with
this exciting initiative, follow @TWT_Now. Lewes CLP puts on
both an annual ideas event and an annual practical activism skills
workshop, keep up with both @LewesLabour.

Wondering how to get organised 'from below'? Pretty much
the set text for this is Becky Bond and Zack Exley's *Rules for
Revolutionaries: How Big Organizing can Change Everything*. A really
good introduction to essential activism skills is provided by Michael
Segalov's *Resist! How to be an Activist in the Age of Defiance*.

Change 'from below' will invariably begin at the local level,
in communities. Aditya Chakrabortty's *Guardian* series 'The
Alternatives' is an inspiring survey of what is possible. For a sense of
how the Labour Party is seeking to facilitate such a process, follow
Labour's new Community Organising Unit at @LabourByTheMany.

It is hard to make sense of modern trade unionism without at least
some reference to the past that came before us. *Live Working or Die
Fighting: How the Working Class went Global* by Paul Mason is a short
but indispensable history of progressive strands in workplace self-
organisation. The classic account of the post-war decline of militant
trade unionism and the rise of sectionalism, and the debate it ignited,
is found in Eric Hobsbawm's 1981 book *The Forward March of Labour
Halted?* Read Hilary Wainwright and Dave Elliott *The Lucas Plan:
A New Trade Unionism in the Making?*, also published in 1981, for a
practical, and inspiring, alternative to sectionalism; 'socially useful

production', an idea that couldn't be more relevant today, when we need to reorient entire sectors of the economy towards sustainability. The emergence of a 'precariat' is explained in Guy Standing's *The Corruption of Capitalism: Why Rentiers Thrive and Work Does Not Pay*. The online journal www.notesfrombelow.org is a good source on the state of this precariat and movements towards resistance. The Brighton-based campaign against unpaid 'trial shifts' is a textbook example of the latter, follow @NoUnpaid.

From outside the activist subculture, try a useful practical insight into how to fuse branding with purposeful politics: *Do Purpose: Why Brands with a Purpose do Better and Matter More* by David Hieatt, the man behind the clothing label Howies. Stephen Duncombe's *Dream or Nightmare: Reimagining Politics in an Age of Fantasy* sets out the need to reinvent how we communicate our ideas and ideals as a vital part of any radical political project. Such a project will need to be every bit as visual as verbal; follow @LabourDesign for inspiration and help. Watch the @VoicesLabour films, breathtakingly good, short and punchy, making the case for Labour. The tragic death of the project's founder, filmmaker Simon Baker, in June 2019 was a huge blow – this is precisely the kind of communicative culture Labour needs. Lynne Segal's *Radical Happiness: Moments of Collective Joy* gives an inkling of how such initiatives cannot be just about producing niftier graphics; they must be about how we do our politics too.

Justin Schlosberg's reports 'Should He Stay or Should He Go? Television and online coverage of the Labour Party in crisis' and 'Labour, antisemitism and the news: A disinformation paradigm', the latter co-authored with Laura Laker, should be enough to convince of the scale and nature of media bias against Labour. Both are available as free downloads from the excellent www.mediareform.org. uk. Justin is of the school of analysts who, while recognising this bias, also accept that it is nowhere near sufficient to heap all blame for Labour not getting a fair hearing on a simplistic (and sometimes conspiracy-theory-based) construct designated as 'the mainstream media'. The new, Corbyn-era edition of the classic work *Culture Wars: The Media and the British Left* by James Curran, Ivor Gaber and Julian Petley is a suitable corrective.

A flavour of a Corbynism-inclined online media can be acquired via daily visits to the ideas-producing website www.newsocialist.org.uk.

For a more traditional Labour left but Corbyn-supporting view, see www.labourhub.org.uk. For a broader pro-Corbyn view and a whole lot more perspective, see the video and audio output from Novara Media. On a smaller scale, but no less impressive, is the almost daily intellectual output of the 'All that is Solid' blog authored by Phil Burton-Cartledge; www.averypublicsociologist.blogspot.com. Add in a daily trawl of sympathetic (to varying degrees) Twitter feeds too, from the editor of this collection @markperryman, to @owenjones84, @misselliemae and @paulmasonnews, via Richard Seymour's @leninology and @jemgilbert – plus, if you can face it, a view from the Labour right, @lukeakehurst.

Of course none of this reading, writing, tweeting and the like will amount to very much if Labour loses elections. Some amateur psephology might, therefore, come in useful. To start yourself off try a regular dose of statistics, poll tracking and election results at www.britainelects.com, and a compendium of votes and poll results at www.electionpolling.co.uk. Then, to help understand what all this amounts to, seek the help of some really smart and accessible psephologists; the pick of the bunch being @p_surridge, but also Ian Warren at @election_data, and Patrick English at @PME_Politics. A means of interpreting votes and polls is provided by @LeftieStats. For the practical side of things, look out for local #LabourDoorstep sessions and 'Unseat' days of action in Labour's target seats, invariably led by the indefatigable Owen Jones.

For many, pluralism is a key test of any kind of politics from 'below'. Not easy to enact in practice, Compass, which describes itself as 'a home for everyone who wants to be part of a much more equal, democratic and sustainable society', has had a better go at being pluralist than most. A range of their publications has sought to develop a plural politics, including Neal Lawson's 'Beyond monopoly socialism' and '45° change: Transforming society from below and above', while Ken Spours, Frances Foley and Nick Mahony have co-authored 'Common platforms: A new stage of alliance-based and participatory politics'. All three are available as free downloads from www.compassonline.org.uk.

Two outstanding books outline the broad socio-economic-cultural context in which Corbynism has emerged: *Nervous States: How Feeling Took Over the World* by William Davies; and the latest from Paul Mason, *Clear Bright Future: A Radical Defence of the Human Being*.

Of course, none but the most party-chauvinist would claim that Corbynism is the only space in which a 'politics from below' might break out and take shape. Jodi Dean's *Crowds and Party* is a useful introduction to the interface between social movements and existing left party structures, and what the latter might become.

Making the case for the enduring need for the left, and associated movements and campaigns, to keep the pressure on Corbynism, not simply from below, but from outside the limitations imposed by Labourism, is Chris Nineham's *How the Establishment Lost Control*. Paul Foot's *The Vote: How it was Won and How it was Undermined* provides the history, while Ralph Miliband's *Parliamentary Socialism* is the classic critique of a left trapped within the Westminster bubble. A current, and internationalised, version of such a critique, drawing on Miliband's intellectual antecedents, is *The Socialist Challenge Today: Syriza, Sanders, Corbyn* by Leo Panitch and Sam Gindin.

Whenever the era of Brexit impasse comes to an end, we will in all likelihood see an acceleration in support for a populist right with racism at its core. *The New Authoritarians: Convergence on the Right* by David Renton offers an excellent framework for understanding this. Satnam Virdee's *Racism, Class and the Racialized Outsider* explores the importance of formulating a politics of popular anti-racism for any kind of project rooted in class politics. For inspiration to resist and invaluable lessons for today, read *Reminiscences of RAR: Rocking Against Racism 1976-82*, edited by Roger Huddle and Red Saunders. The messaging, content and means to help develop this kind of popular anti-racism that is so urgently required now can be found in Akala's *Race and Class in the Ruins of Empire*, and in spoken word artist Potent Whisper's *The Rhyming Guide to Grenfell Britain*. See *Brit(ish): On Race, Identity and Belonging* by Afua Hirsch to understand the histories that have constructed the past and present of a nation largely in denial about where racism comes from. At the core of current discourses of populist racism is the issue of immigration: Maya Goodfellow's *Hostile Environment: How Immigrants Became Scapegoats* explains both how and why. Any opposition to racism cannot simply be against, it must be for, too. *Back to Black: Retelling Black Radicalism for the 21st Century* is an account by Kehinde Andrews of a hidden history of black radicalism, offering this as the basis for a politics of black and white together that is not only progressive, but liberatory.

Strange Hate: Antisemitism, Racism and the Limits of Diversity by Keith Kahn-Harris is a contextual argument that an anti-racism which is selective is no kind of anti-racism at all. Paul Keleman's *The British Left and Zionism: History of a Divorce* is similarly contextual, a rare and invaluable aid to understanding the political shift among the British left from supporting the foundation of the state of Israel following the Holocaust, to showing solidarity with Palestine. For an insight into a childhood filled with both Jewishness and socialism, which will make you laugh, a lot, try *So They Call You Pisher!*, Michael Rosen's memoir of growing up in the Jewish East End in a Jewish Communist family. Amongst the best sources of material, research and education on antisemitism is to be found at the Pears Institute for the Study of Antisemitism, www.pearsinstitute.bbk.ac.uk.

How the EU referendum result and the eruption of the Leave vs Remain divide shapes the present and in all likelihood the future of British politics is accounted for by Anthony Barnett's superb *The Lure of Greatness: England's Brexit and America's Trump*. Add *Heroic Failure: Brexit and the Politics of Pain* by Fintan O'Toole to complete the picture. For the long view of how we arrived at the point of Brexit, read Danny Dorling and Wendy Tomlinson's *Rule Britannia: Brexit and the End of Empire*. For a broadly correct view that avoids demonising and infantilising the half of the UK population that voted Leave, see the Compass report 'The causes and cures of Brexit', available as a free download from www.compassonline.org.uk. A key theme of the report is the question of England and national identity, including how an idea of 'Britishness' has shaped the Labour Party, notably through a dogged defence of the union. Labour unionism remains a largely neglected subject; helping to redress the balance is Gerry Hassan and Eric Shaw's *The People's Flag and the Union Jack: An alternative history of Britain and the Labour Party*.

For a short but richly thought-provoking narrative of how we might escape the mire of the political present into a better political future, there is none better than *For a Left Populism* by Chantal Mouffe. Adding some impetus – or should that be 'momentum'? – to making that happen through change 'from below' is Graham Jones's revelatory read *The Shock Doctrine of the Left*. More often than not this process of change is described in age-group terms:

Keir Milburn's *Generation Left* describes the characteristics of millennial socialists, and outlines what they have in common with those whose politics were formed more in the twentieth century than in the twenty-first. Political organisation is being transformed by social media, and where it is not, it will die. *The Digital Party* by Paolo Gerbaudo sets out the potential, and pitfalls, of this transformation.

Above all, a 'next left' will be measured by its ability to develop and popularise a sustainable economic strategy. Naomi Klein's latest, *On Fire: The Burning Case for a Green New Deal*, sets out the reasons why, and then some. The Labour part of this campaign can be found at www.labourgnd.uk.

What would a Labour government look like with Jeremy Corbyn in Number Ten? Christine Berry and Joe Guinan's *People Get Ready! Preparing for a Corbyn Government* is a very good assessment of the problems and prospects. Edited by John McDonnell, *Economics for the Many* is an insight into what policies we can expect from next door at Number Eleven. For a round-up of the campaign 'from below' in favour of those policies, follow, for starters, @Labour4DayWeek, @We_OwnIt and the new think tank Common Wealth; www.common-wealth.co.uk.

Revolutionary Keywords for a New Left by Ian Parker is a helpful addition to our A–Z of Corbynism list, with useful essays on the 'isms' and 'ations' that make up the language of modern left politics.

Getting our language right, and finding good means to discuss the ideas it represents, is best done as part of a collective endeavour. This book's focus has been on politics 'from below'. Why not use these books, journals and magazines, websites and Twitter feeds to bring together friends and colleagues to transform your local Labour Party? Constituency Labour Parties should be spaces where individual contributions are shaped into a collective; where we find a conversational party rooted in locality and community, nurturing the ideas and action to make change possible. The local Labour Party as an organic intellectual: now there's an idea.

Afterwords

Notes on Contributors

Mark Perryman edited *The Corbyn Effect*, the collection that preceded this book, and since its publication in 2017 he has been speaking at local Labour Party events to open up a discussion around its themes and arguments. He looks forward to doing the same with *Corbynism from Below*. For his own local party, Mark has helped pioneer an ambitious series of large-scale day events combining ideas with campaign skills training. In these ways he has been putting into practice some of the thinking in *Corbynism from Below*. Mark is a member of Lewes Constituency Labour Party and Momentum. **@markperryman**

Lorna Finlayson writes regularly for the *London Review of Books*. Lorna is a lecturer in philosophy at the University of Essex with research interests including political philosophy and its methodology, critical theory and theories of ideology and feminist philosophy. She is author of *The Political is Political* and *An Introduction to Feminism*. Lorna is a member of South Suffolk Constituency Labour Party and Momentum. **@LJFinlayson**

Andrew Gamble is the author of the classic account of politics of Thatcherite conservatism, *The Free Economy and the Strong State*. Andrew was one of the pioneers of *Marxism Today*'s analysis of Thatcherism in the 1980s. Since then, his writing has tracked the political impact of the 2008 financial crash on the progressive project, most recently in his book *Open Left: The Future of Progressive Politics*.

Phil Burton-Cartledge blogs at 'All That is Solid', and is currently writing a book on the political crisis of the Conservative Party. A lecturer in sociology at the University of Derby, his research interests include social theory, social movements and the critique of political economy. Phil is a member of Stoke Central Constituency Labour Party. **@philbc3**

Jeremy Gilbert pioneered the term 'Acid Corbynism' first in *Red Pepper* and subsequently at Open Democracy, in the *New Statesman*, and elsewhere. The original writings can be found on his blog. The Acid Corbynism podcast is hosted by Novara Media. Jeremy's latest book is *Twenty-first Century Socialism*. He is a member of Walthamstow Constituency Labour Party and Momentum. **@jemgilbert**

Jess Garland recently completed her PhD on Labour's multi-speed membership at the University of Sussex, a subject she has written about for a number of publications, including the journal *Renewal*. A former Senior Political Adviser to a Shadow Cabinet Minister, Jess is currently Director of Policy and Research at the Electoral Reform Society. **@JessicaJGarland**

Adam Klug co-founded Momentum and worked as its National Organiser until June 2017. During the 2016 labour leadership election, he was head of volunteer mobilisation on Jeremy Corbyn's campaign. Since June 2019, he has been Director of Member Mobilisation and Activism for the Labour Party.

Emma Rees co-founded Momentum and was its National Coordinator until November 2017. She now works on progressive, volunteer-driven campaigns in Britain and abroad. Emma is also part of The World Transformed ideas festival core organising team. **@emmavrees**

Heather Wakefield is formerly a full-time national official for UNISON and candidate in the union's General Secretary election. Now a Visiting Fellow attached to the Work and Employment Unit at the University of Greenwich, Heather is a member of Lewisham Deptford Constituency Labour Party and Momentum. **@hibiscuits1**

Anne Coddington is Course Leader in Magazine Journalism and Publishing at London College of Communications, University of the Arts London. Anne has extensive experience in left publishing, including as a journalist on *LA Weekly*, editing the fortnightly newspaper *New Times*, and as Deputy Editor of *Marxism Today*.

Neal Lawson is Executive Director of the ideas and campaigning organisation Compass and author of several Compass publications, including 'Beyond monopoly socialism: Why Labour needs to learn to live with complexity and seek power with others, not over them', and '45° change: Transforming society from below and above'. During the 2017 general election, Neal was an organiser and spokesperson for the Progressive Alliance. **@Neal_Compass**

Lindsey German is a convenor of the Stop the War Coalition. Lindsey has written a number of books on extra-parliamentary movements, including *How a Century of War Changed the Lives of Women* and, as co-author, *A People's History of London*. Lindsey helped to found Counterfire, a revolutionary socialist organisation. **@LindseyAGerman**

Satnam Virdee is a professor of sociology and Founding Director of the University of Glasgow's Centre for Research on Racism, Ethnicity and Nationalism. He is the author of *Racism, class and the racialized outsider*, and his research interests include racism, class and social movements, as well as theories and histories of modernity.

Gerry Hassan is the author and editor of more than two dozen books on Scottish and British politics. The most recent include: *The people's Flag and the Union Jack: An Alternative History of Britain and the Labour Party*, a historical study to the present day of Labour's failure to develop an alternative idea of Britain; and two studies of Scotland's past twenty years, *Scotland the Brave? Twenty Years of change and the Future of the Nation* (on culture), and *The Story of the Scottish Parliament: The First Twenty Years Explained* (on devolution). **@GerryHassan**

James Meadway is an economist and writer. He was formerly economic policy adviser to Shadow Chancellor of the Exchequer John McDonnell and, prior to this, chief economist at the New Economics Foundation. A regular contributor to Open Democracy and Novara Media, James is currently writing a book on 'Corbynomics'. **@meadwaj**

Paul Hilder is founder and CEO of Datapraxis, a European political consultancy, and he has worked with left parties and progressive campaigns across Europe. Previously, Paul co-founded Crowdpac, Open Democracy and 38 Degrees. He has twice been a candidate to be Labour's General Secretary, and is a member of Lewisham Deptford Constituency Labour Party and Momentum. **@paulhilder**

Paula Surridge is Senior Lecturer in the School of Sociology, Politics and International Relations at the University of Bristol. Paula's research focuses on social and political values, both their links to positions in socio-demographic space and their influence on political behaviour, using large-scale quantitative data sources to investigate how these values influence voting patterns. **@p_surridge**

Hilary Wainwright is co-author of *Beyond the Fragments: Feminism and the Making of Socialism* and *The Lucas Plan: A New Trade Unionism in the Making?*, and author of *Labour: A Tale of Two Parties* and *Arguments for a New Left: Answering the Free-market Right*, four books from the 1980s which made the case for 'bottom-up' socialism. Her latest book, *A New Politics from the Left*, returns to this theme. Co-editor of the magazine *Red Pepper*, Hilary is a member of Hackney South and Shoreditch Constituency Labour Party and Momentum. **@hilarypepper**

Acknowledgements

My previous collection *The Corbyn Effect* was published in September 2017 and launched at the The World Transformed festival in Brighton. Ever since, I've been on the road, mainly in south east England, where I live, speaking at events inspired by the book. These, more than anything else, have informed my thinking for *Corbynism from Below*, because events like these are, in practice, a politics from below; the party, 'turned upside down'. Thanks, therefore, to the following Constituency Labour Parties (CLPs) for having me: Chichester, Eastbourne, Lewes, Reigate, Somerton and Frome, Tunbridge Wells, Wealden, Woking and Worthing West. Labour Party branches too: Evelyn, Hassocks and Hurstpierpoint, Henfield, Lewes, Seaford, Newhaven, Alfriston and Polegate (SNAP). Momentum groups hosted 'Corbyn effect' discussions in Bath, Brighton and Hastings. Southend Trades Council put on a special 'Corbyn effect' event for local trade unionists. Counterfire organised an entire day of discussion around the themes of the book, and the annual Marxism festival held debates with me on it too. I'm now looking forward to doing discussions on *Corbynism from Below*: to host an event get in touch via Twitter; @markperryman.

Similarly, #LabourDoorstep and other campaigning since the 2017 general election has been a vital influence on the formation of this book, as I campaigned with Crawley, Hastings and Rye, and Worthing West CLPs in the local elections of 2018. I'd like to especially acknowledge Emily Clarke's inspirational community campaigning in Lewes, and her 2019 local election campaign for Castle Ward.

This is an original collection, nevertheless I am enormously grateful to the *London Review of Books* for granting permission to Lorna Finlayson to base her chapter in part on existing material published there. Likewise to *Renewal* for Adam Klug and

Emma Rees's contribution, and Open Democracy for Andrew Gamble, James Meadway and Jeremy Gilbert's chapters. Not only do I appreciate their ready co-operation so that the rewrites could be done, but all three publications in print and online are a constant source of ideas and good writing that I relish and value. Thanks.

Peter Brawne and Sophie Gibson have been hard-pressed collaborators on the design, and a whole lot more, for various Lewes Labour projects, and following a pixellated Jeremy for *The Corbyn Effect*, Peter's inspired further subvertisement of an existing COR-BYN subvertise has done the text proud.

Thanks to the unknown photographer whose picture of the Durham Miners' Gala we use uncredited on the book's back cover. We tried to find you, but without success. If you see this, get in touch with the publisher and we promise to credit you on any subsequent editions.

Lawrence and Wishart responded readily, and positively, to my suggestion for a second collection. Books editor Katharine Fletcher has been faultless with her editing, and necessarily patient with me too. Long-standing friend, comrade and former Lawrence and Wishart Managing Editor (retired) Sally Davison did her best to edit out my own chapter's verbal and political excesses. Marketing manager Kate Potts has devised a superb promotional plan for the book. For aspiring left authors I would recommend the small but perfectly formed L&W, without hesitation.

In Lewes Labour, we are pioneering our own version of 'from below' via an annual ideas event and activism skills workshop. Thanks to Belinda Chapman, Emilia Ransom, Jane Thomas, Lin Heyworth, Richard Baskott and Teresa O'Brien from the CLP for their support. And to those who have helped make the events happen, including Adam Gearey, Barbara Hayes, Claire Scanlon, David Hendy, Gill Scott, Henrietta Gill, Keane, Michelle Porter, Paul Grivell, Peter Faulkner-Murphy, Sean Tunney and Tony Adams.

Of course it should go without saying, but I'm going to say it anyway, a huge dollop of gratitude to all the contributors. Responding positively to the idea, accepting my commissioning brief, sticking to the deadline (mostly, ahem!), enduring my edit. And thank you to

Karen Dobres for the idea of an A-Z to help decipher the coded language Corbynism can on occasion speak, and write, in, and for checking my final version of it.

Throughout the editing, Edgar has been a constant source of much affection and distraction, admonishing Daddy for any inclination to vote tactically, loudly telling me I should always vote for what I believe in, and quite right too. Best of all, Edgar promises me that the red star biscuits he's a dab hand at baking, with Mummy's help, will be ready for the launch of *Corbynism from Below*. Can't wait.

Mark Perryman, August 2019.

Index